Mama Said

Vera Jo Strickland

Enjoy my heart ♡!

Love,

Vera Jo Strickland

"Mama"

Is. 55:1

Contents

Preface

Deuteronomy 6:6-7 "And these words that I command you today shall be on your heart. You shall teach them diligently to your children, and shall talk of them when you sit in your house, and when you walk by the way, and when you lie down, and when you rise."

Over the years of my life, there have been many young folks enter through the door and walk right into my heart to be there for a lifetime. When they came around talking about their own lives, the decisions they were needing to make and the questions that plagued them as they grew up, they sat with me at my table, or on the porch by the pool, even in the living room when the other rooms were filled with our family, and voiced the never-ending thoughts that tumbled from their mouths. These are the responses I gave to them as they grew and started becoming the men and women that the Lord called them to be.

These are my efforts to teach my family first, then others, the Word that guided my own life through happiness or pain, through feast or famine and through early and late years. This book of devotionals is meant to bring comfort and cheer, as well as, joy and courage to those living in the real world where pain and sorrow live too. It was developed through eighty-plus years of experiencing the wonder and joy of newborn babies and the unbelievable pain of standing by the many gravesides that have been a regular part of our living.

May the thoughts that this "Mama" is sharing in each page bring a greater understanding and acceptance of God's plan for you. May it be a light to God's pathway, and to having a heart full of love for others who are part of your lives. May the central thought always be on Jesus, the Author and Finisher of your faith. May it help bring restoration to broken relationships and bind up the wounds that hurt you and keep you from being all that God has planned for you to be. And always remember that "being" is far more important than "doing" for the Lord. Let his Spirit fill you with power to do what He calls you to do so that it will bring blessing to your door.

And may you honor his Name as you pass on these thoughts to those whom God puts into your realm of influence. Listen to his Word, hide it in your heart that you might share it daily that your world will know more about Him. Mama said!

Acknowledgements

When I began the thoughts of doing "Mama Said" devotional book, it was so long ago and existed as a dream only. There were so many hindrances to going forward. One major hindrance was the lack of computer skills, even the inability to type! A young man in our Grace Sunday School Class, Ken Burton, promised to bring me, albeit, kicking and screaming, into the twenty-first century of computers. Thank you, Ken, for your willingness to take on an old woman for such a daunting task. Without your beginning there would be no previous cookbook, From Seed to Feed, From Plow to Chow, much less this endeavor of devotionals.

The ones who continually encouraged and helped to put it together are: my children, Alicia, Elizabeth, Yvonne, and daughter-in-love, Lesli, wife of my only son, Daniel, along with my "other children," Amy and Wendy, with each of their husbands who shared spouse-time with me. Those who did editing and computer work were more valuable than they'll ever know. Thank you, Norma, Betsy, and Karen. Most of all, this book would not have been possible at all without my granddaughters, Hope, Claire, Carly, and Shelley, who did the massive work of the final put-together of the finished work, including the publishing preparations. The greatest appreciation is to Buck, who strengthened me and struggled through reading each devotional.

There is no work in life more rewarding than that which gives the opportunity to be with those who mean so much. This book is meant for ALL my children and grandchildren, even to my great grandchildren whether you bore our family name or not. I pray you will hear me talking to you as each word is read and know that I am still sharing my heart though I am no longer with you. I have loved you and appreciated the "who" you are as God meant you to be, knowing he will one day complete his good work in each. Thank you, Lord, for this opportunity, given by these wonderful family members.

Foreword

Our ears are drawn to certain voices during seasons of our life. Sometimes the voice takes the form of a teacher who encourages us in an exceptionally difficult class. Sometimes the voice is a coach who seems to push us a little harder than he does anyone else. Sometimes it's a friend who gives advice during a particularly dark time in our life. These are the voices that guide, rebuke, console, and train. These are the voices that tell us what we need to hear even if we don't want to hear it. These voices help prepare us for a future that they themselves would most likely never see. But it's a future that is eerily similar to their past. Their words are so timeless that we are shocked with their accuracy.

These voices never really go away. Standing on the ledge of making a bad decision we hear, from the recesses of our minds, the correcting voice of our father. While mourning the loss of the end of a relationship, we hear the consoling voice of a friend who has long since passed. The voice sounds so close and so real that we snap our head around to see if they are standing behind us. This is the power an influential voice has in our lives, It echoes, for years, in our soul.

Sometimes this voice sounds like a great-grandmother from Parrish, Florida. Vera Jo Strickland is a woman who exudes wisdom and discernment from every fiber of her being. Her voice is soft enough to comfort the most delicate of souls, yet strong enough to bend the hardest of hearts. As you read these pages, you will smile at the homespun familiarity with which she writes. You will get a glimpse of the depths of life experiences from which she draws her guidance. Her words so piercing and so applicable you will wonder to yourself how she knew you needed to hear that.

What stands out the most from this book is her voice. It's a voice that will stay with you the rest of your life. It's a voice that loves you so much she can't wait to celebrate your next achievement. And it's a voice so kind she can't bear to watch you make the next mistake. Listen for the voice in these pages. Let her words sink deep into your soul. You will find her past eerily familiar with your present. You will find your ears drawn to her voice. But most importantly, you'll find her echoing the voice of Christ and His love for you.

Phillip Hamm
Senior Pastor, First Baptist Church Palmetto

Mama Said

January 1

1 CORINTHIANS 9:24, 25, 26A, 27A

"Do you not know that in a race all the runners run, but only one receives the prize? So run that you may obtain it. Every athlete exercises self-control in all things. They do it to obtain a perishable wreath (crown), but we an imperishable. So I do not run aimlessly … but I discipline my body and keep it under control …" ESV

We, as believers in the Lord Jesus Christ, as followers to the end of our days that God has given us, are to run this race where we are each day with the goal in mind, with that goal in sight continually. We need not to be distracted easily, but to stay in the Word of God that he might lead us onward all the way. We cannot know his will for our lives if we do not read the love letter he has had written and preserved for us.

It is my desire that this book of devotionals from a life time of following Jesus will encourage and strengthen you to keep on keeping on throughout your time he leaves you on this earth as his witness, as his hands and feet to aid those running with you. I am not perfect by a long shot. Not even near! But I learn daily how to press on, to run when I am tired or tangled in the pain of living in a fallen world. His joy is given to help this runner. His strength is mine as I lean on him moment by moment. I cannot walk or run without his Holy Spirit being there to guide into the Lord's truth.

This book is from a mother's heart to her children, whether they were brought up in my household or not. They are a copy of a lifetime of mistakes, of falling down and getting up with the encouragement from his Word daily that my mistakes do not stop my Lord from loving me or wanting me to learn from the places where I fell and sinned. He desires me to keep his goal in view. May they encourage, strengthen and teach you that he wants you to go the entire way with him, for without him we can do nothing. But with our Jesus we can do all things he calls on us to do and be. Remember always, the "being" is so much more important than the "doing." The "doing" is the outgrowth of the "being" a child of the King, our God. His goal is the Crown we get for running the race he has set before us daily. Run, dear child, run for the crown!

January 2

2 TIM.2:22B

"... Follow righteousness, faith, love, peace ..." ESV

There is always someone following behind us to see, to emulate what they see in us. Am I easy to follow toward goodness and mercy or do I leave a crooked path of meaninglessness for others close on my heels? As each day opens, I must make choices in every moment of every day that I must then live through. Some will have no great consequences. Others will have grave ones for me and those who come after me. As I climb into this last season of life, and it is a climb, I want to ask myself another important question. Have I chosen to follow my Father, my Savior, to walk in his ways every moment of every day? Of course, not! None of us do every moment, every day. Poor choices are made, repeatedly. But his forgiveness and restoration are wonderful, refreshing and encouraging. And I can start another day fresh with better choices as I learn from his hand. But the choices are there early, in the beginning. I must make them then, that I do not have to make them under the pressure of the obstacles that day brings.

Lord, give us wisdom as the day arrives to seek our daily bread, to rest in your promises and plans, to be able to face the problems you've allowed to grow us, to perfect us, to strengthen us for your glory that those who follow may see You from a straight and narrow path. Thank You for forgiveness for failures. Thank You for restoration and the energy to start over. Thank You for your perfect plan all the way to the end.

January 3

DANIEL 1:8

"But Daniel resolved that he would not defile himself with
the king's food or with the wine that he drank." ESV

Here's a key to making those very important decisions that we all
must make at one time or another. The prophet Daniel purposed in
his heart, that is, he made a strong decision that he would not change
with other people's opinions about this decision. He thought deeply
and came to a sound choice that he knew would please his God. He
was not to be easily persuaded to do differently on this one thing. It
was not so much about the food and wine as it was that this was one
choice Daniel could make and show his allegiance to his God.

There are always choices to make in every day. Some will have
no great consequence and some will have grave consequences. But
choices must be made. Here is a good way of dealing with those
important ones. Think deeply about the choice. Consider all the
possible options available to you. Think through the fallout of each
option. Do not be easily changed without really looking at any
change that another presents to you. When you finally decide your
line of action, make a plan. Write that plan down in black and white
so you can go back to the plan as it unfolds. This helps to keep your
mind set on your goal and the avenues you have lined up to get to
that goal. Set a time line for your plan as Daniel did. His was for ten
days that he worked out with the supervisor over him. He did not sit
like a child throwing a tantrum but discussed his plan with the one
in charge. And then the plan was left in the hand of his God.

Choices are to be made. Be wise as you consider each one. And
trust your God to deliver you to your goal as you follow your well-
thought-out choice to its end. Keep your goal in sight. Keep your
heart resolved, set on that goal.

January 4

DANIEL 5:27

"… you have been weighed in the balances
and found wanting." ESV

There will come a day of judgment for this world with all of its ungodly behavior. Those who have not accepted the sacrifice offered by God's perfect plan will be found wanting, short of the balances being equal to the sin. They think it doesn't matter how they choose to live, whom they decide to destroy, and whom they chose to take what they want from in this life.

But there is that day coming whether they realize it or not.

We need to pray for our world and those who live here. We need to believe that God desires all humans to be saved. It is up to us to share the love of Jesus with our world. No one else is going to do what God has given us the opportunity to do. Do you know those who are living apart from our God? Do you care that they are loved by the Father? Do you want them to hear the Good News of Christ? You may be the only words they will receive in the way you choose to live. Listen to the Father's words of promise as he pours out his love on you that you may carry that love on to another.

Turn your eyes straight upon Jesus. Look at his love expressed in his gift, his sacrifice. You can share that with your realm of influence that you move among every day, whether at home, work or in pleasure. This is the day you have to do so. Be obedient to his call. Your world is waiting to hear.

January 5

DANIEL 6:10

"Now when Daniel knew that the writing was signed, he went home. And in his upper room, with his windows open toward Jerusalem, he knelt down on his knees three times that day, and prayed and gave thanks before his God, as was his custom." NKJV

The prophet Daniel knew the decree had been signed into law that would stop anyone from petitioning any god or person other than this earthly king in this earthly kingdom. He knew what he was going to do was not going to be popular. He knew it was not going to be tolerated long. He knew there were those who would see him and report him. But he did as was his custom from early days of his life. Daniel went home to his upper room, knelt and prayed to his God.

How about you? When we believe our behavior will not be liked, or will not be tolerated by our earthly "king or kingdom," will we still do as is our custom is and seek the face of our faithful God? Or will we hide our belief from the world around us that is threatening to us? Daniel walked home, opened his window for any to see, knelt down before that window and prayed. In this land we call home, the U.S., we can still pray openly. At least, at this time we still can!

Pray, dear child of the Faithful God who has delivered us from darkness. Pray that our land will stay open to our God. Pray for his mercy to be ours and for our land to repent of her sin of unbelief. Pray that God's people will remain true to him, will serve him openly and faithfully. Pray as Daniel did, three times daily for his ways to be our ways. Pray, child, pray!

January 6

DANIEL 6:26

"(King Darius) 'I make a decree, that in all my royal dominion
people are to tremble and fear before the God of Daniel, for
he is the living God, enduring forever; his kingdom shall never
be destroyed, and his dominion shall be to the end.'" ESV

It would be nice, I think sometimes, to be able to make a decree that
everyone is to bow before the living God of Daniel. But he doesn't
want that kind of surrender to him. He wants us to willingly give
our obedience to his word out of love for him because he first loved
us. He has shown himself to be a caring, loving, faithful God, but he
will not look on sin, not yours and not mine.

The prophet, Daniel, had just been taken out of the lion's den
where he was expected to die at their jaws. But his God had delivered
him and King Darius was delighted at Daniel's God's choice in this.
So, since he saw this God as the greatest God, he wants all to see
that too. He recognizes that Daniel's God will be God forever, His
kingdom forever. His dominion over all is forever too. A pagan king
can see the reality of God.

We need to stand in awe of Daniel's God, the living God of
forever. We need to believe he has the power to deliver even from
the mightiest of lions. But he does so only in his wisdom for each.
He is not bound by our ideas or notions. We can rest assured that
he reigns over all. May those around us be able to see he is our living
God. We trust him as such and serve him because he has given his
great salvation to us. We make the personal choice to do this. It is
not decreed by any other.

January 7

DANIEL 12:3

*"Those who are wise shall shine like the brightness
of the firmament, and those who turn many to
righteousness like the stars forever and ever." NKJV*

When you have received Jesus yourself, there is no greater calling, when given opportunity, than to share him with those around you. Be found faithful to speak the Name of Jesus every time you can that others might hear with their ears and respond with their hearts to him too. God has promised that those who share their knowledge of Jesus will be shining like the heavens! What a beautiful idea to contemplate!

With the opening of your mouth, with the understanding of the power of the spoken word of God to your friends and family, you can speak life to those most precious to you. It is still up to each of them to receive that living word. But faith comes from the hearing and opportunity is given to take that word into the inner heart and mind to be received to salvation. If you would be as a "star" in this world, share Jesus!

As for those who hear and accept, their world is forever changed. When they receive, they are turned from unrighteousness to God's righteousness, the only true goodness for anyone. Let your light shine, child of God. Offer the true bread. The world is hungry and is in darkness. Do not let fear or laziness stop you. Choose to be a "star" for the Lord. Mama said!

January 8

PSALM 23:5

"You prepare a table before me in the presence of my enemies;
You anoint my head with oil; my cup overflows." HCSB

Since I love to look at beautiful tables set for guests, I wondered when I read these words about the Lord setting a table before one of his own and just what such a table would be like. I thought about golden bowls filled with heavenly foods. I saw gleaming snow white dishes with silver place settings laid beside those plates. I saw crystal glasses which sparkled as the light of the Lord shone on them. I saw many places set for many guests at this dinner much as a huge banquet table would hold.

And then reality set in & my eyes were opened to these words. This table is my personal table set before my own enemies! It is the very table that the Lord brings me to sit with him regardless of the world around me. His blessings are mine to the point that my cup held in my tight little fingers overflows with all that I need from his hand. And then I realize that my Lord sets this table that he shares with me alone with love before anything else. Point taken: Set your table with love before you set it with dishes! This mama says!

January 9

DANIEL 6:22A

"My God sent his angel and shut the lions' mouths,
and they have not harmed me …" ESV

An amazing story of how God delivered his prophet from a den of wild lions where he had unjustly been thrown. You need to read the balance of the story in the sixth chapter of the book of Daniel. It is so full of God's justice and kind revelations of who he is and what he is able to do for his children.

One of the notable facts is that God has his angels to do his bidding for him to have his will carried out in this world. He has no lack in seeing to it. God knew that Daniel was not guilty of any sin against him or of any bad deed against King Darius. His justice is right and his timing is perfect. He can send any number of angels to aid his people but it is his choice as to when, how many, or not to do so at all. In his wisdom, he deals with us all.

It is another fact that he rules over the nature of animals as well. He had no problem shutting those wild hungry lions mouths to keep his prophet safe all night. He was not bothered by the length of time Daniel was in the den with all of them either. In fact, he is not cut short of anything by the world he created. Our God is able! When you are down in that den with what you see as hungry lions, look up. There may be an angel standing at the door of each lion's mouth! Trust him whether you can see or not in the darkness that overcomes your eyesight. He sees even in the dark!

January 10

DEUTERONOMY 8:11A, 12-13B 14,18A

"Beware that you do not forget the Lord your God by not
keeping his commandments ... lest, when you have eaten and
are full, and have built beautiful houses and dwell in them ...
and all that you have is multiplied; when your heart is lifted
up, and you forget the Lord your God who brought you out
... of bondage ... you shall remember the Lord your God, for
it is He who gives you power to gain wealth ..." NKJV

God is reminding his people how he brought them out of slavery and
bondage. He is also telling them how easy it is to forget him when
we have a belly full of food, a bank with lots of money in it with our
name on the account and a great home to call our own. Ease makes
for poor remembrances of just who it was who gave us the ability
to earn those possessions. We can become so careless and prideful,
thinking it is ours, it was made by us and it is all our own, not someone else's, that our minds vacate the knowledge that God is the one
who made it all possible.

Those are the times when we must be most vigilant over our
hearts so we still live by his commandments and follow his judg-
ments and statutes. Ease makes for a laziness of thought and purpose.
It becomes a way of life instead of his way of living. It is too easy to
say, "My power and the might of my hands has delivered all this to
me." But God is the giver of all good gifts including the gift of making money. Use his gift wisely.

January 11

DEUTERONOMY 6:18

*"And you shall do what is right and good in
the sight of the Lord …" NKJV*

How often we are told to do what is right in any given condition. That seems right on its face. It sounds good to our ears. What the greater question is, what is right and good? Let's take a closer look at this thought.

Do we listen to our world as to what is right? Do we listen to parents always in determining the right and good? Do we do as our teachers have taught us about being right and good? Each of these should be right…we think. But each of these can lead us astray in knowing exactly what is right and good. Where is the best answer to our question of what is both right and good?

The last part of this quote from the book of Law as Moses put it down for us is the answer to our thoughts. God said to do what is right and good in the sight of the Lord…every time, in every circumstance, in every situation here on earth.

Therefore, we are to go to the Word for our decision making that we might be obedient to his Word, to what he has already said about this time, circumstance or situation. He is always right. He is always good. He has made it possible for us to be both right and good also. He has given us what he thinks so we can know how to live every day. Ask what he says before you make a decision that will seem right and good but that will be according to another way than to be the Lord's way… the only WAY of blessing. Do what is right and good in the sight of the Lord! And you will be both right and good.

January 12

ACTS 9:10

"Now there was a disciple at Damascus named Ananias. The
Lord said to him in a vision, 'Ananias.' And he said, 'Here I
am, Lord.' And the Lord said to him, "Rise and Go …"'" ESV

The Lord is calling you and me into his fields to witness to his world
about him, who he is, why he came to earth and how they can know
him as Savior and Lord too. He has a plan that only we can carry out
in his name. We have a choice, as we do in most things. We can be as
Ananias was and answer with the words, "Here I am, Lord." Or we
can refuse to hear and decline the opportunity to obey.

How wise we would be to be ready to hear, ready to get up and
ready to go. There are many things that cause us to be wary of his
call. There are many persons who would cause us to wonder if we
heard right. We can let finances hold us back. We can listen to family
members or friends who fear our leaving them or of our being hurt
or killed. We can allow our own fears to hinder us and our own lack
of confidence lead us to deny the place of service. We also can move
away in our hearts and mind to close the door to our being able to
hear with our ears.

But the wise will hear. The wise will answer, as Ananias did, with
an affirmative of hearing our name. When the Lord calls, he calls us
by name! God used Ananias as an instrument in the Apostle Paul's
blindness to restore sight.

He can use you too!

Hear the word of the Lord today. Answer with an open heart
that knows your Savior will never call you where he will not go with
you. His promise is secure.

January 13

ACTS 10:24-26

"And the following day they entered Caesarea. Now Cornelius
was waiting for them, and had called together his relatives
and close friends. As Peter was coming in, Cornelius met him
and fell down at his feet and worshiped him. But Peter lifted
him up, saying, 'Stand up; I myself am also a man.'" NKJV

Cornelius, a centurion, was answering God's call to him by receiving
Peter at his home. He was so excited about God's message being
delivered by Peter that he had invited family and close friends to hear
too. His home had become a platform for God to use, an instrument
of God's peace, not only, for himself but for many others also.

Our family and close friends are so often the very ones we have
trouble speaking with about Jesus. They know us too well. They
know our frailties and our sins. Perhaps Peter's words would be a
good starting place. It's not about us. It's all about him: Jesus, and
his forgiveness that's available to all, you and your family and friends.
Never deny your need of Jesus and his forgiveness. You are just a person, a human with difficulties before you and sins too often at your
life's doorway. That's why it's so important to show Jesus' salvation
you received, not because you deserved it, but because you needed it.
That's what mercy and grace is from the hand of Jesus.

Start today with one of your family or friends and speak the
Name of Jesus with that one. God had spoken with Cornelius before
Peter arrived there. Perhaps God has spoken to this one you love
already too. Become an instrument of his peace today. Tomorrow
may be too late.

January 14

COLOSSIANS 2:5-6

"… though I am absent in body, yet I am with you in spirit, rejoicing to see your good order and the firmness of your faith in Christ. Therefore, as you received Christ Jesus the Lord, so walk in him, rooted and built up in him and established in the faith, just as you were taught, abounding in thanksgiving." ESV

When you have Christ, you have everything you need to complete this life here on earth, a land that is fallen, that awaits the redeeming of the Lord in his day. It is important to remember that he has equipped us to meet life as it is, where we must walk in the contamination that sin has brought to it. He chose not to remove us from earth but to leave us here to be his witnesses to those he has placed in our realm of influence.

Over the course of this time together, whether at our table or couch, in a Sunday School class or Bible study somewhere, or in the pages of this devotional, I have continually taught you that Jesus is my all in all. He is the specific of my salvation; no other has delivered me from sin or will present me faultless before the throne of the Father except Jesus.

He is the Morning Star when all I see is the darkness of my night.

Jesus is my Strength when I am filled with nothing but weakness.

My Lord is my Joy as my heart breaks with sorrow.

My Savior is my Hope each time I must face defeat.

He is my "Press On" when I am tired.

He is my Shelter when my steps are slow and halting.

He is my Lift when I am overthrown by the waves of my personal storms.

This Jesus is my Sanctuary when I am fearful.

He is my Strong Tower where I can run to it and be safe.

My Christ is my Head when I need wisdom.

He is my True Substance when there are shadows around me.

This Jesus is my Worth when I am unworthy.

Jesus is my Redeemer when I desperately needed redemption.

There is no philosophy nor great persuasion that can take me away from him.

Whether face to face or here in these words, when you have Jesus, you have everything you need! This mama loves you as my Jesus has loved me, completely and unconditionally. Press on, my child!

January 15

2 PETER 1:5-7

"For this very reason, make every effort to supplement
your faith with goodness, goodness with knowledge,
knowledge with self-control, self-control with endurance,
endurance with godliness, godliness with brotherly
affection, and brotherly affection with love." HCSB

FAITH
    Goodness
    Knowledge
    Self-control
    Endurance
    Godliness
    Brotherly Affection
    Love

Our faith is sufficient for salvation. Yes. But wisdom is supplementing our faith with this life style that follows from our faith and ends up exhibiting a pure love for those around us who follow Jesus too. Enough said! Choose today to be found faithfully growing in the Lord all the way to that pure love. Make every effort to fulfill this Scripture, every day.

January 16

EPHESIANS 6:1,4

"Children, obey your parents as you would the Lord, because this
is right ... Fathers, don't stir up anger in your children, but bring
them up in the training and instruction of the Lord." HCSB

Over the years I have witnessed so many times when children have
been disrespectful of parents, but I have also seen many more times
when parents were just as disrespectful of the personage of their kids.
Neither of these is good!

Let's address the kids first. The simple fact is that your parents
are your parents. They are not always right, nor are they always easy
to get along with every day. Parents get tired too. They draw down
into their bucket of patience until suddenly there is the bottom of
that bucket. You end up receiving the dirt on that bottom. But when
we cut them some slack and give what your parents need, respect,
it can be amazing how much they can be changed into delightful
beings. Now I realize that is not always the case! Sometimes parents
are just trying for kids, aren't they? But the bottom line is this: obey
just as you would if it had been Jesus telling you what to do. Can
you think of it that way? That is Jesus talking to you! At least, think
of it that way!!

Now parents, it's your turn. Actually, it bothers me more when I
witness a parent harming a young one with harsh words and jerking
around. That parent has the power of life and death in the words
spoken to that child or teen. Children were given to you to train
as the Lord trains his children, with patience and love, spoken and
delivered with life-giving appropriate hugs and pats on the shoulders. Gentle but firm sentences spoken with respect brings so much
more respect from a child than does yelling and jerking. Our words,
our touch says to our child they have value and have thoughts with
value too. They need an opportunity to express them safely with us.
They may have a hard time keeping their voice down when they are

excited or angry too. After all, they haven't had as much practice as we as parents have had! Start today to give your kid room to grow as they learn (yes, it's a process!) to converse with you about their behavior or dreams. If they never get the chance to talk about their misbehavior beyond being criticized by you, they will probably never let you into their dreams and hopes either.

January 17

EPHESIANS 5:18

"And do not get drunk with wine, which
leads to reckless actions …" HCSB

I have known many folks who could drink moderately and not ever get to the stage of being drunk. But in my family on both sides of the tree there are several alcoholics who made many a fool of themselves, wreaking havoc in their households. One was close enough to be my maternal grand-father who died when I was only four.

As a teen, I thought really hard about a few choices I was old enough to make in life. They were choices I would live by and receive blessings or curses, according to what they were. My father and two brothers smoked heavily. Two of these three died with lung and bone cancer. These two thoughts I had early: if I choose to never smoke nor ever to drink, I would never have to worry about becoming a "smoker" or "alcoholic." It was an easy choice for me. It was never about the "look" of being either. It was never about my church. It was all about the choice to be as healthy as I could be.

We each make choices about our lives, some unwise and some wise. I made these and have never regretted either one. I made a few others too…the choice to live a lifestyle that could lead others to Jesus. My life is not perfect. Never was. Never will be. But it is about leaning on the arms of Jesus whether I do any given thing or not. Some things are not wrong to do I decided not to do because of love for another person who might consider that thing wrong. It's not about eating or drinking or smoking. It is about putting another above my own wishes. I do not want to lead someone else down a path toward anything that could harm them. Life is too short to bring hurt to another person's heart of hearts.

January 18

EPHESIANS 6:11-12

"Put on the full armor of God so that you can stand against
the wiles of the Devil. For we do not wrestle against
flesh and blood, but against the principalities, against
powers, against the rulers of this age, against the spiritual
hosts of wickedness in the heavenly places." NKJV

When we are assaulted by others that we work with, live with, even worship with, or move among in this life, how often we blame them for the pain we experience. It is true they played their part in making life hard. But it is also true that others are most often used by the unseen forces of darkness, of evil that the Devil, our true Enemy, desires to rain on us to turn our thoughts and hearts away from the Lord. This is how he brings anger to our minds, desires of getting even with our tormentors into play with us.

Next time it happens to you, look instead toward the real Enemy and see just how those who are working against you are being used by that one, the Devil, who tried to deter our Lord from his journey in this world to be our Savior. He has a plan to destroy you if you allow that. Keep your mind set on heavenly things, on the Author of your faith who will finish it in his timing. He has not left you to live alone where the Enemy still is. The Devil will get his due when our Lord comes back as Victor and King. So, instead of reacting to your hurt, put on that armor of God provided in his word for you. And know that the Devil is alive and well on this world stage. Turn to the Lord for your victory too.

January 19

EPHESIANS 6:13

"Therefore, put on the whole armor of God, that you may be able
to withstand in the evil day, and having done all, to stand." NKJV

Because we fight not against flesh and blood, we need to learn to put
on the whole armor that God has provided for us to fight the good
fight of each day. It is wise to do this early in the morning before
you become "Lucy-in-the-chocolate-factory" with your life racing on
with you trying to keep up. Daily life has a way of stressing us with
the next thing to be done whether we're finished with the last thing
on our list or not.

If you are to stand and having done all to keep standing, be
ready as God has prepared you to be. The Enemy is out there waiting for the unsuspecting to waltz by thinking all is well. You can get
blown away that way! Just by not being prepared to face him, as you
surely will. That Enemy is ready for you. Are you ready for him?

Read the rest of these verses for the full understanding of God's
gift of preparation for battle. The battle is the Lord's but we must be
ready to stand with everything we have that our Redeemer has made
available for us to keep standing. Stand, my fellow Jesus followers,
stand!

January 20

DEUTERONOMY 33:25

"As your days, so shall your strength be." NKJV

No, we none know how many days we shall have on this earth for this life. None can say we have even tomorrow. But one promise we can be assured of is the one found in this verse. It is a good thing to know when my days are long and they are painful or full of sorrow.

As the years have progressed for me, I realize that we all get older, our strength weakens and draws near to the line marked empty. We wander when even trying to walk a straight line! It is a privilege to grow in years, but there is a price we pay for that privilege!

Somewhere on each person is marked an expiration date. Thank God, he doesn't allow us to view it. But it is there just the same. So, we wake every morning and look in the mirror and see that we are not the same as we were yesterday. One day makes a difference at this stage of life. But we are still here and still need to finish this one day following the Lord's Word with joy and sweet peace.

How can we do this when we know we are tired and, sometimes even weary? This promise is what keeps me going on those mornings when I feel too weak to do what's on my agenda. This gift from our loving and gracious God is a strong set of words of strength equal to this one day that keeps on giving for all the days he has marked for me. There will never be a day that comes to my life that he has not already promised the strength to make. It doesn't matter what any day holds for me. He has seen it, known it and gathered the strength I will need to go through it and gives it to me one moment at a time. Thank you, Lord. You, too have this promise, child of God. Walk on. Your strength is equal to your days.

January 21

EPHESIANS 6:10

"Finally, be strengthened by the Lord and
by his vast strength." HCSB

The joy that I find in these few words that gather up my days and bind them together with the knowledge that my God is strong with a vastness that my mind cannot really understand, is immense. But it is strength that I can count on in every day, every occasion, every situation, every relationship, every problem and every way that I must walk to get through this life as he has called me to do.

The heart of the matter is this: I can go to him when my day is long. I can make it through any job I must do. I can remove the worry from any occasion or situation that arises that must be dealt with whether I want to or not. I can rethink any relationship that hurts and bring to mind the words he has spoken to me about living in harmony with others. I can know his heart is for me, with me and will be with me forever. That is joy, my friend!

And the biggest part of that joy is that his strength is vast. That means beyond anything I have to face as I make every day, all day. The end of each one of those hard days does come and brings with it the satisfaction that he was with me. He never left me to draw on myself alone. He held my arms up in praise and thanksgiving as he held them up in victory. I am so glad when each day closes, true. But I am so grateful for his strong arms being there when I couldn't see them or even feel them. I depend on the word saying they were there! His word is delight. It is a wealth of stamina for me. Draw on his strength, not just your own. Call out to him for his vast expanse of strength, equal to your days. Joy unspeakable for you!

January 22

EPHESIANS 5:18B,19-20

"… be filled by the Spirit: speaking to one another in
psalms, hymns and spiritual songs, singing and making
music to the Lord, giving thanks always for everything
to God the Father in the name of our Lord Jesus Christ.
Submitting to one another in the fear of Christ." HCSB

Consider these few words found here about what life can be with each other. Wonder how different our homes could be if we stayed the course outlined here for each other and our actions toward one another. The idea of making music from our hearts toward those around us, whether in the house of God or in our personal homes, is an exciting thought.

This does not carry the form of making beautiful music to each other. It does bring to mind the joyful noises we make as we rock our little ones. It has the connotation of laughter in our music, encouragement for the other as we sing our hearts empty with the fulness of love. It makes praise easy and thanksgiving a rapid delivery from our hearts to our mouths to our loved ones and friends. It brings us closer to accepting the fact that we each make grand mistakes and need forgiveness.

It covers the huge thought of mutual submission to one another as we walk through this thing we call marriage. It shows us that it is not about being "right" in the situation. It is about being "righteous" toward the other. It is about giving place to the one you love. There are some folks who have to be right about everything. They will lead a lonely life because that's hard to live with every day! Whatever you choose to do, be certain to do it with the main thought of acting in the name of the Lord Jesus. That would stop a whole lot of thoughtless actions, wouldn't it?

January 23

EPHESIANS 5:31

"For this reason a man will leave his father and mother and be joined to his wife, and the two will become one flesh." HCSB

The newlyweds seldom grasp this beautiful thought expressed in God's word about the union of two people to become one flesh. How can such a thing be? Only by the grace of God as he joins them! What a wonderful expression of pure love, of acceptance of another person to be you! What we learned over the years is that God does this in his way. He establishes the union, full and complete that day, and then he teaches the two of you how you do it!

It was hard to come to realize what love really was when we were young. Oh, yes, we knew what the term was, what it was supposed to be and just how it was supposed to work out. But putting it into practice was different. It meant learning (process) to put the other person first. It was like giving the last piece of cake to the other. Or putting the only steak on his plate without even cutting yourself a little piece first. Then that other person would cut you a piece and share! Or not!! Sometimes we didn't do as we were supposed to do. Sometimes we chose for ourselves! It took time for us to get used to thinking about that other one first.

I saw the man in my life start moving toward me with giving to me first, with sheltering me first, with taking the place to die first to me! It was a leadership I could follow more easily. It was a learning about real love, true love from him as I walked the way of life with him. He was a good teacher. I learned to trust him just as I learned to trust my Savior. And as he left all behind for me, I was able to walk with him into our future. God made us one flesh. It was our job, our opportunity to learn what that really meant. You can have that too. Give yourself first and let God show you how to do the rest.

January 24

ECCLESIASTES 12:1

*"Don't let the excitement of youth cause you to forget
your Creator. Honor him in your youth before you grow
old and say, 'Life is not pleasant anymore.'" NLT*

How wise we would be if we listened to this simple advice! How many regrets could be avoided in those last days, the days of old age, if we paid attention to these few words while still in our youth. But, alas, we too often think those days of age are way down our line of vision for our future. We can't see too well how very soon our youth is spent and the years have piled up to our dismay.

Age comes to all. It will arrive at your door as well, sooner, far sooner than you expect. I used to tell my friends that I went to bed one night and I was young. I got up the next morning and I was old! I was not too sure just how it happened that quickly. I don't know where all the in between days went. I was busy, I suppose. That's what we usually say about the passage of time, isn't it? I was too busy to watch it pass by me. But it does pass, ready or not!

It would be good to consider your ways today. Right this minute. It might to be too late if you tarry. If I think through the wisdom I already know from God's word from early Sunday School days, there are many choices I probably would not make. There are a few things I would never learn to do, things that bring harm to my body. There are some I would make certain I would do more often, acts of kindness, generosity and friendship. These so often come back to us from others who appreciate such thoughtful behavior. But whether I received them back or not, I would still want to behave in that manner. Such a life lived is a joy to experience going through it. Take time to think before you act in your youth. Remember the words of your Creator and respond to them wisely, for old age is at your door waiting to be let in! It will be insistent. It will not wait for you.

January 25

EPHESIANS 5:22A

"Wives, submit to your own husband as to the Lord …" ESV

A little lost thought from this famous verse is the part of submitting as to the Lord. When I decide, yes, that's make a choice, to submit to my husband, I am making a choice to submit to my Lord Jesus as well. It is much easier to do when I think in those words, for I want to submit to Jesus' leadership! I know he has my best at his heart. I trust he loves me unconditionally and completely.

That's where I need to begin this willingness to submit. I am to trust my husband as I trust the Lord, though I realize that man has feet of clay and makes mistakes! Wow! But Lord… He says to honor that man, and to give that man to him to develop into the man he created him to be. Can I trust the Lord to do that? Yes, if I'm willing to give God time to do this in his own way, in his own timing. Lord… even though I think I want that now!

That's when Jesus says to get my own act in gear before I start trying to do his job on my man. I can honor my man because I honor my Lord to make me into the woman he created me to be. I can give grace where due because he gives grace to me. I can forgive when needed, for I have been forgiven. I can answer in kindness when receiving unkindness because Jesus was kind to me. I can wait upon the Lord for my joy to be complete while he makes us both into his image. He teaches and exemplifies love. May we both accept his perfecting of us in this relationship we call marriage.

January 26

ACTS 4:19-20

"But Peter and John answered and said to them, 'Whether
it is right in the sight of God to listen to you more
than to God, you judge. For we cannot but speak the
things which we have seen and heard.'" NKJV

These two men, Peter and John, had just been told not to speak nor teach in the name of Jesus. How would you handle such a demand? These two disciples simply replied they could not keep from speaking and teaching in that Name of Jesus! Why? Good question.

They had seen. They had heard. And they were changed forever by this man Jesus. Their mouths could no more be closed than they could stop breathing. It was life to them! It was their beginning; it was their ending; and it was everything in between. Note that their enemies continued to threaten them. It made no difference to these two.

Have you met my Jesus yet? Is your life changed with the things you have seen and heard? Are you willing to open your mouth with the truth of this one Man? Will you let his Holy Spirit fill you with the truth to be shared by all you meet? Sit down long enough to search your heart to learn where you stand with the Lord. There is no better time than right now!

Peter and John had decided on Jesus and they opened their mouths with the truth of God regardless of the consequences, even to the death. Like Paul, a later disciple, to live is Christ and to die is gain!

January 27

2 PETER 3:4A,9

"… saying, 'where is the promise of His coming?' … The Lord
is not slack concerning His promise, as some count slackness,
but is longsuffering toward us, not willing that any should
perish but that all should come to repentance." NKJV

Man has tried to decide for a long time whether the Lord's words
were true when he said he was coming back again. Because it has
been such a very long time since he came the first time, many have
determined they were just words and he won't ever return, even that
he can't. These words from the pen of the Apostle Peter are decidedly
saying he will be coming back again!

As believers, we must be about our Father's business sharing the
truth that Jesus is the Messiah, the Son of God who came to save
the world the first time. He is longsuffering these words remind us,
so that all who will may come to know Jesus as Savior. He will not
leave one single one out who accepts that gracious offer of eternal life
through the blood of Jesus.

We cannot be complacent, sitting idly by as the world passes
up the best life they could ever have. Jesus has called us to share the
Name of Jesus everywhere we go, with all peoples wherever they are.
Are you being obedient to that calling? Choose to move among your
personal world and speak his name easily and regularly that any who
hear will have the opportunity to receive it. It is our challenge. It is
our choice.

January 28

EPHESIANS 6:17-18

"And take the helmet of salvation, and the sword of the Spirit, which is the Word of God; praying always with all prayer and supplication in the Spirit, being watchful to this end with all perseverance and supplication for all the saints." NKJV

Included in this verse are all three of the points of the stool on which rests our growth.

First, the Word of God: after he has given us the helmet of salvation, he gives the sword with which we may slice life so we can know what to do, how to do and when to do. His word is clear and his Spirit is there to give understanding. He has preserved that Word for us.

Second, we are to pray always in the Spirit, diligently, that is, paying attention to details, about everything. There is nothing too small for your God. There is nothing too large for your God. Jehovah is able!

Third, we are to pray for our fellow believers, which is our fellowship with each other. The saints need our prayers! We are on this pilgrimage together and we must stand shoulder to shoulder with one another or we can fall, getting run over by our own! We are critical to the Family of God.

Be a good member of his Family. Read his Word, pray diligently for each other, upholding our brothers and sisters in Christ. Stand as one fellowship in one Lord. Get together at your house and have a great time living your faith. And pray about everything, that is, ALL THINGS … REALLY! Why? Cause mama said!

January 29

1 PETER 1:15-16

"But as He who called you is holy, you also be holy in all your conduct, because it is written, 'Be holy for I am holy.'" NKJV

We are to be as obedient children to our Father God. We have been given the life style within which we are to conduct ourselves as sober minded and hopeful of the day of the revelation of Jesus Christ. That day will occur right on time as the Lord counts time, not as humans decide about time. There are several things to remember as we await that day.

First, to have holy living, we must live a disciplined life that is led by disciplined thinking. Set your mind on eternal things, on heavenly settings instead of the earthly things that distract us so easily. We need to keep the vertical thinking going. When we look around at the horizontal life, we are moved too easily by things we want or things we see the world involved with that seem so interesting.

Second, we want to keep our thinking clear. Sin clouds our minds and sight. When we miss God's perfect mark for us, and we all do, quickly repent and agree with the Lord about this sin being real sin. There are no little sins. Those things we call big may have many more consequences than what humans term little sins, but they all harm our communion with our Father. But he is willing to open his arms for his erring child who doesn't try to deceive him about sin! God never is the one who moves in breaking our relationship. We do. When we sin, we are the ones who pull away to keep from having to admit our sin. The world will deceive us if they can about this. Be vigilant. Choose holiness!

Best of all is the last thing to remember. Rest your mind in the blessed hope that Christ Jesus will return one day to take us home with him for his glory because he has redeemed us by his own blood, as a Lamb without blemish or spot. He is holy. We are to live as holy too by keeping our thinking disciplined, vertical and clear, and resting in this blessed hope in Jesus. Look up! Our redemption draws near!

January 30

1 KINGS 19:4A

"But he himself went a day's journey into the wilderness, and
came and sat down under a broom tree. And he prayed
that he might die and said, 'It is enough!'" NKJV

Elijah had just finished one of the great moments in his life in praying for God to withhold the rain (He did) and then praying for God
to let it rain (He did!). Bu when King Ahab's wife, Jezebel, threat-
ens Elijah, he is scared to death…literally! He is totally discouraged,
tired and depressed with the whole thing. He wants to give up and
die. He says, "That's enough!"

There are times when even the mightiest of believers get down,
tired and worn, especially after great things have been wrought by
the Lord through them. None of us are above becoming so. We have
weaknesses that leave us weary. But God still had a plan for Elijah
and he does not let him die. God answers him in his need, and sends
help. Read the next four verses. God sends an angel to minister to
this servant of his. It is glorious to see how the Lord moves Elijah
into his plan again.

God will sometimes allow us to go into the wilderness of life at
these times. But he is able to bring us through all the way to victory.
Trust him, when you are in your own wilderness, to lead you out and
back into his plan for you. He is not finished with you yet!

January 31

1 COR. 16:14

"Let all that you do be done in love." NKJV

Do you realize how many things we would leave undone if we simply put the test of love to them? Words would be locked up tight in our mouths and never let be heard by anyone if we considered what they would sound like from another's viewpoint. Looks would be squelched before they were turned on someone else. Our Body language would be moved out of our thoughts before they could become real and be seen be those we say we love. We would become more perceptive of other's responses to our thoughtless words and actions. We would read their unspoken language, their body movements, their eyes, as they try to hide what hurts. A good question to ask ourselves before we do or say anything is, "Is what I am about to do or say redemptive, is it kind, is it true, remembering just because a thing is true does not mean it should be said to another always?

Yes, there is a time to speak the truth, the whole truth, but only as I can speak it in love, genuine love. When my speech will be vindictive or in anger, I must always stop and quiet my heart, my emotions, long enough to get myself in control. When my mind is still for a while, it gives rise to my obedience to this law of love. Then I may speak with the understanding that God is the one to make judgment (that is, the condemning of the other person). I can know an action is wrong and judge that action. But I do not condemn that one, just the behavior.

Turn the spirit of love loose on the ones you have the opportunity to interact with in the place where God has placed you. His love is able to move in another's life to produce a changed life. Become a channel of his massive love to those around you at each opportunity. Let all that you do be done in love!

February 1

DEUTERONOMY 32:7

"Remember the days of old, consider the years of
many generations. Ask your father, and he will show
you; your elders, and they will tell you." NKJV

Everyone has boxes of old pictures. Some have names on the back; some not. But for some reason they have been saved in these old boxes for a future time. Usually, by the time we get them out to look through, we cannot identify many of them. I took one of those that I have and started going through it, sorting them according to those I could identify. The pictures went back four generations on both sides of my family.

There were some really funny ones; some very sad, even pictures of times gathered at funerals. Three of these were folks collected around a huge casket of a loved one none of us knew. But I did know many of the mourners, my mother's family. One had the whole group, one had no children, and one with just the very old folks. I noticed how intense they all looked. There were no smiles even on the kid's faces. But then, it was a funeral!

That's when I began remembering the stories my grandmother had relived for me when I was a child sharing a bedroom with her. From her memories, life seemed very hard and cold. I'm sure there were times of laughter and warmth, and times of special occasions when there was music, for my grandfather was a fiddle player at the square dances held on weekends. But then, he was an alcoholic so that might not be a good example! Perhaps that's why her memories seemed hard.

Now would be a good time to seek out parents or grandparents to close the gap of who is who in your old family albums. Old pictures are streets of memories to avenues of learning more about yourself. Not just the old folks! Our forefathers were instructed to share their experiences so the young could begin to know what the

Lord had done for them. How else will they learn? Family history is important. As you learn from that generation, you will be able to see how God has redeemed them. It will help you to trust God to work in your generation. It will take a moment to connect but then you will have a lifetime of thoughts to lean on for many years. Last of all, tell your own children about the way God has moved in your life. Pass it on!

February 2

DEUTERONOMY 24:16

"The fathers shall not be put to death for the children,
neither shall the children be put to death for the fathers;
every man shall be put to death for his own sin." ESV

Our children will be a lot like us as they grow into adulthood. Their gene pool is set before they are born. Their environment is set by us. So much of who they are is decided by God from our genes in his selection and by us as parents in arranging life in their environment. It is an awesome responsibility we have in doing this. If your child is by adoption, you are responsible only for the environment. Genes and environment are two very strong parts of who we become. But neither of these are impossible to overcome. There is the "I will' piece of self that, with the grace of God and a strong determination, God can strengthen us to be overcomers of both.

One of the first steps to this outcome is to stop blaming others for our choices and our behavior, especially a parent, for our genes or the way we were brought up in their household. These are circumstances over which the child had no control. But a child does have a choice at this point. It is that one's choice! No other can make it. (It's always about a choice, isn't it?)

A second step is to recognize that we each must stand accountable to God, both parent and child. Some of my children's choices were learned at my knee. Some were not. But the day comes when they are no longer accountable to me but to the Father. Sometimes this is learned in teen years, some learn much later and some never learn becoming victims of their lives.

If they have grown to know God and that his watchful eye is over them, they will understand that Mom and Dad are no longer their "keeper". God is! And he is always there seeing and hearing. They can have the abundant life that Jesus promises to those who are his. They can be overcomers of all the past. And they will stand alone before God, just as the parent does.

It is helpful to forgive yourselves, both generations, for mistakes made and promises broken, for love covers a multitude of sins.

February 3

DEUTERONOMY 32:7A

"Remember the days of old; consider the years long past." HCSB

For my birthday, my late twenties grand- daughter gave me a tumbler with big sunflowers scattered around it with the words," You Are My Sunshine " on the side. Yes, it is pretty, but the exciting thing about it was not its beauty, but the remembrance that it represented. When she was a toddler and then a preschooler, she often stayed with me as the need arose for her care while mom was busy. The part that meant so much for me was that the tumbler let me know she remembered the songs I sang to her when rocking or lying down for a nap.

You know that I was not gifted with a lovely voice for singing, so it was not the pleasantness that caught her heart. It was not my great list of songs for my concert. I sang only that song, Amazing Grace and Jesus Loves Me. It was not about perfect pitch; it was about perfect love, spelled "TIME" with her alone. Yes, I kept all the different grand children at one time or another, both the girls and the boys. Sometimes I kept several of them at one time. But each one knew I loved them because I spent time with them.

You can do the same for you children, grand-children or great-grand-kids, whichever is appropriate for you. If you do not have any of these yet, find a young child, perhaps a nephew or niece, or other young adult who needs a little extra care and respect to begin to blossom. You will be pouring the oil of your encouragement over the dry sponge of their lives. All the world needs someone to spend time, giving breath to the lungs of youth to fill them with shouting joy. Do it today!

February 4

"And now, Israel, what does the Lord your God require of you, but to fear the Lord, your God, to walk in all his ways and to love him, to serve the Lord your God with all your heart and with all your soul. And to keep the commandments of the Lord and His statutes which I command you today for your good." NKJV

Seems simple enough, doesn't it? What it really is saying though is that your God will be number one in every part of your life. There can be no other before him. Not family or friend. No other thing can take his place in the very depths of your being. He is always to be first. It is as simple as that, but oh, so hard to do. We allow so many people and things to usurp his throne in us, to sit where no other is to sit, to fill a place no one else is to occupy.

What God is requiring is everything about us to be his and for us to follow his commandments as they are provided for us in his word. But why are we to do this? The last phrase is the key. It is for our good. It is not that God is being hard on us for no reason. It is that his plan, his way is the very best way you can have. It is the way of rejoicing and peace, whether there is pain or sorrow included or not. Those are a part of living in a fallen world. His way leads through these to his victory in Jesus, the completion of his plan. Follow with all your heart. Love no other more than you love him. Serve no other but him. Let no other into your heart and being. It is for your good!

February 5

DEUTERONOMY 25:4

"You shall not muzzle an ox while it treads out the grain." NKJV

When someone is working with you to help you to get what you need done, it is important for that one to know he is rewarded for his work. In our day, we pay a person for the hours worked. An animal does not get paid the way people do. An ox is paid by the care he receives, the food he eats. That care and food is what keeps the ox able to go on working. We are to be good caretakers of those who work helping us to maintain our lives. It applies to these animals that help too.

You can tell a lot about a person by the way that person tends to his animals whether working ones or pets. Watch out for those who are unkind or abusive. They will abuse people easily too. The way one uses a hand in touching pets and folks reveals whether there is respect for a living creature residing inside the heart or not. Listen to the voice. Is it harsh and demanding? Notice the tightness with which the hand is used. See how the animal responds to that one. If the animal is afraid, stay clear of such a person.

God wants his people to be kind and generous with those who work for them. The ox was allowed to eat whatever he needed of the grain as he worked. It kept him healthy and hard-working. Remember to be kind to those who help you too. Let that ox partake of the grain as he treads the mill that keeps you in bread!

February 6

ECCLESIASTES 11:3A

"If the clouds are full of rain, they will pour
out rain on earth …" HCSB

When we look to the horizon and the clouds are building with heavy darkness through them, we can assume there will be rain. Sooner or later. As they keep piling up over themselves, shooting upward in billowing spouts, getting darker and heavier looking, we can know it will be a big rain. While we need rain, there are sometimes when it gets to be too much for us and it's difficult to move around to do what is necessary.

In our lives it's that way too. It is not the rains that makes life harder. It is when the rains are overwhelming, bringing floods and hardship with it. It is when we are caught under them with no way out of the downpour that we cave to the pressure of living through them. So, I want to take a lesson from the rain and my own yard.

When there have been copious rains every day from a tropical storm, we chafe under the difficulties of maneuvering in them. But I look out at my yard that was almost dead a few weeks ago from a drought and now that those hard rains have let loose, the grass, the flowers and the shrubs are so lush and green. The blooms are coming and the leaves are proud, standing so full in the light wind of today. The very rains that were cumbersome to me is what gave them all new life. If there were no heavy, dark and ominous clouds, there would be no life in that yard.

It is the rain clouds of hardship, of difficulties and pain that bring the promise of the rainbow. God's promise that destruction is not the purpose of rain shows in the beauty of those colors that exist all the time in the heavens. We just can't see them without the rain clouds! Those very things are what God uses in our lives to give us strength for the next day, grace for today and joy in the morning. See your personal rainbow above your life. It is there whether you can see it or not. Take the storm and give it to our Lord. He can reveal your rainbow clearly.

February 7

"I perceived that whatever God does endures forever, nothing can be added to it, nor anything taken from it." ESV

Would that people would read and learn from these few words! When God has done it, it is finished. End of story. We try so hard to determine how to undo some of the things he has determined will be. We believe we know best and can decide what is truth and what is not. Oh my, we know so little in the grand scheme of life, but give ourselves a high grade for our ignorance!

We need to explore our world, our heavens and our own existence. There is nothing wrong with any of those choices to see just where we are, what's "out there" and why. The problem comes when we decide God has nothing to do with any of these. It would be good if we chose to start with God and proceed from there to explore all that God has done. We cannot add to it. It is finished. But God opens the mind of folks to look under the door, so to speak, to see behind the curtains that hide a fuller understanding of what he has done, what is really there in the glorious parts of his creation that make the whole.

Enjoy what you see, what you learn and what is still available to learn about this place we call earth and the beautiful, bountiful expanse over us. We have touched only the surface of it all. There is so much more to see, to learn. He wants us to know. But the greatest knowledge he wants for us is the knowledge of himself! Open your heart to know that God made it, finished it and said, "A job well done!"

February 8

ECCLESIASTES 11:1

"Cast your bread upon the waters; for you
will find it after many days." ESV

Have you ever stood on the edge of a beach and held something in
your hands that you let go of into the waters? It drifts away and it
is gone. But occasionally, that same item will drift back toward you
with the movement from a wave that turns it around and tosses it
toward you. On quiet waters, it will often return right away, sliding
on a ripple back to where you stand. If we are willing to let go of the
things God has graced us with in any given day, to ease it into the
streams of people that are before us, to share it with the ones drifting
along the shore, we also find that God pushes the grace back into
our hands from another source, from another's hand. As we share,
without thought of getting a return on our gift, we often do get
that reward. Not because we deserve it for the sharing but because
God is gracious. We don't share to receive. We share because we have
been shared with by someone else. As we have been given, so give to
others. God does not always return in like coin. Many times, it is in
a totally different coin. But a blessing it still is to us. When in need
ourselves, is a good time to be willing to share what you have with
another. Theoretically, it is always possible to divide any item.

There was a time early in our marriage, when I had a chicken
breast, a thigh and two drumsticks for lunch. There were the two
of us and our four year-old daughter, Alicia. A young man was
helping us with a project outside and Alicia asked if he could stay
for lunch too. Of course, I said yes, wondering how I would divide
those pieces of chicken. Somehow, I cut that breast into four pieces,
deboned the thigh, cut it in two and fried them all. Made mashed
potatoes to go with them. Believe it or not, we actually had one piece
left over, and no one went hungry. I don't know if the blessing was
for stretching the chicken or in filling the appetite to "full" before it

ran out! But we did cast our "bread," or chicken in this case, on the table before the three of us and our guest. It was wonderful! That young man died early in life. I am so glad we shared that one day, that one meal with that one man.

February 9

ECCLESIASTES 3:11A

"Yet God has made everything beautiful for its own time." NLT

What a good, an excellent job, God did when he made all things that were ever made. There is nothing without purpose and plan. When he surveyed his creation, he even said it was good! But good was not enough. Here he says through King Solomon that everything was beautiful too.

Let's look at this a few moments. As I look at pictures of the animals of the world, it is easy to see that God even had a sense of humor as he put them all together, each in the exact place he planned for them. Nothing was left to chance. Think about the kangaroo, the mouse, the snake, the worm or the giraffe, the elephant or the gorilla. What a hoot they each are in their habitat. And to each his own, they are beautiful to one another. And there are so many!

Then look at the flowers, whether a plant that flowers with huge blooms or a bush that springs forth in tiny, tiny buds. Even weeds often have the most wonderful flowers making them a beauty to behold when in the right place. He has made no mistake in any of these. He has brought forth their beauty and fragrance at the right time for each. Wild flowers shine all along the highways, planted by no hand of any human. They know where to sprout and bloom. They are hardy and strong to withstand the winds and rains that blow through them. They are all beautiful in their time.

Look at the humans around you and be amazed at the uniqueness of each. There are no two exactly alike. Even twins can have minute differences. Do you think God had a sense of humor here too? I do! It is great that he has said the animals, the flowers and the humans are different, but still beautiful, each in its own way and own time. His purpose is complete in all that he has done. He delights in all of his creation. We can do so too and praise him for the beauty of each. Rejoice with him today as you look around in wonder.

February 10

ECCLESIASTES 7:14

"In the day of prosperity be joyful, and in the day of adversity consider: God has made the one as well as the other ..." ESV

Everyone loves the day of prosperity. We all like to be on top! All enjoy the good things of life as we say. But that is not all of reality. There is more for man than just the easy way to go, the way of fulness and beauty.

Over the years, there have been some wonderful times on the farm when the crops were great, the price was good and the day of joy was there. It was fun and all enjoyed being able to have possessions we had not had for a while. That's the way it is on a farm. There are the really good crops and there are the crop failures too. We always said that farming was either feast or famine!

But the important words are that God made both, the feast and the famine! We can be assured that he is present at the table of both. He does not leave us when life gets really hard, nor does he forget his children when our very breath feels as if it is being pulled from us. He teaches us great beauty in every circumstance he leads us through. His heart is set on us and he desires for us to make it to the next step before us. Keep walking, dear friend. You are not alone.

February 11

ECCLESIASTES 5:4-5

"When you make a vow to God, don't delay fulfilling it, because
He does not delight in fools. Fulfill what you vow. Better that
you do not vow than that you vow and not fulfill it." HCSB

This is talking about your relationship with God. He is not impressed with your rash vows or your loud promises that are made without a second thought. He demands that you do what you say you will do!

But I would like to think in this same vein about our relationship with our children, our family. There are too many times when we rashly promise what we cannot do, or we vow what we have no intention of doing! We are careless with our families and do not follow through on the words we lay out to them. But we must remember, words have consequences for all.

Children, I am so sorry for the many times I disappointed each of you with words quickly spoken that I knew right away I couldn't deliver. Also, for the times when confronted with a conflict between a promise and an upcoming event, and I didn't know all I should have known before I spoke, I gave respect to the conflict and not to the family. It is the expectation that the family should give way to the conflict; that is wrong. We place them in second place behind others in our world. Please, forgive.

Today is a good time to straighten this out with your family too. You need their forgiveness. None of us is perfect. They don't expect perfection. But they do want honesty. If God doesn't take lightly the rash vow, neither do they.

February 12

ECCLESIASTES 4:9-10

"Two people are better off than one, for they can help each other succeed. If one person falls, the other can reach out and help." NLT

Loneliness is a terrible thing. Folks will do all sorts of foolish things when they are lonely. They will spend money, whether they have money or not. They will seek out another person, good for them or not, and make crazy choices. They will go places they wouldn't normally be caught in otherwise or hide at home for weeks on end, perpetuating the pain of loneliness. As I said, loneliness is a terrible thing!

The Word says that two together are better, for they have the opportunity to aid each other in hard times. If one falls, as we all do, the other can reach over to steady the one fallen or help to lift that one to a higher place. How important a family member or friend can be at such times. How important a spouse can be to the faltering partner. I know Jesus is always there with us. But it is so good to have that side by side one whose arms are there where they can be felt, that one whose heart is touched by the same feelings we are experiencing at that moment.

To fall and be totally alone is trouble indeed. How sad that it happens too often in life. When you see one who is weak and weary, when you realize there is not a person to aid in that case, God has earmarked you to touch that one with his arms and his heart to help as only you can. It is a divine appointment for you to meet. Be there as though Jesus were there, filling the need of the lonely for a friend. Don't walk away as though you're not aware. Step up and love as he has loved you.

February 13

ECCLESIASTES 3:11A

"He (God) has planted eternity in the human heart …" TLT

When we are young, we decide that the future is a long way off, too far for us to be concerned about it. We have to live long enough to learn that the future is really only around the corner. But even when we are thinking it is far down the road, around many bends that we can't see just yet, there is something way back in the recesses of our mind that speaks differently to us about this future.

Those thoughts occur once in a while that tell us there is a place, a distance from us that is more than we can imagine. We resist pondering on that future for a little time, but then, it creeps back to the front of our wonderings and we engage the idea of an eternity somewhere. It will slip in and out of our thoughts. It will come unbidden to the top of our mind and we take it out to examine just a little. Then, one of our friends or family will pass, whether old or young, and it comes back with a rush not to be put aside.

God has made certain that we all have those thoughts about eternity. He wants us to know there is more to this life than what we experience here. It will not be put away forever. He has planted it, firmly, way down deep so we have no excuse for deciding to foolishly waste this opportunity in this world to know him. He is our Creator and desires to have us be his in eternity also. Consider your Creator in the days of your youth before you have let so much of the joy of living in his love here slip over the horizon into old age.

February 14

ISAIAH 58:7

"Share your food with the hungry, and give shelter to the homeless. Give clothes to those who need them, and do not hide from relatives who need your help." NLT

When I was growing up, still living at home as a very young girl, I was always surprised at how my mother could turn a cabinet low on groceries into a supper for, not only our six, but also, for another family who needed extra food, whether eaten at our house or taken to their home after we ate. She seemed to always be able to stretch our meals to cover any who showed up at our table.

There was also room for others to spend the night, even if, the kids had to sleep on quilts on the floor to give our beds to the guests. And she never appeared to mind the extra ones at breakfast the next morning. There would just be two pans of biscuits to go with the eggs and bacon. Mother used to say that we farmers planted, worked the crops, gave God the first from that crop and he gave the increase. I think he increased our food on the table too!

Mother was quite the seamstress, making all of our clothes herself. So, she could make my dress and have enough material left over to make something for another kid too. Again, I was amazed at her resourcefulness. Of course, chicken feed sacks weren't the most expensive material in town either!

I remember relatives who came to our house occasionally to ask daddy for help. I don't remember him ever turning any of them away empty handed. It seemed that God blessed that and gave the increase there too. Friend, don't be afraid to divide your life's goodies with others. There will be enough for you and them. Trust God with your needs and share what he has given to you. Blessings will be yours. They may not always be in like kind, but there will be blessings to you or in your house; and when you clothe the poor, God notices and clothes you with splendor of pleasures…his pleasure.

February 15

HEBREWS 13:15-16

"Therefore, by him, let us continually offer the sacrifices of
praise to God, that is, the fruit of our lips, giving thanks
to His name. But do not forget to do good and to share,
for with such sacrifices God is well pleased." NKJV

The praise from our lips, the ability to do good to others, the willingness to share what God has given us daily, are all sacrifices we can
joyfully give to our God, even when we are facing crises in our daily
living. Here are a few things to remember when facing any crisis:

1. There is an end to it.
2. There is a purpose to it.
3. There is a limit to the circumstance. It cannot go beyond
   the limits God has set over it.

First of all, ask God about the purpose to this circumstance. Go
to the Word to see what he is saying to you. Look for Scriptures
that deal with life situations, asking the Holy Spirit to open your
mind and heart to receive his purpose. He does not take lightly your
struggles.

Second, remember that the Enemy cannot go beyond what God
has set for this. If you believe it is from the Enemy, draw near to God
and he will draw near to you (James 4:8). Submit to God, that is,
humble yourself. Resist the Devil and he will flee from you (James 4:7).

Third, start praising your God, for he is able to overcome in you
all the way to the end, and begin to do good and to share as you
offer the sacrifices of your lips and behavior. It will come to an end,
eventually, by God's design.

Last, think on these things: things that are true, noble, just, pure,
of good report, virtuous, praiseworthy (Philippians 4:8). Do not
let your mind run away with you, but go to him in diligent prayer
concerning your circumstances, knowing that he will never leave

you nor forsake you (Hebrews 13: 5b), but will see you through this. Trust the Lord of the universe…he cares for you (1Peter 5:7). Delight yourself in the Lord and he will give you the desires of your heart (Psalms 37:4). Most of the time the Enemy beats us between our ears (in our mind). Many times, it helps to have a close friend or family member who will pray with you and stand with you in the gap. Seek out that one and pray with all your hearts. Our God is able to walk all the way through this circumstance with us. Then, praise him with your lips, for he is well pleased with this.

February 16

"As one whom his mother comforts, so I will comfort you …" ESV

When I was a child, it was so easy to run to my mother when I was hurt, disappointed, distressed or fearful of what I could not see, but felt was there to bring pain to me. She was always the same, quietly holding me to still my frightened heart and with strong hands would run her fingers gently over my face and arms to sooth my tears. She was my tower of safety. She was my net to remove any unseen danger that she would scoop up into that net to cast it away.

My God is that way too. She was just a picture, a very small one at that, of who he was and what he could do to rescue me from the fears before me, the terrors behind. He loves infinitely more than she ever could. He is to be trusted far more than she was able as another human who makes mistakes. But she was a good picture of him, and his word shared more insight into who he is, was and evermore shall be as I learned at her feet about him.

In these few words, God shares his promise that he will comfort me in my world as I move in and out of the streets that I must walk here on my way to his plan for me. Thank you, Father, for these words of comfort themselves. You will not disappoint. You will be there as my world shakes and you will steady me as I go on unshaken into my future. Even in old age, I can trust your word to comfort me, when I am weary and sad, when my body betrays me with weakness and it is hard to stand up. His promise is for you too, friend. Trust it. You will be comforted!

February 17

JOSHUA 9:1A

"And it came to pass…" NKJV

How I love this phrase that is so often found in the Scriptures. It is God's promise to me that life moves on to accomplish God's plan. He will not be thwarted by man, beast or the Enemy. Thank you, Lord, for moving us closer to you through this space we call life.

There are disappointments, pains, sorrows and discouragements along the way. There are wondrous events and good days too. There are exciting times and sad times. But they are all in your timeline for all of us. You perfect us through each occasion you allow in our lives. How gracious you are to your creation.

Thank you, Lord, for "…it came to pass" that we are on our way to you through Jesus Christ. Your love is immeasurable and steadfast. Your promise is secure to us forever.

February 18

ISAIAH 5:20

"Woe to those who call evil good and good evil, who
put darkness for light and light for darkness, who
put bitter for sweet and sweet for bitter." ESV

How mixed up our world is getting when leaders and judges alike switch truth for a lie and turn the minds of people into a mush of never being able to sort the truth out from the lies. The sad part is that leaders on both sides of any idea do this with no regard for what is best for humans in the land. It is always about winning, not about being righteous. They desire to be what they call, "right," not righteous. And it doesn't matter whether you are to the right or the left!

God has pronounced judgment against those who do this. And how awful that judgment will be when he measures it out to each! Those of us who stand on the sidelines need to be concerned because we often receive the pain these leaders bring on themselves as the fallout spreads a long way! One thing we each can do is pray for our leaders diligently. Pay attention to the details of what is being said and recite them to the Lord God for him to take action on in his timing. Trust our God to deliver his people from the snares these in charge set for us. Look to him for wisdom on how to pray and how to live in these times where truth is denied.

We must be a part of God's plan to bring good leaders to the front. When you pray, make certain your sins are confessed and your life is in order. He wants us to be his shining light in this dark world. Darkness cannot abide when Light is present. Shine, folks, shine!

February 19

ISAIAH 55:10

"The rain and the snow come down from the heavens and stay
on the ground to water the earth. They cause the grain to grow,
producing seed for the farmer and bread for the hungry." NLT

When the rains are slow about coming from the heavens, we often resort to using our sprinklers and our well to make up for the lack. The last time we did this after a very long time with no rain, we were amazed that the grass turned green before our eyes as the water covered it with each succeeding round of the sprinkler head.

We realized anew just how dependent on water our earth is, not to mention our own dependency on it. It seemed that the flowers shimmied in delight as the water glistened on each leaf and bloom petal. They were so in need! And it took only a moment to position the hose and sprinkler, turn the well on and watch the life return. Our God is a Living Lord. He is the Living Water that covers us with his mercy and grace, his unfailing love that causes us to shimmy in delight as he gives new life to us. Only when he waters our soul with his Word can we grow into all he has created us to be. His Word is life to us. It reveals his plan to us and enlightens our brain with steps of obedience.

Let the Living Lord water your life today. You can become that seed that grows into his grain that feeds those around you with bread, the Living Bread of Life. He is ready to water you into vital, green shoots that can lift another onto a higher plain where they too can become all that God has created them to be. Be delighted in him and "shimmy" before your personal world for him with new life gained from his Living Word.

February 20

HOSEA 8:7A

"For they sow the wind, and they shall reap the whirlwind." ESV

When we are standing before our world, deciding just what we want to do with each day of the rest of our lives, we often make the choice to do as our desires dictate rather than choosing those things that are within the realm of God's best for us. We settle for less, thinking that its better than others think, wiser than many realize and more interesting than being caught in a boring life.

These people, who claimed to be God's children, had deserted him, were making idols from their silver and gold and were choosing those that they would serve under as leaders without even consulting their Lord. They could not understand they were building idols that would destroy them in time to come. They did not want to follow any rules from God. They wanted what they wanted, when they wanted it, how they wanted to have it, regardless of any possible consequences. They deliberately chose rebellion, spurned the good God would have had for them and called their creation "god." But the only God said, "It is not God!"

We cannot fool the Living God. We may think we have, and rush on into the wind. But when that wind we have sown becomes the whirlwind, we will falter and be laid waste by the very thing we have created to our destruction. Do not forsake your God. He will not let it slide. Repent quickly, today, and turn from rebelling. Choose to follow your God with a glad heart. It is not too late! Today is the day to start. It's always about choices, isn't it? Be wise. Choose obedience.

February 21

HABAKKUK 2:1A

"I will take my stand at my watch post and
station myself on the tower." ESV

The world you live in, the place you occupy, is your special place to be a watchman for those around you. It is your very own to be able to help because you have seen what is coming beyond the wall of today. You are one of those who can see over the wall at the enemies there. Many others cannot see. Their eyes are clouded and blinded by the sin within and the sin without. They need your sight!

There are many reasons why we choose to ignore those around and the sin beyond. We are too busy. They will not listen we think. We have our own to think about and care for each day. There is not enough time. I am too weak and not knowledgeable enough yet. Someday I will do what I know to do. Just not today.

But today is the only day you really have. There is no tomorrow; there is only today. You cannot change yesterday. You don't live there anymore, as I've told you before; remember? You can never enter tomorrow. It is an illusion that we desire and never reach. It is about choices. Oh my, how many times have I said that? So, my friend, you must choose today. Will you be the watchman for those who so desperately need your sight? Open your mouth and let God fill it with his warnings and encouragement for those who follow you. Leave a clear path and wise legacy for them to follow you. There is no other who can do what God has called you to do.

February 22

HEBREWS 12: 1-2A

"… Let us also lay aside every weight, and sin which clings so
closely, and let us run with endurance the race that is set before us,
looking to Jesus, the founder and finisher of our faith …" ESV

In this world in which we must sojourn and occupy until he calls
us home, there are sins, and heavy weights that make our progress
forward so very hard. If we are to move into the place of obedience
to our Lord, we must get rid of some things that pull us downward.
The writer of Hebrews shows us four things that need to happen for
us to be able to run this race successfully that is ours.

The first item on our "to get rid of list" is the weight that is too
heavy to bear. If we could just understand that sin is a millstone
around our necks so heavy that we lose the ability to walk, much less,
run this personal race. Sin brings a strong burden onto our shoulders
as we try to overcome what we've said or done, or by trying to hide
it from the eyes of others. We've all been there and done that! It can't
be done and that is a load indeed.

The second is the sins themselves that harbor pain, shame and
guilt, causing us to pull away from the very one who could make a
difference in this…our Savior. We find them clinging to us, wrap-
ping around our legs, our minds, our hearts, pulling us with a weight
that drowns us in self-pity at our weakness. But the Savior continues
to wait for us to turn back to him.

But the answer is in the third and fourth items that belong on a
separate list: the one for victory. If we would be victors instead of victims, we must run with endurance, keeping our eyes on Jesus, who
is the beginner and the ender of our faith. We cannot be continually
looking back at the trail we've left behind. Nor can we let our gaze
ramble around from side to side, being distracted by everything the
world and the Enemy will place in our path. Neither the world nor
the Devil want us to be overcomers in this life! But our Jesus does

and has made a way for that to be ours. Our part is the endurance and the eyes. They are to be that which keep us on the right track, the straight and narrow and on the goal before us: our Lord waiting at the end of the race. Look on to the goal. Run, believer, run! And when you think you can't run anymore, run, run and look up. He is there, drawing you on to the victory that's waiting.

February 23

JAMES 4:8

"Draw near to God and he will draw near to you." HCSB

In an earlier verse, James reminds us to submit to God and to resist the Devil. Those are some very powerful words. Understand that we cannot live a fruitful life if we keep insisting on our way of everything. God is very certain about how he feels on the idea of pride. He will not tolerate it for long! There are two wonderful promises in these few words though.

The first is, when we draw near to him, he will draw near to us. To know that the Almighty God, the Creator of all that exists, the Master of all is willing to come even a little closer to me is amazing. Me, a sinful creature who is careless so much of my time. Too often I am one who sits in life turning all things toward myself where possible. But he says to submit to him, draw near and he will meet me where I am, as I bow to his authority over me. But we don't like being subject to anything or anyone, do we? Surrender is a bad word for most of us. But it is the price of being close to our Father.

How can we draw close to him? We can start by seeing what his word shares with us about his nature, his character and strive to be more like our Father. We can hide his words deep in our minds and hearts to be able to bring them out to encourage us, to strengthen us and to make us more as he is. We can seek out a fellow believer who will stand with us as we move to follow his words here. We can kneel to listen to God as we pour out our need before his throne on grace.

The second promise is that when we resist the Devil, he will flee from us. What a promise! Like a soldier of the cross, we must resist his advances toward us. Take the field of battle and pray for God's way out of the Devil's pull. Stand firm, with the Sword of the Spirit at your call. Do not turn your back on this Devil. Face him with the assurance that God will fight the battle if we give him the opportunity by submitting to him swiftly. Submit, resist and draw near. Simple, true battle cries. It is always about a choice. Choose wisely, dear children.

February 24

HEBREWS 13:3

"Remember the prisoners, as though you were in
prison with them, and the mistreated, as though
you yourselves were suffering bodily." HCSB

What it means to have empathy for another: When a dear friend of ours called with the news of the death of her grandson, it was devastating to her, of course. But what I felt was not sympathy for her pain. It was empathy because we too, had experienced the death of our young baby many, many years ago.

It was not the same as hers, but it was immediately the remembrances of that time in my life. The shock, the breath stopping pain, the unbelievable desire for it not to be true. What I felt that day was the memory of my own pain…that's empathy! The writer of Hebrews says to feel as though you were there as the one experiencing that hurt, that same pain.

When you are the one called on to be with a friend or family member who has just received such hurt in their life, think as though you are there in the same experience that day, that the difficulty is yours, not just that one's. You are needed. Be there for them, because sometimes life hurts!

February 25

ISAIAH 1:7

"The whole earth is at rest, and it is quiet;
they break forth into singing." KJV

In my "yesterday" there was a storm. It was not a big one, particularly. Although there was some damage done! There will be bigger ones I'm certain. That's the way life comes, isn't it? But today it is quiet in my personal world, the place where I must walk each day.

Thank God for the in between times that get quiet! They give us a time to breathe, to stay still and be glad. These short breathers give time to recuperate from the stress of the yesterday's storm. The quietness gives us a space to replenish our strength. Quietness is good for a time!

So, take time this morning to breathe. Sit for a spell, as my mother used to say. Have a nice simple lunch at noon and enjoy the stillness. This afternoon, replenish your strength with a nap and start the evening with rejoicing. Be glad that all storms end sooner or later.

Then, when tomorrow is today, move into it with gladness, singing your praises to our gracious God. He did not leave you by yourself even in the quietness. He was there all the time. We have the quiet and we have the storms. That too, is the way life comes. Accept the storms and enjoy the respite of the in between times of quiet. That too, is God's plan. Press on, child, press on!

February 26

"For the earth will be filled with the knowledge of the
glory of the Lord as the waters cover the sea." ESV

One day, this will be. One day he will have the earth covered, completely, with his glory and all will know that he is the Lord. There will be no one who does not know. How we as believers in him long for this day. But, until then, we must occupy this fallen world and be a reflection of his glory to those around us. But how can we be this light of God's glory here?

Let's think for a moment. Everyday your life intersects with those around you whether you want it to or not! You have a world of influence before you in each and every day. Again, whether you want it to be so or not. There are little eyes that see you and your actions. There are small ears who listen to the words that pour from your mouth like an ever-flowing stream. There are those who follow in your steps, close on your heels to be just like you!

Therefore, there is a choice we must make in every moment of every day. Will I be a stream of life-giving water? Will I be a strong tower for those who are fearful to run to that the power of the Lord may each them with peace? Will I be a broad shoulder to lean on for those who are in great pain? Will I be a food vendor with the Bread of Life in my hands to share that Good News? Will I be a channel of his blessings to others? Choose wisely. But choose today.

February 27

HOSEA 14:1,2B

"O Israel, return to the Lord your God, for you have
stumbled because of your iniquity; say to Him, 'Take
away all iniquity; receive us graciously, for we
will offer the sacrifices of our lips.'" NKJV

These words were written to the nation of Israel, but they apply to us as well. Iniquity is an old- time word for a real-time problem: sin! When we choose to sin, and yes, we do choose it, we need to return to the Lord and agree with him it was sin. His forgiveness is available but we must return.

Then we have the opportunity to give him the sacrifices of our lips, that is, our praises. You will notice that word is plural! God is so gracious to his children every day. He forgives, he restores and he loves with a forever love. He lifts us above our sins, out of the deep pits we dig for ourselves repeatedly. He sets our feet firmly on a higher plain with a hope that fills us with joy. He walks with us through the daily routines of life and through the storms that roll over us. He is forever there regardless of our circumstances or choices. While it grieves his Holy Spirit when we fail, it does not remove that Holy Spirit. What grace! What love!

Take a few minutes today to make a list of his kindnesses to you. Fill it with all the times he has been there for you and with you. Add the occasions when he kept you from harm. And take note of the grace he has spread over you again and again. Then make the sacrifices of your lips by sharing all those with the ones around you who need to know of his mercies. He has never failed me and he will never fail you. You are his child through Jesus his Son. He loves you and this mama loves you too!

February 28

HAGGAI 1:7

"Thus says the Lord of hosts: Consider your ways." ESV

What a somber set of words for God's people to hear. "Consider our ways." If we are to do this, what are we to do? Just what does it mean to take time to consider? I have thought about this and decided that is just what I am to do, to take time. To think deeply, to observe, to deliberate over my ways of doing things, to see where my priorities lie as I make choices for my life is my idea of considering my ways.

I believe it is good to set aside a time to reflect, to come to any conclusion that will lead me to make any changes that need to be made. Therefore, I cannot do this on the fly or when I am pressed for time with the things that have taken up my life. That in itself might be a reason why I need to consider my ways! It is too easy to let things get in my way that usurp the importance of real life, life lived to its fullest.

What are some of these "things"? It is going about without any follow through on what is stealing my time away. It is spending the morning without purpose or planning. It is going where others have planned for me to go. It is slipping in and out of my day without consulting my God about any of it. It is looking at my clock after the day is over and realizing there was nothing meaningful in it.

Basically, it is about making choices that are about the calling God has on my life first, not after the fact of time lost. It is looking for God's divine appointments he's scheduled into my day as they appear, not when they have passed me by and I know later it was an opportunity missed. God wants his family to think about him first and his choices he's laid before you. Take caution, my fellow believer. When the day is being planned, there must be room in it for him. It is always about choices, isn't it? Consider before you choose. Thus says the Lord of hosts, Consider your ways. While there is still time to make a difference. Time is lost one moment at a time. It is also lived one moment at a time. Redeem the time!

February 29

HOSEA 14:9

"Who is wise? Let him understand these things. Who is prudent?
Let him know them. For the ways of the Lord are right;
the righteous walk in them, but transgressors stumble in them." NJKV

The world talks of wisdom and prudence. It remarks that those of the world are both. But they do not want to listen to the words of the Lord or walk in his ways. They raise a tone of righteousness that they think is good and wise, but they have no real idea of what either is. This world is blinded by the Enemy who wants all to perish. That old devil is ranting and roaring around looking for any who think they are wise and don't take the word of the Lord seriously.

It is time for those of us who call ourselves believers, who hold to the Lord's words as life, to start matching our words of righteousness with deeds of righteousness. It is not enough to say we follow in his ways. We must show the way of obedience to the lost world. They will not hear unless we speak with the love with which the Savior wooed us. When we tell of God's love, we must reveal that love in us for those around who need it.

Speak today to those you love, and to those whom you have the opportunity, about God's great love for his creation. He desires that all should be saved. You can be the instrument of his peace to those with whom you walk daily. Choose to be that chosen vessel of truth, of love and peace with God. He will use you if you will make yourself available to him. Be wise and be prudent.

March 1

HAGGAI 2:4

"'Yet now be strong, Zerubbabel,' says the Lord; 'and be
strong, Joshua,' … the high priest; 'and be strong, all
you people of the land,' says the Lord, 'and work: for
I am with you, says the Lord of hosts.'" NKJV

The time had come for Zerubbabel, the leader of this group of the
people of the Lord, along with Joshua, the high priest, to begin
to rebuild the temple of the Lord. There was much to discourage
them, enemies that were against this rebuilding. There will always
be enemies against the Lord's people. There will always be work to
do, sometimes more than we think we can do. But God tells them to
work for he is with them. He commands them not to fear, but to be
strong. He repeats those words, to be strong! The phrase that God is
with them is so important in this setting of a job too big for a small
group of folks.

What do you do when you feel unable to do what's right in front
of you that you know you must do? Do you take a nap? Do you drive
away to somewhere else to keep from looking at the task? Do you
stop and lay out all the reasons why it can't be done? Do you think
through the project and lay it aside to mull it over for a few days? Just
what do you do? Where do you go for enlightenment?

God sent his prophet, Haggai, to these two leaders with God's
message for his people. The message was clear; it was short. '' I am
with you!" was the Lord's declaration! When God says it, it's a good
thing to listen and respond in obedience to that declaration. God
is with his people in every generation. As the people of God, we
need to be praying for our leaders, both political and spiritual. Begin
today to pray God's wisdom in each. Pray without ceasing.

March 2

HEBREWS 11:40A

"God, having provided some better thing for us …" NKJV

The writer of Hebrews has just spent many verses about faith here through the "Roll Call of Faith", the list of men and women who came before who had not seen the coming promise of the Messiah. Many had even died for that faith in the promise. God was giving the current believers the opportunity to know they could trust what the early witnesses had stood and died for before them. He was sure to give what was necessary to make it understandable for them also to stand on the certainly of that promise. And earthly lesson for me to learn.

I have a magnolia garden filled with roses all around the stately magnolia. Sometimes I get behind with my weeding. One day I did not get finished with my weeding. I was willing. I was able with the God-given strength and tools to do it. But as I advanced around the north end of this area, I ran into a huge ant bed under the heavy grass & weeds. The big man (the husband) came and put the ant poison on the offending bed. Therefore, I had to give it time to die. Thank God for the ant bed! You gave me the ability to do this, but you showed me there was a good reason to back off and give the ants time to move. You know they never really die; they just move over! I had no idea they were there. I had the belief that I was on the verge of finishing what was before me that day. My faith was still intact. But I had met a deterrent to my faith. The wave of ants was definitely a deterrent! But I also realized that I could wait a time and come back to this project. I could live to fight another day, or pull weeds without ants another day. They will pass as they run from the poison. And I can rest and regroup as I wait. I believe that God often gives us a reprieve from the task at hand as he makes a better thing for us. He does not mean we must never go back and finish it. He means, we are to come away and rest to regain strength and desire. We can spend time with him to do this. Did we do everything we planned? Did we do it all? No. But when we lie down that night, we can know, whether we finished every task or not, that we have done what we could, when and where we could, for whom we could. And that God has given meaning to that day because of it. Life is not lived in one day. That's how it comes and it is a moment by moment occurrence when it comes. But the big man and I had some extra moments together, a special treat we would not have had without the ants being in my way. Thank God for the ants and the wisdom to walk away when it was wise to do so. I was given the better thing for that one time. Jesus is our "Better." Don't let the "ants of life" distract you from the "Better" thing!

March 3

ISAIAH 35:1

"The wilderness and the solitary place shall be glad for them;
and the desert shall rejoice, and blossom like the rose." NKJV

Restoration is a beautiful thing for humans to witness. And when God restores all his people, all nature will rejoice and be glad. The wilderness and the lonely places will be filled with contentment and laughter. What a day that will be!

This morning at eight a.m. I was in the yard finishing that magnolia garden. Those ants were half dead. The top of the hill was gone but they were tenacious, because the whole bottom was lively and mean. But that was not a deterrent to me and my trusty hoe now. I backed up a little and swung the sharp hoe with all my strength. With two swings, it lifted that bottom of the ant hill slap out of the ground. It was nestled in a huge clump of crab grass that was holding it together. It looked as if the whole earth had come to life as they scrambled up. On yes, I did get four or five bites, but I was victorious over those bad ants. I was "badder"! The big man (husband) came home from breakfast abroad (restaurant) and retreated them. He was the "baddest"!

And then I stood back and admired my garden that God had created when he made all the beautiful plants and flowers, and gave me the desire and willingness to put it together. He plans work for us to do and for us to enjoy what we see develop from that work. The roses were still wet with dew, the Magnolia was shiny from the sun spilling over the tree tops and the mulch was renewed with my hoeing it around as I cleaned the area. There was a tiny green frog settled down in one of the roses hidden from view unless you were right on top of the petals peeking close. I let him be and went to my other rose garden to disbud them. There was another little green frog there in a rose too. Nature is amazing! But one day our God will draw his special people back together according to his plan, purpose and promise. And how the earth will rejoice then! The places of seemingly nothingness will sprout and blossom. Oh, my. Until then, I choose to rejoice and be glad in this one day, my only day and wait expectantly for his promises to be fulfilled in his perfect timing. And I sing, to myself you'll be glad to know, the praises of my Father and his Son. Come sing with me too. You can sing out loud.

March 4

GENESIS 39:2-3A

"The Lord was with Joseph, and he was a successful man;
and he was in the house of his master the Egyptian. And
his master saw that the Lord was with him and the Lord
made all he did to prosper in his hand." NKJV

The young man, Joseph, was a bought slave to his master the Egyptian. There was really nothing he had and nothing he did that was of his own choosing. Everything he had was owned by his master and he received only what his master was willing to give him. He was "owned" by another human being. That was not a great place to be: a slave in a foreign country! Life definitely was not fair nor to nice to Joseph.

Notice how Joseph responds to his situation. He does not berate the master. He does not disobey him either. He does not try to flee his surroundings even once. He does do as a man who trusted his God to be with him in the place where he was not in control of the slightest part of his life. He was a successful man in spite of his circumstances. He lived as though he were a free man. And he was in his heart. He did have some choices. He could be obedient or not. He could receive his food or not. He could dress as he was given clothes to wear or desire more in his heart, making himself discontented. It wouldn't have given him anything any different!

But the word says the Lord was with him inside of his personal set of circumstances. He was still a slave; he was still not free. He still had to wear the clothes, and eat the food that was given to him by another. But with God there beside him, he chose to be what he should have been: an obedient slave. The result of his behavior? His master saw that the Lord was there with him. He realized that Joseph's God made him to prosper regardless of where and how he was.

Joseph found favor in the eyes of his master. How different our lives could be if we learned Joseph's lessons! He chose to be who he was, a believer in the one true God wherever his God had allowed him to be. He trusted God with everything about himself, his food, his condition, his clothes, his very life. He became the best slave his master could have. And God honored his life. Thank God we don't have legal slavery anymore. So, give your circumstances over into the hand of the Lord. He will be with you wherever you must be.

March 5

HABAKKUK 2:4

"Behold, his soul is puffed up, it is not upright within him, but the righteous shall live by faith." ESV

The Lord is so clear here about how he feels about pride! It is a magnet that draws the foolish into a net that embroils them with strong binds that are hard to break. As long as we see ourselves as the benefactor of our greatness and possessions, the creator of it all, we are filled with pride. Remember that the Lord hates pride and will humble the prideful. We don't want to be in that position.

Instead, we are to live by our faith in the God who did create us, the God who gave us life, who upholds us every day, the God who loves us now and loved us first! He is the center of our universe. He is the One we follow because he is trustworthy and leads us to his green pastures to feed, who takes us to the still waters to drink that we may be filled with his joy no matter what we encounter along the way he leads.

Our faith is to remain strong whether we can see the depths of the water before us or whether we can know the green grass of his pleasure is just over the hill, or not. Faith is not about seeing. It is about believing. It is about trusting even though the way seems dark and we halt before the road that leads around the bend. He is just beyond that bend. He bids us come around the bend to see his hand extended for us. In those moments when we can't see, trust and advance to him.

March 6

MATTHEW 11:28-29

"Come to Me, all you who labor and are heavy laden, and I will
give you rest. Take My yoke upon you and learn from Me, for
I am gentle and lowly in heart, and you will find rest for your
souls, For My yoke is easy and My burden is light." NKJV

The invitation that Jesus offers for us is for all mankind. It is for the
believer and for the lost too. He calls us to come to him for the much-
needed rest that we all hunger to have. He knows how difficult it is
to walk the roads in this fallen world. He knows our frailties, our
weaknesses. He knows and cares.

Jesus gives us two thoughts in this invitation. First, is a command to, "Take" his yoke on ourselves. This part we must do each
day. We must reach out and choose to take up his way of living this
one day to give glory to our Father. It is always about a choice, isn't
it?

The second is to realize we can learn from him, for he is a gentle
teacher and meek in heart. That is, he has a quiet strength to do his
Father's will. To learn is a process. It does not happen in one day or
one year. It is a continuous process in every day for all of our lives.

And lastly, he reminds us that his yoke is easy and his burden
light. When the lead ox is in control, he bears the heavier burden
forward to the goal. We are the weaker of the two "oxen" pulling life
toward our goal. Let Jesus bear the heavier load as he leads us onward.
Take his yoke and let him teach us, lead us to holiness and purity that
we may glorify our Father too.

March 7

GAL. 5:16

"… I say then, Walk in the Spirit, and you shall not fulfill the lust of the flesh." NKJV

Once, when I had my annual physical a few years back, my doctor asked me if I walked or not, to which I answered quickly, "Of course, from the house to the car, and then back from the car to the house!" I was rather proud of myself for being so quick-witted with my answer. Since then I have thought so many times about that funny answer. I really think that sometimes we think we can pull a funny on our God about this walking in the Spirit-thing. We try to believe that a short distance "in the Spirit" takes care of our spiritual growth, just as we think a short distance walking to and from a car is going to make us healthier. Neither one will work, will it? We miss the idea that "Walking in the Spirit" is a continual movement of my will. And it is only that kind of walking that will enable me to keep from fulfilling the lust of the flesh.

The lust of the flesh is ever ready to slip into my daily walk and cause me to slip into old patterns of living that are not to be my way anymore. But, if I walk in the Spirit daily, the fruit of the Spirit is developed in my life by the power of the Spirit making it possible for others to see Jesus in the way I behave. You see, It's really not about me anymore…it's all about him, Jesus. Walk a mile in his shoes today and then get up and walk a block or two for our earthy bodies. Doing that day after day will improve both our body and our spiritual lives…all to his glory and our good.

March 8

GENESIS 29:15B, 18, 20

"Then Laban (Jacob's uncle) said to Jacob…'What should your wages be?' … Jacob oved Rachel; and he said, 'I will serve you seven years for Rachel, your younger daughter' … So Jacob served seven years for Rachel, and they seemed but a few days to him because of the love he had for her." NKJV

What a love story; what a man filled with passion for the woman of his choice. Jacob was willing, even anxious to serve the length of time he himself suggested for the beautiful Rachel. It was but a few days in his sight. The work was hard, the weather was unpredictable, hot at times and cold at others. The animals were difficult to tend to, but he was willing. And. even though Jacob received Rachel at the end of the wedding week, Laban had fooled him by giving the older sister, Leah, to him first. The only way he did get Rachel was to work an extra seven years for her. Fourteen years he worked for his love. Think those second seven were easier than the first? I doubt it. But he was willing! Fellows, I want you to know what a blessing it is to have a man who is willing to do whatever is necessary to have the woman he has chosen.

Big Buck has served me for over sixty years now. I know how he feels about me because he tells me often. Now, I admit I sometimes must translate what it is he's trying to say to hear the words of love! Every time he fills my car up with gas, or when he shows up with a sandwich for lunch out of the blue, or still tries to cover me up at night when he thinks I am cold, I realize he is saying words of love. You see, all these sixty plus years I have never had to put gas in my car. I know how to do this for myself. But this is one thing he likes to do for me! And, best of all, is when he looks at me across the room and I see the look that says, "Let's vacate this party and be alone." I still see that same look of adoration he had at eighteen! He has never acted as thought the years have been hard. Yet, I know some of them were. I believe that he would feel they were as but a few days. That's real love! Thank you, Buck, for showing your love as Jacob did his love for Rachel with a willing heart to pay any price for her. Let your love know you would be willing to pay any price for her too!

March 9

JOSHUA 1:9B

"Have I not commanded you? Be strong and of good
courage; do not be afraid, nor be dismayed, for the Lord
your God is with you wherever you go." NKJV

The children of Israel had been in the wilderness for forty years and
were on the edge of the Jordan River at the opening of the Promised
Land. There were enemies there, big ones! There was the unknown
there before them. But God has said to cross that river! He has said
that he has given that land to them, regardless of who occupied it at
this time.

For the third time, he has said, "do not fear; be courageous; be
strong." There was a continuation of God's purpose for them. Moses
was gone, but God was not! This was a certain possession to them.
This was God's exact place he had promised to them. There was a
conquering power that was theirs through his power, for he had
promised to be with them. God is able! It is our responsibility to
respond in faith to his command.

Notice: Joshua was afraid. He was weak here too. He needed this
encouragement. Just as we so often do. God reminds him that he is
to live by God's word, the Book of the Law and is to keep it before
the people as well. God didn't require Joshua to deny his fear. He
simply commanded him to fear no more because he would be with
Joshua.

We too, are to conquer our Canaan. We are not to wander in our
wilderness forever! Yes, there are enemies and there are giants. Yes,
there are unknowns to you there. But those are not unknown to our
God. He knows it all and has promised to never leave us nor forsake
us. Arise, folks, and cross your river!

March 10

GENESIS 24:1

"Now Abraham was old, well advanced in age; and the
Lord had blessed Abraham in all things." NKJV

It is upon me, whether I think it should be or not, this "age" thing! I am continually amazed at how quickly it happened. But age brings an opportunity to take stock of my life, a moment to look over those wonderful blessings that God has given to the two of us. It is too easy to forget when we stay so very busy with the everyday sort of things. The beauty of his kindness is lost among the laundry, the food prep, the yard weeding, the trimming of hedges, the cleaning of the garage or barn, the…well, you get the idea.

Today would be a great day for you to look at the days of yesterday and be surprised at how far the Lord has taken you into his presence in priceless times of pleasure and in the extreme times of exhaustion and pain. See where the Lord is to be praised and where he is to be thanked. He is faithful whether you always realize it or not. When you couldn't find him, he was still there! When you thought you were abandoned, he was holding you above the darkness.

For us, praises are there when God stood by us in loss, in crops that weren't great, in times of desires being fulfilled and when they were left empty. He was there when the second and third daughters were born after the death of the first daughter. He was there when we saw our last daughter and only son for the first time and he let us know instantly they all belonged to us. They were ours for a lifetime. He was still there at the gravesides of those we loved.

He will never leave you nor forsake you. He is faithful. Mama knows. He has been faithful to me!

March 11

1 THESSALONIANS 5:24

"Faithful is he that calleth you, who also will do it." KJV

Along about Thursday I begin to look forward to the end of the week I am living in as I work in the yard to do away with all those weeds that just keep reappearing all the time. I usually weed early in the morning when I am fresh, or at least, more so than later in the afternoon. That's when I try to "empty my ocean with my bucket" as I tell the kids. The weeds are relentless, but I am just as determined to destroy every single one of them, no matter how often they sprout back. I just have to keep at it. I'm often out there in the yard before 7:30 in the morning as the hot sun does me in as it starts raising the heat about ten o'clock.

Tomorrow I want to be finished. After all, it will be Friday and the end of a work week. But I begin to think about how tired I will be by the time I get anywhere near being finished with my ocean. I wonder how I will make it. I being to wilt in the ocean before me. And it's just Thursday! My mind begins to play on my feelings. My thoughts begin to betray me. I begin to believe that I must quit and wait for Monday to start over. I realize I am making provisions for my flesh, in advance! I begin to make excuses for myself. I talk myself into choosing to throw my bucket into the garage for Monday, another day, any other day but today.

That's when I begin to think how grateful I am that God doesn't give up on me so fast. In fact, he doesn't give on me at all. He is always faithful, always there, always lifting, always holding out his hand, always leading us onward to his goal for us. He never slips, never sleeps, is never too busy to hear our heart cry or to take time for each of us. What love, what endurance, what patience, what mercy and grace. And tomorrow, if you give me tomorrow, I will start my day with you. And when you have given me strength for my day, I will go out to my magnolia and rose garden to weed those "growth-to me-given-from-your- hand" pesky little weeds. I will con-tinue to "empty my ocean with a bucket because I will keep at it until my day is gone." Thank you, Lord.

March 12

GALATIANS 6:1

"Brothers, if someone is caught in any wrongdoing, you who are
spiritual should restore such a person with a gentle spirit, watching
out for yourselves so you also won't be tempted." HCSB

Oh, my friends, how I wish those who deem themselves watchdogs
over the rest of the fellowship could grasp what is being said here!
Too often I see our fellow believers being attacked by others in the
name of correction.

Anytime we see our friends who name the name of Jesus as Lord
making a serious mistake or even a deliberate choice to sin, before
we decide to go into correction mode of them, may we stop and
remember that could have been us! None of us are without sin. May
we keep an attitude of gentleness toward them as we use words of
correction with a grain of tenderness and a whopping mess of love as
we try to aid and not destroy a weak child of God.

May we reach out in mercy to touch those who have fallen into
sin and keep our eyes on Jesus as we move toward them with grace
and strength. May we be the breath of fresh air that helps our fellow
sojourners in this walk to become overcomers. May we lift their eyes
to the Lord and aim at restoration of them to the straight and narrow.
They are worthy of our time and care. Never let pride or judgment
stop us from ministering. After all, God has touched us with his
mercy, grace and love! Pass it on!!

March 13

GENESIS 2:15

"The Lord God placed the man in the Garden of
Eden to tend it and watch over it." TLT

When our grandson, Nicholas, was about ten-years-old, he and I were in our backyard looking at the flowers. As we moved a little away from the house, we realized there were two young does approaching us coming from the nearby pasture. They seemed oblivious to our presence. I quickly and quietly told him to stop, to stay perfectly still. The deer kept moving toward us, slowly moving their heads back and forth to watch for danger. The larger one came to a stop, but the smaller doe walked up to Nicholas and stopped. As he reached out his hand slowly toward her head, she did not move away, but came closer to him. He touched her neck and then her ear. Still she did not run away. She edged closer to him, smelling a human's scent but unafraid. His hand moved down her shoulder and the other deer began to walk away. Of course, she followed.

Both young does walked through my flowers eating the tops as they went. They were probably the ones who ate my peas in the garden! Our son's girls came out slowly to watch this unusual event. The little deer jumped the fence of their pasture, eating their way down the fence line. Nicholas easily followed the two. The grand-daughters were amazed as the deer walked right up to them by the fence and the one allowed the girls to touch her too. They "played with" the kids for over an hour before they escaped to the big pasture.

What a place Eden would have been! All of God's creation living in harmony. One more time we had the opportunity to see God's handiwork as it was meant to be…in peace. One day he will return to restore his wonders. But today we saw the beauty of his glory in a never-to-be-forgotten way.

March 14

GENESIS 2:23A-24

"And Adam said, 'This is now bone of my bone, and flesh of my flesh … Therefore, shall a man leave his father and mother, and shall cleave to his wife; and they shall be one flesh.'" KJV

What is it like to married forever? Here are some of my thoughts about our relationship:

For every tear, there has been laughter.
For every fear, there has been strength.
For every argument, there has been resolution.
For every frown, there has been a smile.
For every sickness, there has been medicine.
For every lost sock, there has been found humor.
For every parting there has been meeting.
For every pain, there has been purpose.
For every sorrow, there has been tomorrow,
For every brokenness, there has been wholeness.
For every bitterness, there has been sweetness.
For every difficulty, there has been understanding.
For every hardness, there has been softness.
For every soup, there has been crackers.
For every bread, there has been butter.
For every dream, there has been reality.
For every wound, there has been healing.
For every hurt, there has been help.
For every tear, there has been thread.
For every loneliness, there has been friendship.
For every sadness, there has been joy.
For every emptiness, there has been fullness.
For every birthday, there has been cake.
For every meal, there has been enough.
For every cup, there has been tea.

For every thought, there has been expression.
For every chill, there has been warmth.
For every frost, there has been flowers.
For every dark night, there has been morning.
Thank you, my love, for it all.
Lesson learned: perseverance, people!

March 15

JAMES 1:5

"If any of you lacks wisdom, let him ask God, who gives generously
to all without reproach, and it will be given to him." ESV

All of us need wisdom, far more than we think we do. It would be wise in itself if we took these words of instruction to heart! Our God has plainly said that we can have it, have all we need of it and he won't even mind giving it to us. How much more could we want?

So, what keeps us from asking our God for wisdom? Could it be because we already think we are smart and don't really need wisdom to go with that? Smartness does not wisdom make! Or perhaps it is that we have found no reason to look for it in the life we've chosen for ourselves? We may believe we have it all and need nothing more. Maybe it's because we are deceiving ourselves with not knowing what others really think about us or see in our lives. We may be under the impression that other folks think we are very special! I am quite certain most folks don't think too much about us period. They may wonder why we did or chose a way to go that seemed foolish to them. They may believe that we just don't know any better and should be pitied.

But whatever the reason, we need to reconsider this verse. We have the opportunity to ask our All Mighty God, who created the universe and us, for wisdom for a whole lifetime of living in a world that makes wisdom a necessity. We need it. He offers it. We may have it just for the asking. So, what's your problem? Ask!! And believe him when he says it's yours!

March 16

"In the thirtieth year, in the fourth month, on the fifth day of the month, while I was among the exiles by the Chebar Canal, the heavens opened and I saw visions of God. On the fifth day of the month—it was the fifth year of King Jehoiachin's exile—the word of the Lord came directly to Ezekiel the priest, the son of Buzi, in the land of the Chaldeans by the Chebar Canal. And the Lord's hand was on him there." HCSB

It strikes me just how exact our God was in preparing his word to make certain we can trust him with the things we have to be concerned about. Look at the list of precise information here for us: It happened, it was the thirtieth year, it was in the fifth day of the month, Ezekiel was among the exile captives by the Chebar Canal when the heavens were opened to him and he saw visions of God. In case you didn't catch it so far, there is more! It was the fifth year of King Jehoiachin's captivity. The word of the Lord came to Ezekiel, the priest, the son of Buzi, in the land of the Chaldeans. And it was there that the hand of the Lord was upon him!

Knowing that God keeps such perfect records, aware of everything going on around his chosen, from the place to the leadership to the year and month, as well as the day, makes me know I need not think I can fool him or trick him with anything I try to get away with in my life! He knows me, my actions, my thoughts, my beliefs, my everything. I might as well begin to be totally honest with him and open my heart, mind and body to him just as he opened the heavens to his prophet.

It would be wise of you also to stop trying to blow by God and instead, stand before him in submission for his will to be carried out in your personal being. He misses nothing. He knows you are a sinner, but he also keeps it recorded that you have accepted his Son Jesus for the sacrifice he made just for you. And with that is the blessed thought that we belong to him by the blood of the Lamb of God. Safe, secure and as surely as Ezekiel did, we have the Lord's hand upon us as we follow him all the way. Today is the day of redemption.

March 17

EXODUS 2:2-10 (CONDENSED) NKJV

"…the woman conceived and bore a son…she saw he… was a
beautiful child, and hid him three months…when she could no
longer hide him, she took an ark… put the child in… and laid
it in the reeds by the river's bank. And his sister stood afar off…
the daughter of Pharaoh came…her maidens walked along…the
river's side… and when she saw the ark, sent her maid to get
it… she… opened it…and the baby wept…his sister said, 'Shall
I call a nurse from the Hebrew women… (to) nurse the child for
you…the maiden went and called the child's mother…So the
woman took the child and nursed him. And the child grew, and
she brought him to Pharaoh's daughter, and he became her son."

Several things to notice here. You know the background of Moses.
Pharaoh had ordered all male babies killed, fearing the increase in
the numbers of the Hebrews. But God's plan would not be thwarted.
It's interesting to see that the baby's own mother always remained his
mother, doing the things mothers do to bring up babies. But God
gave this baby an " extra" place to be nurtured too where he would
learn everything he need to know to be prepared for God's future for
him. His sister also remained his sister, able to help with the baby
and interact within the intimate family circle.

But the time came when Moses became another's son too. We are
forever grateful for the way God put our immediate family together,
but we are also aware and grateful of the way He brought so many
"others" into our family circle, some to prepare for another part of
their future, all of them to receive an extra measure of his love and
nurturing, not to imply that anything lacked in their "real" family.
Moses' mother took care of everything he needed for life, but God
knew his plan for Moses. God has allowed us to have many children
of all ages into our "real" family to love, to care for, to laugh with,
to pray with and over, and to challenge, to warn, to smile with and
at, to pray for and with, to stand with at graduations, weddings and
funerals, to hold their babies and have them grow to call Buck and

me "Mimi and Poppi," to become our "sons and daughters" by his hand. He simply increased our realm of influence of which we will one day stand accountable. As a stone thrown into the water sends out circles upon circles far across the water, so he has cast into the "sea" of our time here on earth and brought "kids" into our hearts and under our care within every circle. Everything God does in our lives and your too, is a part of his plan. God did not "take away" our first baby daughter, Deborah Hope, to punish us, to correct us, to cause us great pain. She was a gift that helped us to prepare our hearts for God's future for us. How we thank him for his plan that included so many wonderful kids to love. He always has a plan. Are you looking at your daily life and searching for his hand in it, his preparing of you for that plan? If not, look carefully into your day and see where God has moved you one step closer to that plan.

March 18

EXODUS 3:3-4

"Then Moses said, I will now turn aside and see this great sight, why
the bush does not burn. So when the Lord saw that he turned
aside to look, God called to him from the midst of the bush
and said, 'Moses, Moses!' And he said, 'Here I am.'" NKJV

Moses was busy keeping the sheep on the back side of the desert. It
would have easy to keep walking or to find a bush of his own to seek
shelter in his personal desert. But he was amazed that the burning
bush was not consumed with the fire that was raging in it. He was
surprised that a fire so intense would not destroy what it was covering with heat.

The really amazing thing to me is that from that very burning
bush, God called his name, his personal name. However, it was when
Moses took time to turn aside from the normal experience of tending
to sheep to see for himself, that God called him! God had his complete attention when he was near the non-consuming fire! And with
his seeing and hearing, God spoke to Moses.

When we are in the midst of our own personal firestorm, in our
desert set away from the normal, hurting or afraid, is often when God
has our total attention so that we see and hear. Next time you are in
such a place, listen for the sweet word of your own name to be called.
God wants you to realize he is in both the pleasant times in your life,
and that he does not flee even the painful. He still has a plan for you,
as he did for Moses, perhaps not to lead a great nation, but to lead
even one other to see and to hear from the Lord as they watch that
you are not consumed by your burning bush experience either.

God made a wonderful revelation of himself to Moses. To Moses
response of, "Here I am," God said, "I AM the God of your father.
He desires to use every day of your life to reveal himself anew to you
too. When you can say to God in the midst of those trials, "Here I
am," he will call you by name and remind you, the I AM is with you.
He has heard your cries and he knows your sorrow. Turn aside, child
of God, and see, hear from the I AM today.

March 19

GENESIS 18:14

"Is anything too hard for the Lord? At the appointed
time I will return to you, according to the time
of life, and Sarah shall have a son." NKJV

I have found over the years that the one of the hardest things I have to do is wait on the Lord. He is able. The Word says so. He has a plan. The Word says so. He will flesh out his plan. The Word says so.

When I am having a difficult time sitting still and looking to the Lord for my need, I remember this promise to Sarah, the wife of Abraham. Everything about nature said it was impossible. But the Word had said it would happen! Even Sarah herself denied it could be. Who knew her body better than she? Looks as if the Lord did!

At the "appointed time," God visited dear Sarah and did for Sarah as he had spoken, as he had promised her with his Words. How important are his Words! He was faithful to complete his Words to her, but in his "appointed time".

Wait on the Lord. He is still there. He is still able. His Word asks the question, is anything too hard for the Lord? And the actions that followed with the promised son proved that he is able. Wait on the Lord. Wait for his plan, in his timing. It will be worth it all!

March 20

GALATIANS 4:19

"My little children, of whom I travail in birth…" KJV

Yes, I know what Paul is talking about here, but it so perfectly fits this day in my mind and heart, because this is the day I gave birth to our third daughter by C-section. Our first daughter was born at night and died the next morning. The second was born by C-section at eight o'clock in the morning and was rushed away because of complications for me, meaning I did not see her until much later. But this day, many years ago, I saw this little girl as they lifted her above the divider for the surgery of another C-section, and she was altogether lovely. They laid her across my chest. I touched her face. I rubbed her nose. She was warm and bright eyed.

This daughter, our Elizabeth, has been a joy all of her life. She entered on the first day of Spring. She has excelled at so many things; she sings as the beautiful birds sing in Spring. She sings in joy as I did when I held her those first few moments that were all mine, only mine.

Enjoy the remembering of the entrances of your little ones, sons or daughters, and remember in your joy to thank God who is the only one who gives life. This child of yours is his gift to you for a lifetime. How blessed you are to receive each one. Touch with sweet memory each one as they return to your home, whether as children still or grownups. They will always be your little ones! Mama knows!

March 21

GENESIS 3:8A

"And they heard the voice of the Lord God walking in
the garden in the cool of the evening…" NKJV

Almost every evening just before dark you will find me walking in my
"garden." It is not like Big Buck's garden of vegetables. It is the way
I see a garden, full of shrubs and flowers, with grass sliding underneath the edge of the flowers to form a carpet for them to drape over
and strut their stuff. Deep in the grass you will see little wild flowers so tiny you would miss them if you weren't looking. They were
planted by God's own hand responding to the natural outflow of the
minute seeds that gather from times past of being there nurtured by
the rains and fertilized by the dead bugs or leaves rotting. They need
no hands to aid them to flourish.

"Walking in the cool of the evening" reminds me that God set all
of his world in motion and I'm certain he enjoys watching it respond
to his commands in perfect unison with himself.

I have been told by one of my neighbors that the only difference
between a plant and a weed is where it's planted, or appears. For
instance, around one of my big oaks there is a weed that is beautiful
for months until it gets to its seeding time. Then you can tell it's one
of those terrible stick tights that cling to your clothes. But on its way
to seeding there are small blossoms that line the edge of the stalk for
about eighteen or so inches in the purest pink possible. I try to cut
it back just after it blooms. That way there is only the mother plant.

I still enjoy the weed for a time. But when I miss the right time
to cut it, I have a thousand little plants of those ugly stick tights. Just
shows me there are some things in life that need to be enjoyed for
a short time, but they are not to become a central part of my life. I
must pass on to the more important and leave behind the trivial.
What are you staying too long doing instead of moving forward to
God's best?

March 22

LUKE 18:31

'Then He took the twelve aside and said to them, 'Behold, we
are going up to Jerusalem and all things that are written by the
prophets concerning the Son of Man will be accomplished.'" NKJV

It seems to me that we all have a strong tendency to steer away from
anything that we think or feel will be the least bit difficult in our
lives. We do not like hardship. We want our days to be all mornings
with no hot afternoons or chilly evenings. We like the easy life. We
are just a mite lazy here on this earth. We would rather receive all
daylight hours and no dark nights ever. We fear what we can't see in
the dark. We turn from the cold of defeat or the pain of loss.

But let's explore the actions of Jesus in these dark hours before
him. He is sharing with his disciples, those who have followed him
all the way and learned to love him as they have walked with him,
that they are going up to the very city that is going to try to destroy
him. He even reminds them that it has been told by the ancient
prophets what will happen in that city. But his face is set to obey
even to the death.

Next time you are faced with the hard parts of obedience to
the Lord, look to Jesus and how he behaved in those hours facing
his own death. To us, death is the final enemy, the last step to the
unknown. But with our Jesus we can be joyful since he has defeated
that last enemy! He was victorious over the fear of the unknown that
humans have. We can walk in total obedience towards even that last
step on this earth. It is not the unknown anymore! It is eternity with
Jesus! Praise him!

March 23

LUKE 19:4-6

"So, he (Zacchaeus) ran ahead and climbed into a sycamore
tree to see him (Jesus), for He was going to pass that
way. And when Jesus came to the place, He looked up
and said to him, "Zacchaeus, make haste and come down,
for today I must stay at your house. So, he made haste
and came down and received him joyfully." NKJV

Now, talk about last minute planning for an important guest!
Wonder what ole Zacc thought about on his way down out of that
tree? I think Zacc was probably so excited about Jesus that he really
didn't mind too much about the condition of the house or what
he could prepare for food. He kept the main thing the main thing!
Which was, of course, Jesus, in his house, visiting with him, talking
with him, accepting him. What joy to include Jesus at his table.

When we are invited to have lunch, dinner or supper with
another family, it is a joy indeed. We are so excited about dining
with them, to have the opportunity to talk with them, to share our
lives with theirs, and most of all, to be accepted by them into the
very inner place of their lives. When it is close to a holiday, it is even
more fun! We appreciate being lifted out of a busy schedule that goes
with all holidays to be covered by their warmth at a meal. Hospitality
at these times is above and beyond the call of duty and rise to the
level of love! Our souls are filled with the beauty that comes when
shared around a dinner table.

Look around your world, choose a simple meal, set a simple
table and pour your love over those folks. They will be forever your
friends because you expressed love to them in such a warm way. Be
like Ole Zacc. Don't worry about the house or the food. Prepare it
in simplicity and serve it with love. That's the best acceptance of all…
across your table.

March 24

LUKE 10:20B

"…rejoice, because your names are written in heaven." KJV

If I could choose the best gift my father ever gave to me, it would be this one. He was my greatest example in knowing that he had eternity written in his heart because he had chosen to receive Jesus as Lord and Savior as a young man. He had assurance of his eternity because of this; he knew his name was written in the Lamb's Book of Life.

Because I could see Daddy's imperfections, and I realized pretty early that I was not too perfect either, I saw that it was his trust in his Lord that gave the quiet spirit about his heavenward journey. It was not about Daddy being perfect. It was about Jesus's sacrifice for Daddy. Yes, it was that personal, for Daddy!

If your father was a good example, follow that and become ever better at "daddy-ing." But if he was not the sort of example he should or could have been, forgive him first and then rise above the example he set. Good news! You are not bound by your heredity nor the environment you were brought up within. You can overcome both and are given that power and privilege by your Lord. He is the deliverer of those in chains from the past! It is the "I will" that he works inside of you, the ability to make a choice. What a joy he established in man when he gave him that ability. Choose to break the cycle of poor parenting and become all you can be by his grace. Choose freedom in Christ!

March 25

JOHN 20:26

"And after eight days his disciples were again inside, and
Thomas with them. Jesus came, the doors being shut, and
stood in the midst, and said, 'Peace to you!'" NKJV

It is not hard to identify with Thomas, the disciple most known for
his sense of doubt when told of Jesus' being alive. We look at our
circumstances, our broken relationships and we falter at the unbelievable truth of Jesus being able to make a difference in any of them.
We think it is impossible for anyone to lift us over what we are experiencing at the time.

But, like Thomas, we too can learn that Jesus is not hindered
in coming to us, regardless of a door being shut. No longer do we
have to fear those closed doors that hold us captive from his heart
we think. He can step through whatever the Enemy, old Satan, or
folks who would harm us can throw our way and reach us with his
love. He can still stand in the midst of your storm, your unyielding
pain or sorrow.

It is not always that he will remove us from those situations.
Many we will need to persevere in for a season. But there does
come an end to what we are being buffeted by in this life this side
of heaven. At the final end, there will be his heaven for us. What a
complete victory in Jesus. What a joy will be ours. Persevere, friend,
persevere to the end.

March 26

LUKE 1:13B; 31B

"Elisabeth will bear you a son, and you shall call his name John…
The angel said to her, 'Mary… you will conceive in your womb
and bring forth a son, and shall call his name Jesus." NKJV

There is no doubt in my mind and heart that our God knows us by name. The 119th Psalm proclaims he saw us before we were formed in our mother's womb. What a delight to know that the God of all creation calls me by name. Several years ago, I wrote these thoughts about being called by name.

"When He calls Me:"
I know when He calls me, whether to joy or pain,
It's not another's I bear; He will call me by name.
When His voice I hear, I will answer His call,
For I know that His voice will carry through all.
His promise is sure. His voice is so clear,
Breaks not the bruised reed, nor calls to life drear.
He fills me with grace, His will to bear.
Prepares me to face, complete in His care.
Walk down the road, No matter the load.
If fashioned in pain, He's there for my gain.
Never falters, nor slips, Tho' days are like blips.
Walks not away; Never leaves me alone
He beckons me, "Come" to touch Cornerstone.
He fills me with love, knowing He keeps.
That One who watches, nor ever sleeps.
He hears my cry; my heart ever weeps.
He is my Source of pain-equaled strength.
He goes all the way, Life's days-equaled length.
When this is finished, This journey I'm on,
I've answered each call and sing in true tone.

The way that He's brought, tho' often so dark,
To the victory on, 'til the victory be won.
To life ever new, and never the same.
It's life there with Him who calls me by name.

March 27

JOHN 20:19

"Then, the same day at evening, being the first day of the
week, when the doors were shut where the disciples were
assembled for fear of the Jews, Jesus came and stood in the
midst, and said unto them, 'Peace be unto you.'" NKJV

How often have I shut the doors of my life against those things outside that I was fearful of meeting inside of me. And how delighted
I am to know that the closed doors were no hindrance to my Jesus.
It matters not that I do fear. He speaks to me not to fear. His voice
calms my heart and stills my trembling. He understands that I am
easily dropped into a fearing mode. He simply reaches out to me
with his sure hand and quiets that fear as he sets my feet on a more
stable ground than I was standing on there.

And as he speaks, the sureness in his voice brings the peace that
can come from him only. I draw back from the thoughts that have
filled my mind and replace them with his Word that I might call on
him for his promises that speak, not only peace, but also, his steadfast love to me. He tells me I am his own, never to be forgotten or
replaced. No one else can take my place in his heart, because he died
for me. Yes, for others too; I know. But in my place of living, it was
for me completely. He left nothing over to be dealt with later. He
tended to it all.

Therefore, I stand with him trusting him to deliver me safely to
my Father in heaven at exactly the right time. It is enough that he
has spoken peace to me!

March 28

JONAH 1:1-2

"Now the word of the Lord came to Jonah…saying, 'Arise,
go to Nineveh, that great city, and call out against it, for
their evil has come up before me. But Jonah rose to flee
to Tarshish from the presence of the Lord." ESV

Everyone knows about Jonah and the large fish that God had prepared for Jonah's poor choice to flee instead of following God's clear direction. But there is far more here than the big fish story. Let's examine a few.

First, God was very clear when he called to Jonah. He called him by name. It wasn't a message for another person. Jonah understood that the message was for him alone, for he wouldn't have decided to flee if he thought God was trying to send another. He also grasped that it was God calling, not another god. It was his God. He was told where to go, when to go and the "why" to go. A great city was evil and in need of the opportunity to repent and be saved from God's wrath.

Second, we learn later that Jonah knew his God and how merciful and gracious he could be. He didn't want these evil folks to get away with anything. He wanted them condemned! He wanted justice where it concerned them.

Third, one thing Jonah wasn't aware of though was that he could not successfully flee from his God! His God was everywhere. Read the rest of Jonah's story. You'll find yourself there!

Lessons: Recognize God when he calls your name. Hear his command to arise and go to share the light of your God with folks in need of forgiveness. You were once that person in need. Don't flee. Go! God has a plan for you. Obey, so he doesn't need to prepare a big fish for you! That's it, folks: RECOGNIZE, HEAR AND OBEY! Today is the appointed time. Choose wisely.

March 29

ISAIAH 59:1

"Listen! The Lord's arm is not too weak to save you,
nor is his ear too deaf to hear you call." NLT

After church on Easter the family will come for dinner and for the grand- children and great-grand- children to hunt Easter eggs for fun. Of course, they know why we celebrate our Lord's resurrection, but they also have fun with the eggs stuffed with change and confetti or candy.

The next day, on Monday, I will go out to the patio to survey the confetti and candy scattered over the blocks. The change they all take home! I will sit down in the swing there to think about each one and the way they each are planning to go into their future. That's the way Easter dinner goes at our house.

I am glad I have time to read this Scripture in Isaiah that reminds me that my God has no trouble hearing their cry or saving them when they call to him. I am assured that when each one comes to the Lord with the confessions of each heart, the Lord hears and reaches out to lift that one to salvation. I am so happy that he is never too busy, never too tired, never too anything, to touch that one with mercy and grace as that very one needs it to have the Father save. Our God is able and he cares enough to pay attention even when that one child cries. Sins confessed are forgiven and that one is restored. Praise God from whom all blessings flow!

I pray for each grand and each great-grand- child by name. As often as they come to my mind and heart. You too, can pray diligently for yours. Call out their names to our Father that he will see how much you love them too. Be as Job in the Bible was. He prayed and made sacrifices for his children. Never miss an opportunity to hold them to the throne of grace with the Lord. His love is everlasting. Let yours be also.

March 30

JUDGES 14:1-2

"Samson went down to Timnah, and…saw one of the
daughters of the Philistines…he came … and told his
father and mother, 'I saw one of the daughters of the
Philistines…Now get her for me as my wife.'" ESV

Yes, I realize the customs were different in those days, since the parents arranged the marriages, but I'd like to draw attention to his attitude about getting his desires fulfilled. Samson was a man for the moment; he wanted what he wanted, when he wanted it, no matter the consequences, whether it was good for him or not. It is so easy to become like this! Consider how we are today.

Years ago, there were catalogs to show us items we could use and we could send off for them. It took a little while to get them to you. Then there came along TV which showed us items we could have, how to use them and what others already had of them. I kind of think that last part is what got us: what others had! But we needed a way to buy them. Enter credit cards! There was the power to buy them available to almost anyone.

Now we have customer service for anything on every device we have. Wonder how many of us have entered the rat race paying off things we didn't need, don't use and couldn't afford? Oh yes, we all have! Let's rethink our life and the quality of it, not the number of things we have, but the who we are. Choose to do away with the Samson Complex and learn to wait for our needs and to live a giving life, not a taking one.

March 31

JOHN 6:20-21

"But he saith to them, 'It is I; be not afraid.' Then they
willingly received him into the boat; and immediately
the boat was at the land to which they went." KJV

These disciples had been rowing hard in the storm that was over them. They were taking care to do what they knew to do, but the waves were too much. Jesus comes walking toward them, and they were afraid! He calms their fears with words of comfort, identifying himself to them. In this particular case Jesus brings them immediately to land.

But there are times when Jesus does not do this. There are times when he allows us to go through dark days, not relieving the pain or sorrow. Instead, he walks with us over the waters of heartbreak all the way into his blessed self, carrying us to his peace that passes all understanding of the world. They cannot understand. They do not have our Jesus. These are the seasons of life where we must still trust him, no matter what he allows or brings to our world. It is not when we can see ground through the shallow waters that we must step in faith. It is when we cannot tell how deep the water is, when we cannot see where to place our timid feet, that we must boldly step in total trust, in full faith, that our Lord is still there, not necessarily to catch me, but to make every step I take with me, never leaving my side.

If you live long enough, I can guarantee you will pass through trials. They are part of living in a fallen world. Some he takes through deep waters, some through the fire, but he takes all of his children through the blood of Jesus, giving salvation. Step in obedience to his word wherever your Lord takes you. His comfort is, "It is I, do not be afraid."

April 1

JOSHUA 9:3-4A, 14B

"But when the inhabitants of Gibeon heard what Joshua had done
to Jericho and to Ai, they on their part acted with cunning…
but (the Israelites) did not ask counsel from the Lord." ESV

Joshua and God's people had destroyed Jericho and Ai at God's instruction. The Gibeonites feared the people of the Lord God. So, they resorted to deception to have Joshua make a covenant with them regardless of what God had instructed Joshua not to do. And Joshua falls into their trap because he did not consult his God before doing so.

Believer, the world will not hesitate to deceive you to get what it wants. Remember, the Enemy of God is the father of lies! When you neglect to go to God to see if there is a lie being put on you, you are already in deep trouble. These liars were always a thorn in the flesh of God's people. We are told not to make compromises with the world. We are to walk in this world but not to be a part of it. We are to be a light to those who are being deceived, but if we are blinded by the world's offerings of peace, we will lose the bright light the Lord has placed within us. Your light, my light will not shine forth as it needs to in this dark world. Consult him before you decide where you are to go, what you are to do or with whom you are to agree on matters of your life.

Joshua did not and it cost him and the people he led greatly. God is waiting for your call for directions. Call first! He will not even mind giving you wisdom in the matter! Remember, he loves you.

April 2

JOHN 21:21-22

"Peter, seeing him, said to Jesus, 'But, Lord what about
this man?' Jesus said to him, If I will that he remain till
I come, what is that to you? You follow Me." NKJV

Oh my, how often we look around and want to know why another
is receiving more than we are. How many times have you thought
about why the one next to you has health, wealth and all things fine?
Ever think it's not fair how your friend, or enemy, for that matter, has
gotten a "leg up," so to speak over you?

In this case, Peter is looking around when he should have been
looking at Jesus! Yes, we do that too, don't we? We decide how the
"game of life" should be played and just who should get the first place
of honor. Or, in Peter's time and question, just who should have to
suffer for the Lord the most!

Jesus puts it in the fewest words possible, I think. He simply
reminds Peter that it is not about what others are to be or do. It is
about how I am to be and do! Lift your eyes off those around you
when feeling a little down and raise them to the face of our Lord
Jesus. That is where you will receive the strength to go on into your
dark night of obedience.

In Peter's defense, I have been with him in thoughts before and
wondered about how the Lord was dealing with those around me.
That is not my choice. It is Jesus' to do the way he desires for the best
of that one. But it is my choice to obey whether I understand or not.
I am to follow my Jesus. You are too!

April 3

JOHN 3:16

"For God loved the world in this way: He gave His One
and Only Son, so that everyone who believes in Him
will not perish but have eternal life." HCSB

The world we live in is fallen through the entrance of sin into it.
There is much pain and suffering, sorrow that is more than we think
we can bear. The evil that has invaded these realms is beyond our
imaginings. And those of us who have believed in God's one and
only Son do have that wonderful eternal life, but we are not immune
from the waves of hurtful happenings or painful diseases, or the sorrow of partings with our loved ones. It is part of life on this earth
where evil exists.

But when those feelings of inadequacy to meet the storm before
you head on, or with any sense of peace in victory over it become
more than you can bear, go to the Word, the Living Word of God
for your peace. Rely on God's written word to find your stability and
ability to be an overcomer in this one life you are given. You cannot
do this alone. He didn't intend for you to do it by yourself! He has
given the Word. He has given us our prayer life, our communion
with him. And he has given us the fellowship of the believers that we
may call of those around us to fill our hearts with hugs and words of
peace and comfort.

We need each other for support and strength to keep up with life
in a fallen world. We need the Word for instruction and his promises.
We need communion with our Father for the quiet spirit of trust.
And he has provided all we need to be survivors and victors. He will
never leave us stranded in our storm. He is there all the way through
each wave as they come. Praise our Father for the mercy and grace
for every moment he has allotted to us. God's love is for all. Believe
in his one and only Son for eternal life.

April 4

JOSHUA 6:1

"Now Jericho was securely shut up…" NKJV

The world out there is still in the hand of the Lord. He is aware of the comings and goings of all the inhabitants of this world. He misses nothing. Let us consider a few things concerning this thought of God's control of all.

First, Jericho was an enemy territory. The world is an enemy territory to those who belong to the Lord's kingdom. That doesn't mean there are no good people out there. There are. But it is not about being good. It is about being righteous because Jesus has bought and paid for you and you have accepted that gift of eternal life from him.

Second, Jericho was well fortified from God's people. Yet, the people were fearful of the Lord's folks because they had heard tales of their God. Now they were closed up for their own safety. The world will close ranks against you because they don't trust you and they fear your God. But the world was overcome by our Lord Jesus at the death, burial and resurrection. The world has reason to fear God and his people!

Third, a few verses later God tells Joshua that he has given Jericho, its king, and the mighty men of valor into Joshua's hand! Victory is assured to God's people. It didn't matter how many men of valor there were! God was in total control of it all.

To sum up, go forth into the enemy territory no matter how closed they are to us and march on with the truth of the Living God as God has told us to do. He is in control. March on! His victory has already been given.

April 5

JOSHUA 3:9A, 10A 11, 13-15, 17

"And Joshua said to the children of Israel, 'By this you shall know that the living God is among you, … Behold, the ark of the covenant of the Lord of all the earth is crossing over before you into the Jordan… And it shall come to pass, as the soon as the soles of the feet of the priests who bear the ark of the Lord, the Lord of all the earth, shall rest in the waters of the Jordan that the waters…shall be cut off… and they shall stand as a heap. So it was, when the people set out from their camp to cross over the Jordan, with the priests bearing the ark of the covenant before the people, and as those who bore the ark came to… the edge of the water… and the feet of the priests… dipped in the edge of the water… that the waters…stood still and rose in a heap very far away…then the priests who bore the ark of the covenant of the Lord stood firm on dry ground in the midst of the Jordan, and all Israel crossed over on dry ground, until all the people had crossed completely over the Jordan." NKJV

The river Jordan is the river of judgment that flowed into the Dead Sea. That judgment is sure for all unless God's provision of the ark brought safety by stopping the flow. God's ark rested in the river completely causing the flow to be stopped and to allow safe crossing to the other side. The river was at flood stage at this time of year. It would have been wise not to step into that river. But the promise was tied to the priests stepping into that water for the ark to be able to rest there. Upon faithful obedience, the water rolled back and the priests were on dry ground. Normally the ground would have been left wet, but not this time!

What a living God we serve! Jesus is our ark, our life. He is the safe passage to the other side. In Christ, we are complete, firmly planted in his place for us at this time in our lives. What more do you need to be willing to step out in faith to obedience? The light is for the step you are on right now. Make it! Obedience reveals the second step.

April 6

JOSHUA 6:17

"Now the city shall be doomed by the Lord to destruction;
it and all who are in it. Only Rahab the harlot shall
live, she and all who are with her in the house, because
she hid the messengers that we sent." NKJV

This is the famous city of Jericho whose walls came crashing down when Joshua and the people of God walked around them once a day for six days with seven times on the seventh day. Joshua had sent spies to check out the city and the harlot Rahab helped them. What a reward she received for believing the God these men worshipped.

It mattered not that her reputation was spoiled or that she was not a part of the nation God had chosen to bless all the earth through his plan of redemption. It mattered not that others around her did not believe even though they had heard of this people whose God was the Lord. She obviously was not the greatest choice of folks to be like! It wasn't about her though, friends. It was about the God whom she looked to with these spies whom she helped.

The city is doomed and destroyed. Everyone around is killed, even the animals that belonged to the people of Jericho. But Rahab is spared because she put out the scarlet cord from her window that signified she was to be saved, her and all those in her household with her. Just imagine how excited her family was when they trusted what she told them to do and they came to her home to be redeemed. Her witness to them brought them redemption too. Be sure to share your Jesus with those whom you love, those of your own household who need to know him. Put out the scarlet cord of his salvation.

April 7

JOSHUA 4:20-22

'And the twelve stones which they took out of the Jordan, Joshua
set up in Gilgal…When your children ask their fathers in time
to come, saying... What are these stones? then you shall let your
children know…Israel passed over this Jordan on dry land.'" NKJV

Do you have any stones of remembrances? They are a good thing to
possess. They are those times when God delivered you from the snare
of sin, or from the Enemy's harassment of you. There are times when
you know God has intervened in your life to preserve you or your
family. Can you retell them to your children so they will know how
trustworthy your God has been to you? Have you thought about
them more than once and want to share them but think they will
not want to hear your life experiences? Believe me, they will want to
know how you were moved into safety by your Mighty God.

My Lord has given us peace in the very center of our storm. He
has placed his strength at my fingertips when there was no other to
help. He has moved us into safety when we were surrounded by the
Enemy's deceptions. He has walked beside us when we didn't believe
we could make another step. As we lifted our foot to the stone before
us, he has planted that foot securely on the next stone and the next.
Without missing a beat, he has pulled us from the miry clay and set
our feet on a higher plain. We have crossed over on dry ground!

Gather your personal stones of remembrances and put them
before your family that they too can know your God is a part of
your everyday life. And that you trust him and put your life in his
hand each day. They will never know if you don't share with them.
It's not too late. Choose now to open their hearts and minds to your
knowledge of your God.

April 8

PSALM 78:25

"Man did eat angel's food..." KJV

When the children of God, the Israelites, were wandering in the dessert, God sent them food from heaven to sustain them in his mercy and grace. He's like that. Whether his children deserved it or not, he fed them from his love what they had to have to continue. How gracious of him. He made certain his name was not smeared by failing folks, as though he could not take care of them.

Easter is just around the corner. The family will be getting together, grown children, grand-children and great-grand-children. A delightful experience for the two of us. The older we get, the more we enjoy these times. Our family likes to have Prime Rib (yes, capitals for this) for any holiday. It matters not which one it is. It is just their favorite meat. So, I am certain I will be making all happy when I head the menu with it. They bring everything else, which I like too.

When you get together this Easter Sunday with family or friends, just remember why we are celebrating. Our Jesus is the reason for this season too, not just Christmas. And this season is the apex of our celebrating. It is his sacrifice of his body, our heavenly food, driven by his love and the Father's plan, fulfilled completely, all the way to the resurrection, that gives rise to our adoration, praise and worship. His body, his blood, my life.

April 9

JEREMIAH 1:5A

"…Before I formed you in the womb I knew you, and before you were born I consecrated you…" ESV

The wonder of reading that God knew me before he even started forming me in my mother's body is amazing to understand. I have a hard time realizing that God operates without the constraints of time. He is not bound by the same clock that I am. He has seen all of the time line and knows it all before it even started by this hand.

This would mean that he understands my strengths and all of my weaknesses. It means he recognizes my frailties and feebleness. He looked within the "Me" and said he would have a plan that would be just for me. This plan would excel over any weakness that was mine. It would exceed the boundaries these would place on me. His plan would be perfect for me alone!

He has chosen me to be his and has set a plan in motion to fulfill all he has desired for me. He wants me to cooperate with his plan rather than to fight against that plan. That is my choice to make. He has set me apart for his glory that my world through me and his plan might come to know him. I can work with him in his plan. I must make my choice daily to walk where he walks. It is always about a choice, isn't it? Choose carefully, friend. He knows you and has known you long before you were even formed as a human. Welcome his plan. Walk today where Jesus walked ahead of you.

April 10

DEUTERONOMY 4:19

"And when you look up into the sky and see the sun,
moon, and stars—all the forces of heaven—don't be
seduced into worshiping them. The Lord your God
gave them to all the peoples of the earth." NLT

We are so prone to worshipping the creation of God instead of worshipping the One who is the Creator. The world has so much that is beautiful beyond description. The heavens too. We are only beginning to see and grasp what is out there in space, flung there by a caring and exact God who made no mistakes in putting order into all of his creation.

There are many places where God warns about worshipping other people, places and things. But here it is so clear that we are not to be seduced into this sin. Which reveals to me that there are forces beyond the norm that are wanting us to do just that. The world and the Enemy deceive us, or try to fool us anyway, into thinking there is some force or power that worshipping these objects will enhance our lives into something more than we already are or have. It is not so!

They are placed in our world for a reason: to light the day and the night! And they are for all beings that occupy this realm. Look only to our Lord God and worship him only, loving Jesus for our free gift of salvation in him, thanking God for the Spirit of God in us. He has given us all we need. The world is wrong to look to the heavens for guidance. His Word is there for that with his Spirit's knowledge to open the way to follow. Choose to obey.

April 11

JOHN 9:4

"I must work the works of him that sent me, while it is
day; the night cometh, when no man can work." KJV

The light of day is over, it is gone forever and can never be recalled
to change any part of it. There is still enough left, though quite dark,
to make us think about it and cause us to recount those particular
things we wish we had accomplished, or said. But we know it really
is futile. We then are faced with a choice. Somehow, it's always about
a choice, isn't it? We can roll those opportunities over to tomorrow,
crowding that coming day with more than can be done in one day,
or spread them out over a period of days. Or, we can actually, mark
some off never to do, but, we must make a choice. Keep in mind we
are to work the works of him that sends us into our world while it is
day, because the night comes when we can do no more. And it comes
faster than we realize.

Look at your day and give thanks for it, for it is the day the Lord
made for you. It is the one day you have from beginning to end
to count your blessings. Forgive anyone who needs to be forgiven,
accept the things you cannot change, change what you are able to
and sleep tonight the sleep that is reserved for those who are at peace
with each other and the Lord. The choice is always yours. Make it
early. Make it without reservations or regrets. Do what you can with
good planning. Then, accept the fact you are not perfect or responsible for everything. Put forth your hand to be a blessing to another
and see what God has for you, his good and faithful servant. Work
now and rest after.

April 12

'And when evening came, his disciples went down to the sea, got into the boat, and went over the sea toward Capernaum. And it was now dark; and Jesus had not come to them. Then the sea arose…" NKJV

These men had done nothing wrong. In fact, they had done all the things they were supposed to do. They knew about boats, they knew about the sea and its unpredictability. They were ready to do what they had always done, to go down to the sea in boats. And they set out to do just that.

As so often is the case, they set out to do a good thing, but the dark stretched over them, and Jesus was not so visible for this period of time. They were aware that storms were normal for this sea. These were often very strong storms, wreaking havoc on those at the mercy of the waves, making progress impossible no matter how hard they rowed. The worse part was that their Jesus was not with them! It was dark and scary. It was more than they could bear.

They had been rowing for several miles, but the storm was too much. Then, verse 19 says they saw Jesus walking on the sea, and drawing near to the boat. They were afraid! I love Jesus' words, "It is I; be not afraid." How often I have been in that boat, afraid of my storm and feeling as though I were losing my battle. Even the thought of Jesus coming to me was fearful to me. I was afraid of my storm, afraid of my Lord. Afraid, until he spoke to me in tones of peace, with words of love, with his hand stretched out to me, calming my heart, putting my mind at ease with his comfort. And, suddenly I arrive at my destination: peace in the midst of my storm. The storm was still there, but my life was quiet with the knowledge that my Lord was over my storm, seeing me through this very strong storm all the way to port, his port, safely in his arms. Thank you, Jesus. Love you, Jesus.

April 13

JOB 1:21B

"The Lord gave and the Lord has taken away;
blessed be the name of the Lord." ESV

Two weeks after I turned twenty years-old, I gave birth for the first time to a big baby girl, full term, with all the expectancy ever held for a new baby by a young mother. She was to be my side-kick, to plant flowers, to cook and sew, to learn to read, to play piano and to play with her daddy as all little girls like to do. She was going to ride a tricycle and play with jacks as I had years before in a school yard. Her name was to be Deborah Hope.

But the morning after came and the joyful expectations left. She died and with her death came a whole new world of feelings, decisions and learning. Through most of those hours she lived, I was still out from the anesthesia, but when I was waked by the doctor to let me know of the changes happening, there were no words to pray, there were no thoughts of tomorrow. There was only the unbelievable pain in my heart.

We learned that the Holy Spirit pled our hearts to our Lord every moment of those hours that he gave to her. We learned that love never goes away, and that even when he takes from us, he still gives the joy of reunion with our little girl one day. We learned to bow to his sovereignty in all things. We learned that the Kingdom of God is of such as these little ones. And we saw his mercy and grace at work in our pain, in the emptiness of our arms, in the sadness of "what might have been." Yes, she received her name: Deborah Hope. It is inscribed on that tombstone above her little grave. Even today, there are tears, though it has been so many, many years. But there is not that sense of loss anymore. There is only the enormous joy and expectancy of a future with our Lord and our little one. Is your faith strong enough to withstand the trials and pain of this world? If not, go to the Savior. He is able to make you an overcomer, to lift you to be able to say, "Blessed be the name of the Lord in all things."

April 14

JEREMIAH 7:8

"Behold, (LOOK!) you trust in deceptive words to no avail." ESV

The world is so easily deceived by lying words, whether from doctors, politicians, lovers or business people. We want to hear the words that soothe and comfort us in most circumstances in which we find ourselves. We really do not want the truth. We would rather hear an untruth that weakens our resolve to follow the narrow path in order to give ourselves an excuse for wandering down the wide world before us. It's easier. At least, we think it is.

But God says to look out when we seek those lying words that enlist us to move away from God's truth into a land that is painful and corrupting. There is an end there that we will not want! Don't mix God's truth with the world's lies and call it religion. God will have none of that!

He persistently calls to us. He faithfully sends those to warn us. He reminds us continually to turn back to him. He graciously gives us opportunity to repent and return. But he will not always strive with us. There will be a day of correction for us.

Behold, Look and Be saved from these lies from the world, from the Enemy. Know the Word of God that you may not sin against him. Compare God's words with man's and see that the Lord is good and trustworthy in all situations. He is the Way. He is the Truth. He is the only Life. And he is that Life abundantly!

April 15

"For I know the plans I have for you, declares the Lord, plans for welfare and not for evil, to give you a future and a hope." ESV

These are some of the most comforting words I have ever memorized to be able to have in my heart for all those times when my world seems to be turned upside down and I feel I am walking in circles. These words are a promise that I remember at those upheavals thrown at us in this life. They are life to me.

One important wording here is that God knows the plans, not necessarily that I do. I must trust him to work out the nitty gritty of his plan. It may lead through some interesting and confusing paths as he brings it about for me. It can wander for a season, enough so that I get anxious for it to go on toward the ending that I seek. I usually want it yesterday, as the saying goes. But that is not what is good for me. Easy is not always godly, I've found. My future is in his hand.

The bottom line is always to choose to trust my God with the details that I can't see and therefore, think don't exist. I must remember that trust is not always being able to see. Faith is to go even where I cannot see the ending from where I now stand. Sight is not faith. I can continue to hope in him because he has proven himself over and over to me through a lifetime. He has a track record with me. So today, Lord, I choose to walk in obedience on the one step you have enlightened for me, trusting that you will light the following one as I obey. That's it, Lord: TRUST AND OBEY!

April 16

JOHN 3:8

"The wind blows wherever it wants. Just as you can hear the
wind but can't tell where it comes from or where it is going, so
you can't explain how people are born of the Spirit." NLT

Jesus has just told Nicodemus that we must be born again, later telling him that He, the Son of Man has come down from heaven and,
as Moses lifted up the bronze snake on a pole in the wilderness, so
He too must be lifted up, so that everyone who believes in Him
will have eternal life. He follows that wonderful truth with the most
known verse in the Bible (John 3: 16) about God's unlimited love.

Let me share a memory with you:

Today as I cleaned the room where I have been shelling peas &
snapping beans from the garden, I was looking out at the playground
beyond the porch. I watched the swings there moving back and forth
gently in the breeze, and I thought about these verses. I could not see
the wind. I did see its effects. I could not hear the wind from inside.
I didn't know what moved it to blow just that way to make those
swings move as if a child were sitting in each. I thought about the
children who have sat in them before. I thought about the ones who
fell out of them. Even about the older ones who pushed the little
ones to go higher as they squealed with delight. I remembered the
parents who stood around and talked to one another. Those empty
swings reminded me that opportunities are lost often as they slip
through our hands unnoticed that we could have shared about the
love of God in a natural setting.

The swings are empty more of the time now. The children of this
household are all grown up. Every once in a while, there comes a
child to swing again. Perhaps the swings in your yard are loose now
and you believe you have no more chances to love a little one. There
are so many who need that kind of love blown over them so that the
Spirit can open minds and hearts to Him who loved them so much

that He died for them. They are part of His world that He came to save. We never know when the Spirit of the Lord will blow over His little ones and we receive another opportunity to join Him in blowing over their hearts and minds. You don't have to see the wind blow to know it is. So, blow your love over these. Blow!

April 17

JAMES 5:16

"Confess your faults one to another, and pray for one
another, that you may be healed. The effectual, fervent
prayer of a righteous man availeth much." KJV

The thoughts I have on forgiving one another are not meant to make
you feel bad about feeling ugly toward those who rub you the wrong
way. Your feelings are always your feelings. They are the truth about
the situation, but we choose not act on our feelings. There's that word
again: choice! It's always about a choice, isn't it? Making choices daily,
moment by moment, is the way of which life is made.

Instead, we choose to forgive and to pray for that one who has
offended us. Really, even that is a choice. True, they have given us an
occasion to be offended, but we make the choice to be offended or
not! I have told many of you that there can be no offense intended
if there is no offense taken. You are in control of taking or choosing
not to take offense. The intended offense rolls off your back if you
simply refuse to be offended. But the forgiveness is really for me, for
my well- being. Let's explore that idea.

If I first confess my own faults to another, I have humbled myself
before that one, giving us a level playing field, so to speak, before
each other. When I pray for that same one, it is healing for me. It
calms the anger that brings the high blood pressure of unexpressed
anger, the pressure of carrying around that hurt, that feeling that all
is wrong with my world. It frees me! And then, I can let God do his
work in that other person's life. I can talk to my Savior with all the
hurt that has ever been sent my way. He knows what to do with it
and I can be free indeed. And I can know there is nothing between
myself and my Savior, such as an unforgiving spirit would leave.

If there is anything between you and another in your life, shed
it just as you would an old threadbare shirt, worn thin with carrying that hurt around on your back. Don't just put it in the garbage

though where you can go get it anytime that same person rubs you the wrong way again. Let it go into the hands of Jesus and let him dispose totally of it. And then, fly, fly into a new life of choosing to forgive, as you were forgiven by Jesus, a new you! Who knows, you may even find that other person behaving differently when that one sees the new you.

April 18

PROVERBS 12:25

"Anxiety in the heart of a man causes depression,
but a good word makes it glad." NKJV

Depression is a terrible thing and causes many a tossing night with loss of sleep. It can keep even the strong down for a time. There are many reasons for human's anxieties, but the Word here does not address the why man suffers from his anxieties. It just says he does.

Sometimes a doctor can help those with depression. And that is good. But there are those times when we struggle with the things that bring us down so low we cannot see our way back up, there seems to be no one who is willing to stand with us as we go through this time of strong feelings that incapacitate us and keep us from being able to rise above the deep feelings. That would be a time we can interrupt the depth of the well that is dragging the other person down with what the Bible calls the "good word."

Let's examine what might be a "good word" that could help. Kindness is always in fashion. Try it next time you don't know what to say to a friend in the pit of depression. Just to be accepted then is important to a defeated person. When you are searching for that kind word, ask the Lord to open your mouth with the right word of kindness.

Another "good" word is one that is truthful. You don't have to understand the how or the why of your friend or family member's anxiety. You don't have to try to solve their situation or problem. You don't even have to talk about it at the time. You don't have to say that you "know what they are going through" because you don't!
The best kinds of words in these times are those that encourage the listener with hope. God is your strength. He can strengthen that person too. Look to him to open your mouth with kindness, truthfulness and hopefulness. He loves you and he loves that one too. Accept that life sometimes is hard for you and others. Accept the

fact that you don't know everything nor does anyone else. Receive the mercy of the Lord and let it flow through you to those around you who need his mercy and love. Be a channel of his grace to them. It's always a choice you have. Make it wisely!

April 19

JOHN 16:16

"A little while and you will no longer see Me; again
a little while and you will see Me." HCSB

Jesus is reminding his disciples that he is going to die and their world will be shaken. All will seem to be lost. But it is not! They will see him again…in a little while. Resurrection is sure!

This makes me think about those times in my road, the journey I am on, when I cannot see my Jesus' hand in any of my circumstances or the situations I must go through all the way to the other side. My eyesight is blurred by the tears. My mind is cloudy with the pain I feel. My heart is weary with the strain of "keeping on" what I think is by myself.

I can remember these times the Savior warned his followers about when they would lose their sight of him and would think they were abandoned on the worst day of their lives. They could remember that he told them of that day before it came. And he shared with them that all was not lost, but all would be beautiful when they could see him again. And they would see him again!

Can you imagine their joy as they did see their Jesus after the resurrection? It is the same for you. When you belong to Jesus, when you are a follower of the Lord, you can rejoice in his resurrection, because you too will experience resurrection because of his victory. Death will no longer hold the horror it once did.

So, when your world collapses and your vision is gone, turn to these verses and know it is but for a little while that you do not see your Jesus. He is not dependent on your eyes sight for him to be with you. Here is there all the time! Trust his words. You will see him again!

April 20

JOHN 20:14A, 15A, 16

"She (Mary) turned…saw someone standing there. It was
Jesus, but she didn't recognize him. 'Dear woman, why
are you crying'? Jesus asked her…She thought he was the
gardener… (then) 'Mary!' Jesus said. She turned to him and
cried out, 'Rabboni!' (which is Hebrew for Teacher)." NLT

What a moment in life…the moment of recognition! That time when everything comes together in one word, our name. There is understanding, peace, joy, comfort, love that one recognizes in the very tone of voice of the one who calls out our name. Ah, to have someone who knows us so well, so perfectly, so lovingly that they call us by intimacy of name. They KNOW us and that knowing brings us into communion with each other.

I thought about my grand- daughter who was called by name at her college graduation. It was by name that her degree and honors were granted. They belonged to no other. I thought about my children and how each calls a little differently. The older one says, ''Mother," the middle one and last one say, "Mom," the youngest daughter uses, "Mama." Of course, they sometimes exchange names for me too. But when each says "Mother" in any of its many forms, I know the voice of each. There is a uniqueness that is that one's alone.

When Big Buck calls me, it takes on more meaning that any other human voice. It reveals the deeper relationship of knowing each other from the third grade of school to the now of many years together. It includes the knowledge that one day our Father will call each of us to our heavenly reward, perhaps having to leave the remaining one behind, alone again. But I rest in the knowing that He will make no mistake of timing, or name. That will be my last call from my Lord. I will answer him in joy because I will know His voice. Do you know that voice?

April 21

JOHN 20:14 A;16A

"She turned around…and saw Jesus…Jesus
said to her, 'Mary'." NKJV

I love the thought of Jesus calling me by name.

Today is a day for walking and talking with Jesus. When I looked out at the morning at six minutes before six, God had washed the earth with his rain while I slept. All the colors were brightened by the water pouring over them just before the sun was rising over the pasture across the drive way. It is the one day each week Buck goes to the restaurant for breakfast. The dog is fed; it's quiet here in a semi-dark house. In the piano room, I sit down to play some old hymns for a few minutes to worship alone. And then I turned to Austin Miles heart song, "In the Garden." And there is where I rested for a long time, just thinking about the words that so beautifully express our experience in that garden with our Lord. I realized it is a singular time that we each have with Jesus. The garden is where Jesus first revealed himself to Mary as she came to be near him in this hour of sorrow, as she wept over what she thought was the worst day of her life. Her Lord was dead! I remembered how few his words were to her, but how they became words of redemption, resurrection and love for her that day, that worst day that became her best day. Those words were etched in her memory to become a song in her heart. They were for her, to be known by no other, the sweetest words on earth beginning with her name.

Miles captured such beauty in his lyrics that we sing from the depths of our own hearts, that one-on-one experience: "I come to the garden alone, while the dew is still on the roses; and the voice I hear, falling on my ear, the Son of God discloses. He speaks, and the sound of his voice is so sweet the birds hush their singing; and the melody that he gave to me within my heart is ringing. I'd stay in the garden with him tho' the night around me be falling; but he bids me go; thro' the voice of woe, his voice to me is calling. And he walks with me, and he talks with me, and he tells me I am his own. And the joy I share as we tarry there, none other has ever known!"

As I played the familiar notes and sang the words in my heart, I realized that he said it so much more beautifully than I could ever do. But at the same time, I also knew that the song of redemption with the promise of resurrection, with his perfect and unconditional love, was personal to me and belonged to me alone from my Savior. That's the way Jesus comes to each, personally. He calls us, as he did Mary, by name. And when we hear our name on his lips, we are wooed by such love to answer. Then he gives an amazing command for Mary. He says, "Go." It is the same with us too. We are to tell others about him, about this same personal love that is to be shared. Don't tarry though it be sweet. Go!

April 22

JOHN 10:27-28

"My sheep know my voice, and I know them and they follow
me. And I give unto them eternal life; and they shall never
perish, neither shall any man pluck them out of my hand." KJV

Our Good Shepherd knows us and we hear his voice when he calls
us with the opportunity of following him wherever he goes. But the
best part to me is that no man can pull us from his hand. He gives
life eternal when we become his. That is forever, folks!

When I was in Morocco, North Africa, a lot of years ago, it was a
delight to see real shepherds leading their flock down the road. I was
used to seeing cattle herds "driven" before the rancher's cowboys. But
a shepherd leads his sheep. He is always in front, he knows the road,
for he just traveled it before them…always in front. He is aware of
any dangers and knows where the water and good grass are located.
But the most amazing was to hear the shepherd talk to his own sheep.
They followed his voice. They responded to his call.

When my Savior calls me to follow him into the last journey I
will ever make, I know he will call me by name. There will not be an
apology. "Oops, I meant to get the one next to you!" He is certain of
the days allotted to me. What a joy, a comfort to be able, by his grace,
to obey his call and answer my name. I can trust him to not be early
nor late, but to remember the days of my life that are already numbered in his "Book." Thank you, Jesus, that you have my name, my
life recorded in the Book of Life, written in your blood. Until then,
may I be found faithful that on that day, in that hour and moment,
I may follow you with joy. May my legacy be that I followed all the
way.

April 23

JOHN 15:12

"This is my commandment, that you love one
another as I have loved you." NKJV

Since this is a commandment from the Lord, it means I must make a choice to obey or not. As I've told you before, it's always about choice, isn't it? Here's my process of choosing: I make a commitment to be obedient to love. I make communication with those whom I have chosen to love in spite of their behavior. I decide (a choice still) to have genuine concern for them regardless of how I feel in any given circumstance. Love is not just a feeling. It is a choice. When I choose these things to do, I can know that my love will be real, complete. So, there you have my choices: commitment, communication, concern and complete = LOVE. What it does not mean: I will always agree or approve of another's choices or behavior. It's not about agreement or approval from us.

After all, I am not always right either. And thank the Lord he has chosen to love me in spite of, regardless of, my choices and behavior. That's real love! And then, he chooses to lead me on to still waters as I grow in his love, leaving behind the mire of my poor choices along the way. He asks that I love as he has loved me, with commitment, communication, concern and completely. He has given the ultimate example: himself.

April 24

JOHN 14:18, 27A

"I will not leave you comfortless; I will come to you…Peace I leave
with you, my peace I give unto you; not as the world giveth, give I
to you. Let not your heart be troubled, neither let it be afraid." KJV

It matters not where we stand in the days of our lives. What matters
is with whom we stand. When Jesus is out Comforter, when he walks
the same path we do, when he sees what we see, what we feel, what
we experience, we are in the best company we can be. He shares our
deepest grief and our greatest joys. He misses nothing! He knows us
more intimately than even our mothers, fathers or spouses. What a
Comforter he is. Thank you. Lord Jesus, for your strong promises in
your word. You make it possible for us to trust you, to have peace in
the darkest of days, not the way the world deals with life's difficulties,
but the way you, our creator does, in a creative way, a way of looking
forward, not backward. We do not have to fear the coming day. He
is in that day before us. What a blessing!

Therefore, we can enjoy today's blessings. And we can trust him
with all our tomorrows. This is the day he made for you! Rejoice in
it and be glad.

April 25

JAMES 3:2B

"…if anyone does not stumble in what he says, he is a
perfect man, able also to bridle his whole body." ESV

Oh my, the tongue is a real problem in the human species. It contaminates the whole body with its fire, its ugliness and its pain inflicting power. Every person has a big problem with this little tiny piece of the body. James has some powerful words to say about the lack of control we exhibit with this thing we call a tongue. In verse eight, he tells that no man can bring it under control. It is a restless evil and full of poison. It has both the power of life and death there. He is quick to share that this should not be so!

So, today is the day we must do something about this personally. Of course, we should make this a matter of prayer, but that is not enough. This becomes the Christian "kiss-off," a way of excusing our behavior and never doing anything about it. We know it is a hard correction to make in our lives. We realize it will not ever be easy to change embedded actions that so quickly slip out of our mouths on the sharpness of that little tongue. Its very quickness is also a sharpness that can harm those closest to us.

So, today is the day to choose to change; yes, there's that word. It is time to stop the way we've always spoken so quickly in response to other's words. This is the day we're to shut that mouth, the door that keeps our tongue silent until we've wakened our minds to be subject to our Lord's teachings. It is the moment to choose instead to shine for our Lord with life giving, encouragement sharing and faith building for others. Today, friend!

April 26

ISAIAH 55:8-9

"'My thoughts are nothing like your thoughts,' says the Lord. 'And my ways are far beyond anything you could imagine. For just as the heavens are higher than the earth, so my ways are higher than your ways and my thoughts higher than your thoughts.'" NLT

There are times when I think I have some really great ideas and my way of doing a thing is better than another person's way. I rationalize that I am better prepared to do a certain plan than anyone else or that I am more knowledgeable than the other person in a particular department. It usually doesn't take the Lord long to correct my thinking!

As I consider the world and all that exists in it, whether on the earth, in the sea or in the air, I decide rather quickly that I really know very little about any of it. The more I learn of God's creation, the more I understand that I don't know a lot at all. My learning reveals a limited knowledge or understanding of the most of this vast earth with its heavens beyond it.

The biggest part of God that I am continually amazed at though is the mercy he gives by not giving me what I deserve in any given day or the grace that is mine repeatedly every moment of my life when he gives what I don't deserve in forgiveness and everlasting love. That is beyond my comprehension. Oh my, how kind he is in letting me continue to breathe, to laugh, to cry out to him in my every circumstance. I am amazed at his amazing grace with every thought I possess. What love is mine in him. Thank you, Lord, for another day at your hands.

Give thanks to him all you who call him by Name.

April 27

MATTHEW 6:33

"But seek first the kingdom of God and his righteousness, and all these things will be added to you." ESV

There are so many things we all chase after every day. We need food, clothing and shelter. All of us. But what place it occupies in our hearts is an important part of how we seek after those necessary items for living. Consider this for a minute and search out the place you have made for it.

Are you willing to do anything to get these necessary things for yourself? Are you often placing these above your health, your children, your spouse? Do you take advantage of others while getting more? What about those who need your kindness along the way of amassing toys in your garage? Do you never have enough time to help? When you have "enough," will you slow down and breathe? Do you ever compromise your integrity to get ahead? Or still your conscience when deciding if an action is honest?

It is too easy to want more of anything and everything! But while we are striving to pay bills and buy extras for our family or ourselves, we could stop long enough to see just where it is all taking us. God knows you have needs. God doesn't mind you having extras either. But God wants you to allow him to be the center of your universe, the cradle of your heart. When you let him reign over your life and that of those dearest to you, and desire deeply to seek a life of righteousness, he can be trusted to aid you in receiving your needs too. I suppose it all comes down to this: do you trust him?

The life you put together will never be as wonderful as the one he has planned to give you. It's not about having more than another person. It's about having the best of God's goods for you. They will be tailor made to fit you! Live the life of joy in all things. When hope is high in your heart and obedience is top of your priorities, it is easier to let God reign every day. It's the inside that counts. What's in your "wallet"? You know, way down deep in there where you really live. The inward man, or woman, lives a worthwhile life, working, yes, but knowing where life is coming from to him or her.

April 28

MATTHEW 5:13

"You are the salt of the earth, but if salt has lost its taste, how shall its saltiness be restored? It is no longer good for anything except to be thrown out and trampled under people's feet." ESV

Salt is a very important ingredient in our diets and in our preserving technics. We need a portion of it for our health, not too much, but a reasonable amount. When I do home canning of the vegetables that we've grown all these years, I use non- iodized salt for them. There is no anti-caking agent in this salt. It is pure salt.

We are to be real salt with no additives to us. We are to retain our saltiness, our goodness, that makes a difference in all that we are added to in this life. Wherever we go, with whomever we interact, we are to make life better, more flavorful to be around. We are to be blessings as we move through the pathway of our lives.

Ask yourself, if you are being the salt of the earth, or have you begun to lose your saltiness? Are you fit only for the roadway to be walked upon daily? Are you making a difference in those around you in each day? Does your life give others a better "flavor" that their lives will bring goodness to those with whom they come in contact? As you go from day to day, look to see if your salt is being spread over others, causing them to spread the saltiness they received from you to others still. That's the way the beauty of God is shared with his world. Shake your personal salt shaker. Only you can!

April 29

ISAIAH 40:31

"But those who trust in the Lord will renew their
strength; They will soar like eagles; they will run and not
grow weary; they will walk and not faint." HCSB

These beautiful words are for every age group that reads them. When
we are young, we believe there is no end to our strength and we strive
to outdo others in our eagerness to be the best. It doesn't take too
long though before we catch the idea that even our strength has its
limits and we begin to look for the side trail. So even the younger
ones have a need to see that trusting the Lord is a place to go to have
renewal at our disposal and restoration our goal.

Those in their middle years are starting the avenue of running
out of steam a little faster than before. We find we are not as we used
to be! We would go higher and cannot as we once could. We aren't
weary, yet, just not young still.

But the best joy expressed here is to the older folks who have
long realized they are not what they used to be! We look with pleasure on this verse that reminds us we can know his strength at any
age as we trust him for our lift to soar like those eagles. It is not
for this world's use. It is for those of us who totally trust him for
every age we go through to reach his place of calling. Wherever he
sends, whatever he asks, with whomever he calls, for every task, for
every day, that's his supply. We trust him and we receive that needed
strength. We may be able only to walk now. No more the running
of our youth. It is too often the weary road we travel. But here we
have the promise of renewed strength to finish the race that we can
now see the light that is at the end of the tunnel through which we
must pass. If you are young, look to those ahead of you and offer
a sweet sprit of encouragement. If you are in those middle years,
thank the Lord for the passage that you have already had and look to
those up the road. Offer a smile, and thanks for their clear pathway

left for you. And if you are those among the aged, thank the Lord for the journey and reach out your hand of cheer to the ones running behind you. Trust in the Lord with all your heart as we travel together onward, always onward!

April 30

ISAIAH 64:8

"But now, O Lord, you are our Father; we are the clay, and
you are our potter; we are all the work of your hand." ESV

Years ago, I was in Morocco, North Africa with some fellow believers. We traveled from the northern parts down to the Atlantic Ocean enjoying the friendly people and the sights of places we had never seen. It was quite an experience and I learned so much about how my God sees his creation of earth and peoples. It was an occasion I will cherish forever.

We went to a potter's shop to watch the potter form beautiful vases, bowls and objects of art. One such gorgeous vase was almost finished and we were looking to see him hold it up as he had other pieces for us to admire. Suddenly he threw it back onto the wheel as it came to a stop and continued to smash it with his hands against the bottom around the wheel. We were startled to say the least. It was one of the most graphic visions of God's prerogative in how he molds us to be sure we are exactly what he created us to be. He is the potter, not we. He is the one who knows when to finish the clay as it was meant to be. That clay did not utter a word, not even a whimper. It simply sat where he left it until the potter picked it up again and began to reshape it to his desires, his plan.

May we know today that our God is not finished with us just yet. He is still shaping, forming and molding us to his specifications, not ours. We can resist or we can receive at his hand his pan. The choice is always ours. Choose wisely and receive his blessing of reshaping you. Surrender is the wisest plan to follow.

May 1

ISAIAH 55: 1

"Come, everyone who is thirsty, come to the waters; and you
without any money, come, buy, and eat! Come, buy wine
and milk without money and without cost!" HCSB

God so freely offers the best to his creation, his children. We can have
water, we can even have the spiritual gifts of the milk and wine. We
have had the mighty hand of our God outstretched to us for a long
time but so often we turn away, thirsty though we be. We will go to
buy those things that bring nothing into our lives. We will seek that
which is less and walk away from that which is life giving and free!

If you are one who looks for meaning in the things of this world,
you are seeking what you will never find. If you think God does not
care about you, you are mistaken. If you want but are never satisfied,
start here with the water of life, offered free and clear. It is not too
late, no matter how old you are. God is always available until your
last breath.

Sing with me the joy that is here in his water. He is full to the
brim with that which will overflow into you and bring up the satisfaction you yearn for so deeply. His heart yearns for you. His love
is here for you. His water can fill your cup slap to the brim to run
over to others in your life who are thirsty as well. They are watching
you to see where you find water. Fill my cup, Lord! Let it be a well
running into their lives. Show them who you are, Lord.

May 2

ISAIAH 59:14-15

"Our courts oppose the righteous, and justice
is nowhere to be found. Truth stumbles in the
streets, and honesty has been outlawed." NLT

Oh my, when I consider the outlandish claims and phrases that go out over our airwaves on radio and television, I am discouraged that nowhere is there the truth in any of it. Or, they will take a morsel of truth and mix the rest to suit their plans. Advertisements, campaigns and "news," as it is called today, all are stretched beyond anything really truthful.

Even in our justice system there is a wide variety of what is called truth and justice. Many judges are sadly beyond understanding what it means to seek the truth or to seek justice for anything or anyone. It has always been so I see though when I read the Word. How shameful, folks, that the people in the streets, don't really mind or care about truth. They say your truth is not our truth. But they are sadly mistaken. God's truth is universal! And one day it will be recognized as truth, real truth, for all. God does not make mistakes. He sees all and knows all, no matter what goes on in the courts or the airwaves or the streets.

It appears that being honest is laughed at by the world. Don't be misled by such. God's commandment says not to bear false witness against anyone. Be honest in all of your dealings.

Check your own heart to see if you know truth, God's truth. Jesus is that truth! Check your mind to see if you would bend the truth into a lie to suit your own desires. Be honest, be truthful today.

May 3

JOHN 16:33

"I have said these things to you, that in me you may
have peace. In the world you will have tribulation. But
take heart; I have overcome the world." ESV

What a promise from Jesus who sees all the future ahead of us. He revealed there will be pain. There will be difficulties. There will be humiliation and sorrow. There will be disappointments and discouragement. There will be more than we can bear, we think, here. He is right too! If you haven't experienced that yet, you're not very old!

We live in a fallen world, turned over to Satan a long time ago by our original parents. But God had a plan already in place to overthrow that Enemy, Satan, and he has carried that plan out to perfection. Jesus completed that plan and has offered that gift to us. We can falter under the destruction Satan tries to put on us, or we can accept that free and costly gift of him paying our sin debt in full. The choice is always ours.

But this promise is ours when we give up trying to do it our way. We can reach out for that promise and live in the victory of obedience to his words. Don't let your heart be bowed down, weighted beyond your strength to walk. Take heart he says. Receive his peace. Yes, we will still live in a fallen world where things are not right for now. But one day he will set all things right and bring Satan to his bitter end. Until then, may we choose to be overcomers for his glory.

May 4

ISAIAH 64:6 A

"All of us have become like something unclean. And all our
righteous acts are like a polluted garment…" HCSB

One thing I learned a long time ago is that nothing I do can offset the
unrighteous things I do. You too, my friend! There is no way to balance the scales for us because our God is a righteous God. We have
all missed his perfect mark for us. In fact, the very Commandments
he gave us taught us where we missed his perfection. We needed
One who would be our Righteousness. And in the Lord Jesus we
have that One.

There are times when I think I am pretty good. Then there are
those times when I see myself as others see me and know that is not
so. Then there are those times when I look at myself under the light
of the Holy Spirit and know that I have not attained by myself any
form of righteousness. That's the human condition. We are all fallen
and all in need of God's redemption. Look to Jesus and learn of
him. His word is clear and his love is immense with no end to it. He
makes salvation available through the gift of his life for ours. Thank
you, Lord.

Today you have the opportunity to take Jesus at his word. He
will stand in your place, giving you his righteousness, clean and holy.
Receive from him all you need; let him reveal his love for you by
opening his gift of life eternal.

May 5

ESTHER 2:9,12

"Hegai (caretaker of the harem), was very impressed with Esther and treated her kindly. He quickly ordered a special menu for her and provided her with beauty treatments. He assigned her seven maids … and moved her and her maids into the best place in the harem … before each young woman was taken to the king's bed, she was given the prescribed twelve months of beauty treatments." TLT

Skip the parts about Esther being prepared for the king's bed and hone in on the care she was given preparing for this. I want to share about the first woman in my life in line with this kind of beauty treatments. For this, I must go back to when I was about seven or eight years old. I would watch my mother get ready to go the field, to town, to church, to the grocery or to a neighbor who needed help with a new baby or illness, or to help one who had just "fallen on hard times," as they used to say.

Remember, we had no inside bathroom, so it meant that she would have to take a "cat bath" in a number ten washtub. (Cat Bath= the way a cat bathes…starting at the top and working your way down! They use their paws. She used a wash cloth.) She would put water in the tub, put some on the stove to heat and mix them when the stove water was hot. Where upon she would take a wash cloth and stand in the tub, bathing herself standing up. This part I never saw but I knew how it was done because that's how all of us took a bath. It was great being the baby in the family, since that meant I always got the first ducking in the hot, clean water and towel. There are some blessings to being the last one on the tree.

When she was dressed, she would get daddy's matches out, strike one and put it right out. She would use the black end for arching her brows and the clean end to push down into the old lipstick tube to get the last bit of color to smooth on her lips. It was many years before I noticed that she had a new lipstick and didn't have to dig out the beauty down in the little tube. Now, I know there had to be new ones along the way, but it seemed to me that it was always old tubes she was digging into for her color.

Occasionally, she had one of the women who worked with her in the fields come to the house to help catch up the household. Having three growing boys and one cow's tail of a girl, whom she sewed clothes for all of us, meant she was always behind. She cooked from scratch all our meals, sometimes after growing and harvesting each food. Yet, she managed to look feminine everywhere she went.

Esther was a queen, but my mother was more than a queen. She was Mother, who gave me life, taught me the word of God, both scolded and encouraged me appropriately as each was needed and who even died in my presence. What a glorious opportunity to see her enter heaven that night, knowing full well I will see her again one day. It is almost Mother's Day. If you can still talk to yours, do so. And praise her for the things you never got around to saying thanks to her. Forgive her for the things left undone. Don't wait for the official day. Do it now. Thank you, my Queen Mother, for all you did for me.

May 6

EXODUS 23:25

"You shall serve the Lord your God, and he will bless your bread
and your water, and I will take sickness from among you." ESV

You might think that just bread and water is not a blessing on this earth. But bread is the staff of life and *water is life itself! So often we want food and drink* a little, well maybe a lot, better than bread and water. Each has the ability to sustain life. When you have had nothing to eat for a long time, know that bread will give the strength that is necessary to keep going on into the next minute. When you have been without simple, plain water for hours, even more so, if you've been without several days, it is all you want!

We look all around for something to satisfy our hunger and thirst. We hunt. We travel. We move until it is found. We try everything to fill that emptiness in our bellies. We do anything to settle that gnawing down in there. But the only thing that will fully satisfy it is the Bread of Life found in Jesus, the Living Water that he alone brings to our hearts.

When God shared this with his people so very long ago, it was a foretaste of what was to come in Christ Jesus. It was an opportunity to know that his blessing was for the very existence of humans. He had already proven his ability to provide to his children moving in uncharted trails with the leadership of Moses to show them God's way. God had shown them how to be well under his lead. He even knew how to bring health. They did struggle with life there in that wilderness. But God had a plan. God had a man: Moses. God had a very specific way.

If we would have his blessing on our lives, he said we would serve him, our God, our only God. We would not divide our loyalties with anyone or anything else. He is specific about this. Bread and water are all you need when God has blessed them! It really is life indeed, abundant life! Serve him with a heart of gladness and a singlemindedness that puts him above all else. And then, praise him for his goodness to you.

May 7

MATTHEW 4:1-3A

"Then Jesus was led by the Spirit into the wilderness to be tempted by the devil. And after fasting for forty days and forty nights, he was hungry. And the tempter came…" ESV

When we are weak, weary and worried with life as it comes toward us, the Enemy will be at our door waiting to present us with strong temptation to sin. He will use deception and the Word to fool us into thinking wrong thoughts to move us out of what we think is more than we can bear. These words remind us that Jesus was to be tempted just as we are in this evil day, in the world we must live. It was necessary that he be, since he was our Savior. There is no sin in being tempted by the evil one. Jesus shows that.

He was able to overcome the devil even though the devil used the Holy Scriptures to tempt our Lord. He used them deceptively. But Jesus knew them well, all of the Word. We need to know the "rest of the story" of the Lord's words to us if we are to be overcomers. The blood of our precious Redeemer covers us and we can use the Word rightly when we are stressed and being approached by the tempter as we are loaded with the grief of living in this sinful world. He was able. We can be able to overcome with the Word as well. Read the rest of this chapter to learn more of our Lord's use of the Word to withstand the tempter. He left us the perfect example of overcoming. Follow in his way. Believe and become victorious.

May 8

MATTHEW 9:20

"Just then, a woman who had suffered from bleeding for twelve years approached from behind and touched the tassel on his robe, for she said to herself, 'If I can just touch his robe, I'll be made well.' But Jesus turned and saw her. Have courage, daughter,' he said. 'Your faith has made you well.'" HCSB

Can you imagine the halting steps of this woman who had been an outcast because of her disease? Would you think for a minute how tremblingly, but bold, she was to come into the group around Jesus just to get close enough to touch that hem of his garment? She was not allowed to be there. But the draw of Jesus was more than she could hold back and she moved to reach out and touch, just touch, the edge of that robe that flowed from his shoulders.

And Jesus knew. Jesus always knows when we are there behind him waiting for just a small glimmer of seeing his face or chance of touching his robe. While we keep waiting, walking a little behind him, still looking for him to see us, he turns and there we are, face to face with our Lord. He does not even mind our need or the hand that slightly touches his garment as it moves to receive his blessing. Today is the day of blessing for you. Stay close and your hand can receive his blessings too. He loves even you!

May 9

MARK 12:41,42, 43B

"And he sat down opposite the treasury and watched the people
putting money into the offering box. Many rich people put
in large sums. And a poor widow came and put in two small
copper coins, which make a penny... (Jesus) said to them,
'Truly ...this poor widow has put in more than all...'" ESV

What a contrast between people and their giving to the Lord! Jesus
calls his disciples together to make such a statement to them that
they might understand it is not always about the dollar amount that
one gives. It is about being willing to give no matter what you have
left after your gift. It is about the heart that desires to please the Lord
out of a great love for him. It is about an attitude that all belongs to
him and we are overseers of his gifts to us. Sharing is a blessing in
itself.

Take stock of your possessions and realize they all belong to God
who brought them into your life. He blesses your cheerful heart as
your share willingly with others and to further his kingdom. He
gives generously and kindly. You can do the same. Become his channel to your world. As you have been blessed, bless others. The joy
that reaches you will be one of the greatest gifts you will ever receive.

May 10

MATTHEW 8:14

"And when Jesus entered Peter's house, he saw his mother-
in-law lying sick with a fever. He touched her hand, and the
fever left her, and she rose and began to serve him." ESV

Oh, the joy of the touch of Jesus when we are in desperate need. When Jesus saw the need, he responded with favor and was willing to touch the one who was ill regardless of whatever the disease was before him. He was not fearful of her or the disease. Praise God he was unafraid! How often he warns and encourages us not to fear.

There are or will be times in your life when you are ill and need your Savior's touch. Be willing to allow him to approach you with his healing hand. Do not fear that he will harm you. He knows exactly what you need. It is up to him those he chooses to heal. But notice that when he healed, she rose up and served him with his needs. If Jesus gives favor and healing to you, rise up and serve him with all of your heart. He has favored you to keep running the race he has set before you.

But when Jesus chooses for his own reasons not to heal, still know that he has you on his own heart and loves you dearly too. I do not know why he chooses as he does, but I do know he is in control of all things and loves either way. He knows what is best for each of us. At those times, it is good to "rise up in your heart" to serve him with your praises and honor the one who made you. He will never leave you alone in this life. Trust him.

May 11

GENESIS 12:1,4

"Now the Lord had said to Abram: 'Get out of your country,
from your father's house, to a land I will show you … So Abram
departed … and Abram was seventy-five years old …'" NKJV

I have always said when I reached seventy I would have to admit I
was old. Well, I lied! I didn't do that. I suppose I didn't look in the
mirror very often at that old woman there. I began to notice things
were a little more difficult to do, that I couldn't last as long working
in the yard as I "ustacud." Well, ten years after that seventy, I decided
to see what God thought about being old and finished! Hence, this
Abram story.

God gave Abram a big thing to do when he was seventy-five,
when he said to him, "Get up old man. I have a message for you…
boy, do I have a message for you! Leave your home, family, even your
country, everything you know and let's go to a place I have in mind
for you!" Note: God did not say, "Here, I have a plan with maps and
charts in hand for you. All you have to do is read these and follow
them to this place down the road a bit."

How was I feeling? I wanted to go back to bed that day! I figured
I had earned the right to be tired and weary. Blot out that Scripture
that reminded me to not grow weary of doing good! I thought about
this: Abram's greatest job was assigned to him in old age. In a very
few days I will be eighty. I'm beginning to wonder what God still has
in store for me???

I'm thinking the ending of life, the slowing down, the
strength-losing, the crepe-paper-looking skin around the eyes, the
snowy hair, the rounded belly instead of the rounded thighs of Song
of Solomon, the elbow skin sliding into the arm pit when lifting your
hands, the eyes dim even in bright light, that all of these are simply
the new beginning of life getting ready for the real future, the real
life, my best life to come: my heavenly home. But I am looking every

day for a new message from God this side of that final destination. Dear God, save me from becoming old between my ears. Old is not about how I look and feel. It is a mind-set. Keep me excited about living, Lord! Until…

May 12

PSALM 113:9

"He gives the barren woman a home, making her
the joyous mother of many children." ESV

Yes, I know Mother's Day is just over the horizon, just around the bend of time. Since I can no longer praise my Mother to her face, I thought I would praise her to you by sharing memories of her and what she was to me. For these next few days, up to that special day, taking one letter of the word "Mother" each day I will share her with you. Today is the letter "M."

In my heart of memories, "M" is for the Many times she covered me in the dead of night when it was cold outside. She would pull the sheets and the homemade   quilt up around me and snuggle me down under them, giving a small hug as she did so. The cold wind at the windows made no chill to me. Also, there were so Many, Many occasions she forgave me for thoughtless words or deeds, or even down-right rebellion against her position over me. She never held those growing pangs against me either as I moved on into adulthood.

She was a Memory Maker for me and my three older brothers, cooking special foods we loved, and by sewing our clothes, mine all the way to college. The scraps from those clothes became those home-made quilts in time. She took us the places she could afford and told us about the ones she couldn't. She wanted us to know about God's world and people. My love for books and words came from her I am certain. She became a Mover- Over- Person, letting us come on to shine when she was really the one who upheld our endeavors and strengthened us to excel all the way to completion. What does the "M" in Mother mean to you?

May 13

PSALM 113:9

"He gives the barren woman a home, making her
the joyous mother to many children." ESV

It is not necessary to give birth to babies to become a mother. In this instance, God gives the barren woman a home where she can have many children. It can happen many ways: marrying a man with children, adopting little ones, or simply taking in those who need a place to be loved and cared for as they grow up. Today I will take the letter "O" from the word Mother to share about my Mother, long gone home to the Lord.

The letter "O' makes me think of the way Mother had of helping me see the Options that were available to me in any given situation. She led me to think through things that way so easily. I can now decide many things the way she taught me, looking far down the road to see the law of unintended consequences and where that can go!

She showed me about Others too, for she always had room at her table for others. There was always enough to share. Now I too can share my table, for I realize God can divide what's on that table for however many are around that table. She showed me the Oughts in life. I "ought" to be kind, truthful, honest and reliable. That was simply how one was to be!

My Mother was an Over-Achiever at many things. She could cook, sew, farm, plow a mule or drive a tractor. She was the family carpenter, flower grower and beautiful pie maker. There just about wasn't anything she couldn't do when she tried. When I need to do something I am having trouble doing, I remember what she told me over and over again. If you need to do something, do it! And, if it's worth your time doing, do it well! What does the letter ''O'' mean to you in the word Mother?

May 14

PSALM 113:9

"He gives the barren woman a home, making her
a joyous mother to many children." ESV

I believe God calls many women to be mothers to children not born from their own bodies. He places them next to ones who need "mothering." When they respond in nurturing ways, they become a mother to that one, meeting the need we all have to receive special nurturing in this life. In honor of those mothers, I want to continue the use of each letter of the word "Mother," bringing us to the letter "T" for today.

When I remember my own Mother, the first thought is for Total giving. When she was tired from working on our family farm, there was still supper to make for the six of us, my three older brothers and me with our parents. For several years, my grandmother lived with us too until her death. I would wake up to her taking homemade biscuits from the old oven, wood for many years, eventually gas, then electric. She would warm my clothes on the oven door after this. She made certain everyone else had enough before taking a part of the "last of anything." Mother gave us what we needed regardless of any need she had. That's just the way it was.

But the best thought for "T" is Time. I really have no idea how she did what she did. She would be ironing or sewing when I went to sleep. She would still be doing it when I would get up in the morning. She cooked from scratch, could sew without a pattern, drove me to piano lessons and school occasions, all after her day's doings. She was tireless, or so I thought. Her life was for us and yet, she always looked like a lady when she went to town from the farm. She was a master at managing her Time. What does the letter "T" mean for your Mother?

May 15

PSALM 113:9

"He gives the barren woman a home, making
her a joyous mother of children." ESV

God has delivered to this woman without children the opportunity to have children, the joyous opportunity to have them! When you have not had the joy of birthing children, to suddenly get them is a special day in your life. Mother's Day is just a few days away and I would like to continue the use of the letters of the word "Mother" as we consider what it is being one. Today is the letter "H" for us to think and enjoy together.

The obvious one that is tailor-made for my Mother is Hospitality. She had that one down pat. It was her middle name, as they say. There was never a person turned away from her door or her table. It didn't matter what the condition of the living room was or what was on the dining table to eat. It wasn't about the house or even herself. It was always about making that stranger feel accepted and glad to be there in her Home at her table. If supper wasn't done yet, she could turn out a Heavenly one in a half hour fit for any guest.

Mother had a Heart for the down-and-outer, the down-trodden or the weak folks who needed encouragement. And she was excellent at turning the face "right side up" as she gladdened the Heart of those around her. Her Hand reached out to the poor because she had been poor for many of her early years. She understood the meaning of watching every penny to make it through each week. Her life had been hard and she grasped that others could use a Helping Hand. What do you remember for your Mother's letter "H"?

May 16

PSALM 113:9

"He gives the barren woman a home, making
her the joyous mother of children." ESV

When you have never had the experience of becoming a mother by giving birth to a little one, it is difficult to see the strength of the joy expressed in this verse. To the woman who is barren, it is beyond happiness to be given the opportunity to be called "Mother" as God gives to this woman. It was the gift of Everything. That is the letter to be seen today, the letter "E."

And that is exactly what a woman in this position would feel on becoming a Mother. It would be Everything. It would mean she would become those children's protector, provider of nurturing life, encourager, strength, laughter and the giver of unconditional love. She would be glad to share her life with those little ones. That's what my Mother was for me, each of those things. There were times she was even my corrections officer! She knew when to direct and lead to another path. She saw when it was time to set me on my feet to strive on my own.

My Mother Entered through the door of birth to give me my first breath. Mother Entered into a covenant with God to grow me to know the Lord God, her God. She was my Earliest Teacher of the Word of God. The Word was alive in her methods of teaching and she made certain that I was an apt student of that process. There are no words of gratitude that would be sufficient to thank her enough for her diligence here. What are the attributes of your Mother that would tell me about the letter "E" in your relationship with her?

May 17

PSALM 113:9

"He gives the barren woman a home, making
her the joyous mother of children." ESV

God is so gracious to this childless woman here. He places her in a home where she is the mother of children, not a single child, but children, multiple ones! Joy unspeakable is here! Which brings us to the last letter of the word "Mother," the "R," the finisher of the word.

When I remember my own Mother, long gone into glory to receive her rest at the feet of her Lord, there are several reminders of this letter.

The first is the fact that she was the Remover of Barriers that would hold me back. She was invested with me as I grew. To do this, she would show me ways to overcome barriers instead of trying to go through them. She could navigate them ahead of me, revealing the corners and side steps to take to see around the bend. Together we could tackle big barriers. Together was the key. She led, occasionally pushed, but always with the idea of opening the way for me to go through on my own. So, we Remained together, strong in the face of adversity, always believing in me to arrive at my goal.

She was a master at knowing when and how to Raise the Bar to spur me on to excellence rather than mediocrity. There was that line over which she stretched me to become all that God had created me to be. Did I always appreciate this as a kid? No, of course not. But today I am grateful for her doing so. Through it all, she Retained Love for me, regardless of my lack of discipline some of the time. What characteristics of your Mother relate to the letter "R" in your life?

May 18

PSALM 127:2

"It is useless for you to work so hard from early morning
until late at night, anxiously working for food to
eat; for God gives rest to his loved ones." NLT

This is a verse I have had to remind myself of so many times over the years, for I have a tendency to burn the candle at both ends. Not a good trait to work under! God doesn't like for us to worry about having enough food. Check out the word, "anxiously" in Matthew 6 for his words on this. But he does expect us to work. Remember the Apostle Paul's warning that he who does not work shall not eat! We need our sleep and he has provided for us to be able to sleep. He gave us night to lay aside our troubles and hard work to renew our lives to meet the coming morning with enough to do what needs to be done. We now work every hour of every day with shifts. We were smart enough to learn how to make electricity. With that equation came light around the clock! That does make it very difficult for humans to get proper rest. Decide, that is, choose, to plan for some down time to fill you with a new sense of well - being, realizing that God has a plan for both work and rest. He was quite thoughtful about giving us a day of rest as well.

Today I came home after worship and took a nice long full sleep that I called a nap. Perhaps it was a little over the top at being an hour. But I was so rested when I got up that I could finish the day and feel as renewed as was needed. I didn't need to putter around the balance of the afternoon. I actually could reach out to embrace the day. And when evening came, the sun went down and I knew the day was over, there were no regrets for what wasn't done. I had taken the time the Lord made for me to recuperate and used it as I was meant to do. The day is gone and I am at peace with it. Night, night, friends. Sleep tight…

May 19

PSALM 128:1-3

"Blessed is every one that fears the Lord, that walks in his
ways. For you shall eat the labor of your hands; happy
shall you be, and it shall be well with you." ESV

The career of being a farmer is not like so many other career choices
we make. In fact, I don't believe farming is a vocation at all. I have
seen through several generations of farmers that it is more like a way
of life. It invades every part of the farmer's day and night. It affects
that person from the breakfast table to the bedroom; there is no part
of a farmer's day that the farm is not a thought traveling through that
farmer's head, whether man or woman. As a fact, women now own
most of the active farm based agricultural businesses.

Of this I am certain, a farm is a way where one sees the direct
connection between the "job" to the eating of one's labors. I realize
there are other jobs where this connection is seen too. But the farmer
eats the exact vegetable, fruit, or meat, that is raised on that farm.
He eats the thing that is planted or fed in the barn lot. Remember
too, on a farm, if you feed it, whether through feed or fertilizer, it
eventually feeds you!

An important rule for farmers is this: a farmer does what Is
needed, when it is needed, where it is needed, the way it is needed
to be done whether that one wants to do it or not! And the amazing
part is that the farmer doesn't even mind doing it. That person loves
doing it. Wouldn't it be great if we took that same attitude with us as
we move through our days and are given the opportunity to witness
to others about the love of Jesus? Any farmer I know loves to talk
about the crop, be it vegetables, fruit or animals. That farmer talks
with an animation of voice that lets others know the love that is
expressed in doing it. If we would do what was needed, when it was
needed, where it was needed, the way it needed to be done whether
we really felt like doing it or not, how different our service to God

would be. Keep in mind the farmer keeps the goal in sight. That goal is the harvest. Our heavenly goal is also a harvest. Others can tell too if you love bringing that goal in just as the love the farmer shows as the price is paid to get that harvest into the "barn". It takes time, effort, energy, strength and willingness to finish the crop. It takes all those for the heavenly crop too. Are we willing to pay the price of harvesting with God, our Heavenly Farmer?

May 20

"I remember your genuine faith, for you share the faith that
first filled your grandmother, Lois and your mother, Eunice.
And I know that same faith continues strong in you." NLT

For many years as God kept bringing children in to our lives, I
thought the whole world needed more mothers, women who would
love unconditionally, who would see through a child's or teenager's
actions to read the motives of their hearts and give back, not what
the young one deserved but what that one needed. I still believe that
we need more genuine mothers, but I also realize that we really need
more grandmothers too. Yes, I know that every woman who gives
birth does not a wonderful mother make. That knowledge does not
cut down on the need for more real mothers. And I know that not
giving birth does not hinder one from becoming a genuine mother
or grandmother in every sense.

The ability to nurture a child can be natural or it can be culti-
vated. It's a trait that is grown as we practice it. There are so many
little ones who could use that extra hand reaching down to lift them
up. There are many young mothers who could use an extra hand
with nurturing their young. They will not ask but the need is often
apparent, especially to a grandmother who can remember back to
her youthful days of mothering and would have loved such an offer.

The world of "grannying" is one of the greatest places of service
that I know. Listen to Paul's words to young Timothy. This young
man had a godly grandmother and mother for training in his early
years. That made it so much easier for the older Apostle Paul to build
on their teachings and training of the young pastor Timothy. Notice
that the grandmother is mentioned first! She had taught Timothy's
mother and continued to teach that next generation alongside of his
mother. Notice too that the father is not mentioned here. They were
much like our single parents today. They became a team to give their

child the best they each had. You can be a mother and grandmother too, regardless of biology. You can also be an older man, a grandfather type, in these young lives, just as Paul was to young Timothy. Choose to honor God by spreading your love over a child that God brings your way. Let him bless that one through you as he blesses you through that child!

May 21

ACTS 8:27, 29-30

"As for Phillip. An angel of the Lord said to him, 'Go south down the desert road that runs from Jerusalem to Gaza…' (he does) and he met the treasurer of Ethiopia, a eunuch of great authority under…the queen… the eunuch had gone to Jerusalem to worship, and was now returning … (and) was reading aloud from the book of Isaiah, The Holy Spirit said to Phillip, 'Go over and walk along beside the carriage,' Phillip ran over and heard the man reading… Phillip asked, 'Do you understand what you are reading?' The man replied, 'How can I, unless someone instructs me?' And he urged Phillip to come up into the carriage and sit with him." NLT

We all know the rest of the story, how the eunuch hears about Jesus, understands, receives the Good News and is baptized. But the thought I would like for us to explore is that unnamed and unsung person who gave this Ethiopian the Word written by the prophet Isaiah. None of the harvest reaped by Phillip could have occurred without this person. So many times, we desire to be the Phillip in God's army and ignore the unnamed people who plant the seed, those who faithfully water it, or the ones who regularly fertilize the planted seed of the Good News. We would all rather be the one on the end of the line where we are seen and named. Perhaps, this weekend, wherever God takes us, with whomever He places us or to what place he sends us, we could be willing to do a little gardening and plant that wonderful seed that can be reaped by another of God's army at another time and place into eternal life. What a joy to be one of God's unnamed heroes.

Today is the day to be found faithful right where God has put you for his plan of reaping his harvest. Be obedient. Also, learn from Phillip, when opportunity comes from the Holy Spirit for reaping, ask questions. He knew exactly where the Ethiopian was in his quest. He knew just where to start with answers. Phillip and Jesus both used the teaching technique of asking questions!

May 22

ACTS 4:13

"Now when they saw the boldness of Peter and John and perceived
they were uneducated and untrained men, they marveled.
And they realized that they had been with Jesus." NKJV

Have you ever thought about whether or not people around you
have any idea that you have been with Jesus? As it was with these two
disciples, so it was with Moses when he had been on the mountain
with God in Exodus 34:29-35. The shine on Moses's face was so
intense the people were afraid to approach him when he came off the
mountain. It wanders around in the back of my mind that sort of
thing. Can folks see his brightness in my eyes or know his love from
my speech, or do they know before I touch them that it will be a gentle move of kindness that they will receive from fingers? I confess that
too many times I react in situations instead of stopping and thinking,
then acting. More times than not it is carelessness on my part. What
about you? If I am to be ready and able to step through the doors
before me, that God has placed in front of my face, I would like
to think I will be bringing the Light of the World into that room
instead of any darkness that would cloud my life and others lives.

Today I would spend time with my Savior so that he can shine
up my countenance as he lifts the darkness from me and fills me with
light…his Light. Don't let the cloudiness of the world slide in with
the fog of chilly hearts to dull your brightness from him. Warm your
heart with his Word and shine for him at every opportunity Make
room in your agenda for the divine appointments that only God can
give you. Meet him there.

May 23

LUKE 9:59A

"Then Jesus said to another, 'Follow Me.' But he
said, Lord, let me first go…' " NKJV

You fill in the blanks. Every day we must get and keep our priorities straight. It is always Jesus first. But we so often allow the cares of this life to strangle our heart for him. We put those in line before our Lord. Today we have the opportunity to place Jesus at the head of our day. We can learn a few of his words to hide in our hearts that will keep us from careless sins that so easily trip us up. He has said, "Follow Me." The call from Jesus is to follow him every day, all day. It is a choice, always a choice.

Tomorrow is not here yet. But today is rising with the sun over the horizon as it does each day. As it becomes light, turn your horizon to his face and say, "Yes, Lord, today I will follow you, all day. Keep my mind, my heart, focused on your words, your never- ending love and mercy toward me. As I choose your Way, be my strength to obey your call to follow. May you be glorified in me this one day. There is nothing else I think I must do first!"

PS There is nothing else you need to do first either, folks! Mama said!

May 24

MATTHEW 4:1-2

"Then Jesus was led up by the Spirit into the wilderness to be tempted by the devil. And when he had fasted forty days and forty nights, afterward He was hungry. Now when the tempter came to Him, he said, 'If you are the Son of God, command that these stones be turned into bread.'" NKJV

I want to explore the thoughts about our Lord being tempted by the Enemy. Those temptations were tailor made for Jesus. They were meant to make Jesus unfit to be our Savior. But I want you to realize that the Enemy knows you well too. He will tailor make your temptations also. He can turn your thoughts and mind, your desires and wants into a sin rather quickly!

The best lesson I want you to learn in this setting is that, if Jesus was tempted, was actually led into that wilderness to be tempted, what makes you believe that you won't be tempted too? Jesus did not turn away from the hour of tempting. Jesus went obediently into that wilderness and came out victorious as he used the words of his Father to combat the devil.

Another lesson is to remember that the Enemy came when Jesus was at his lowest physically. When you are weak from hunger or thirst, expect the Enemy's appearance. When you are weak from anger, weary from work, strained from relationships or stressed financially, you become an easy mark for the devil. Be alert. Be on your guard. He is around somewhere at those times in your life. Raise your eyes to look on Jesus then. Fill your mind with the words of our Lord to be able to pull them out from the bottom of your memory bank when he slips into your presence. Jesus overcame the Enemy, that is, the devil. You can too by the testimony of the word and the blood of the Lamb. Rise, believer. Obey!

May 25

LUKE 11:17

"Knowing their thoughts…" HCSB

There were times when I was a child, when I believed my mother had the ability to know my thoughts, especially when those thoughts were not nice! My brother next to me in the lineup of children and I, (there were two older than the two of us) called mother "Sherlock Holmes" after the famed detective from the books we read. We really thought she knew everything we did!

But the Word says that our Lord Jesus knew the thoughts of those around him as he walked in our world as a man. I do not understand how, apart from the Lordship of Jesus. But I don't have to understand; I just need to accept the fact that he did. He was aware of the failings of his disciples, as well as, the evil men who sought to do away with him. He worked with the disciples and he placed condemnation on the evil ones. He chose it that way.

The blessed hope I have in realizing that Jesus knows my inner thoughts, the failings of my mind and passions, is that he worked with those few men and I can trust him to work with me. He carefully revealed more of himself to them as they grew in their understanding of who Jesus was. You and I can lay our hearts open to him, so that we accept his knowing, and his love in spite of knowing, so that he can train us to think as he did. He thought about the ones who would hear his words and believe. He thought about the desire of their hearts to know him better and he taught them consistently how. He walked with them, laughed with them and drew stronger pictures of God's plan regularly. He can do that for us. Take today and offer your all to him to train and prepare you for his plan.

May 26

LUKE 5:27-29

"And after this he went out and saw a tax collector named
Levi…and said to him, 'Follow me.' And leaving everything,
he rose and followed him. And Levi made a great feast in
his house, and there was a large company of tax collectors
and others reclining at table with them." ESV

It is amazing to me how often the table and food enters the Scriptures
to show a change of heart in someone. In this case, Levi, immediately
wanted to share his new mentor, the one he was willing to leave all
for, with his fellow tax collectors that they too could get to know this
Jesus. It was important to him to have others meet Jesus too.

One of the greatest avenues of witness that each of us has is our
home and our table that can become a blessed way of sharing Jesus
easily and often. It does not have to be expensive or fabulous fair
that you sit down at your table to offer a meal to others. And around
that table the opportunities that lead into discussions about Jesus
are many and simple. It does not have to be great discourse on deep
subjects either. It can be the gentle way of telling how Jesus made
a difference to you alone or how that acceptance of Jesus as Lord
changed your life and the life of your family.

Take today to include a few others around that table you sit
at regularly and open your heart and your pantry. It is easy, can be
quick and need never be elaborate. It's your choice. It's always about
choices, isn't it?

May 27

"Whatever your hand finds to do, do it with your might…" ESV

All of the years my mother was with me, she would tell me, "If a thing is worth doing, it is worth doing right!" On learning to sew, she said, "Choose the best material you can afford when starting a dress, shirt or shorts. When you are done with it, it will be worth wearing."

So, these words of King Solomon ring well in my memory for her words. If you are cheap with materials, you will have no good item of clothing when finished, no matter how well sewed. She also said to use the best of food from your garden or farm, not the "culls' when feeding the family. They are worth the best that you have. When making a simple supper, she would serve it on a plate on a table cloth that may have had a hole in it from years of wear, for she seldom threw away anything. She would patch it, press it and use it! But that simple supper would have been served with pleasure. Whatever she did, she did with all her strength, that she could stand back at her finish line and be grateful for the effort.

As, I am partially a product of her teachings, I have shared many of these "sayings" with my realm of influence through all of these many years. They have brought many a laugh from the family! But still, I say, "Thank you, Mother, for your faithfulness, for your example of making life better for those around by using my best for others." You'll notice I didn't say my most expensive, but my personal best. God has gifted you with much. Whatever you find to do today, do it with your strength to your finish line for this one day.

May 28

EPHESIANS 5:22 A

"Wives, submit to your own husbands, as to the Lord, for the husband is head of the wife, as Christ is head of the church." ESV

How often I hear young women complaining about this verse! And yes, older ones too. We have a mental block when it comes to the idea of submission. Sometimes I think we are reading it as "surrender" with all the negative connotations associated with losing. We forget that we are one flesh and as such, we are not against each other. We are not on a battlefield as opposing soldiers!

I learned a long time ago a very good way of looking at this idea of submitting. When we are given a large, heavy shaped board and then handed four squares of lumber, that's what we have: five pieces of lumber! But, if I take the four straight squares of wood and attach them to the large, shaped board, whether round, square or oblong, I have a table, a ONE PIECE useful table that can give many blessings to those who sit around it.

But, unless I am willing to be a part of the table as the squares of wood under that board, I can never have the table. I can wish for a lovely table, I can want one. I can look for one anywhere in my house. But I must be able to submit to that large, heavy piece of board to have the table meant for my house. Without those square straight "legs" under that board, the board is only a board! It takes both of us working together, as God intended, for there to be the right sized, the smooth topped, table desired for my home. But God is not finished with my home yet. Next God talks to my husband! But I must set myself straight before he sets my mate on a right path.

May 29

EPHESIANS 5:25, 28

"Husbands, love your wives, just as Christ loved the church
and gave himself for her... Husbands are to love their wives as
their own bodies. He who loves his wife, loves himself." ESV

To continue the idea of a table with four legs submitting to the top, making that slab of board a table, think of it this way. If the table were to start slapping at the legs that hold it up, or if it were to take a knife and begin to shave down the edges of the square legs, it would be reducing the strength that gives it stability. The more it hurts the legs under it, the more it is removing that very thing that makes it what it is! We need each other even to begin to be who God intended us to be when he placed us together.

The example that God gave husbands to follow is our Lord Jesus and the way he gave everything for his bride, the church, all the way to the cross. His love for her was pure, it was favorable, it was priceless to her. Together they made the church. He the head. Her the body. There is no lack there. There is only loving of the other.

We have a choice, women. We have a choice, men. What do we want, the table from which blessings flow to us, the family and to others outside the home who sit there with us? Or do we want what we want before the spouse's needs are even considered? Husbands, love your wives completely, unreservedly and unconditionally. Wives, respect the man God gave you by becoming what he needs to be the "Table of your dreams"! Alone we are just five pieces of wood. Together, with mutual honor and love, we are the place where God can send delight and joy.

May 30

ECCLESIASTES 12:10

"The Preacher (King Solomon) sought to
find acceptable words…" NKJV

The meaning of the word acceptable is to find words that can bring delight to the ears of the hearers, whether they are words of correction, encouragement, strength, or laughter. Take a few moments to think upon this and begin to learn how to say your words so that they have the ability to bring to your hearers ears the truth of life couched in delightful words that open the minds and hearts of those with whom you are interacting. It can even be a corrective message you are delivering to them.

Anywhere your little feet can take you, you will find that folks listen a lot better when they are not put on the defensive so quickly. I am not suggesting that you fold the truth into a lie or that you take the truth and cover it in false language. I am suggesting that you listen to the Holy Spirit for the right words that can bring an open ear that can bring teachable spirit into the heart of your listener. Neither am I suggesting you mix your truth with a spoonful of sugar. Just think before you speak. Make certain you are able to speak from the position of loving that person before you.

Today is a good day to share delightful words with those you meet, whether your loved ones, your co-workers, those serving you or the stranger in the grocery store. You are the face of the Lord to those with whom you travel this road of life. What is the reflection you are revealing to them about Jesus? Look into the mirror and check out that face you call yours. Then make any changes you need to address! Mama's just saying…

May 31

2 TIMOTHY 2:3,6

"Share in suffering as a good soldier of Christ
Jesus… The hardworking farmer ought to be
the first to get a share of the crops." ESV

On this last Monday in the month of May that we call Memorial Day, remember we are to be good soldiers of the cross of Christ. We are to be those who, like the good warrior, will go wherever he sends, serve with whomever he places us, and minister to any that he brings into our view. We are at his disposal each day.

During World War Two, my father was a farmer and as such, was classified as four-F and not accessible to service duty. It was considered as important to feed the soldiers and our nation as to fight on a battlefield. There is a saying that "an army crawls on its belly"; therefore, farmers were soldiers too.

As we honor those who served or are still serving, those who did not return from their active duty and those who minister as soldiers, in the cause of Christ as chaplains, determine to say a thank you to those whom you meet who wear any uniform of any branch. We are able to be here, safe, because of the many who have paid the price of time and life for us. Never make ugly remarks to them or about them!

Like the hardworking farmer, we reap the blessings of a wonderful country. We have doors that welcome those soldiers into our hearts. Give one a hug today and say thank you!

June 1

"And take heed, lest you lift your eyes to heaven, and
when you see the sun, the moon, and the stars, all the
host of heaven, you feel driven to worship them and
serve them, which the Lord your God has given to all the
peoples under the whole heaven as a heritage." NLT

To take heed is to pay attention to a thing or person. God forewarns his people to take heed lest you, that is, for fear you will, carelessly start doing that wrong act. He does not take lightly his people worshipping his creation over the Creator of those heavenly bodies, for any reason. Watch out, dear folks.

In this day, there are many who challenge you, who entice you, who desire you to worship these bright objects scattered around in the heavens. These people believe they have great powers over you to guide you into a better life, a more productive and gainful way. They are wrong. Verse 24 in this chapter reminds you that our God is a consuming fire, a jealous God. He will not share his glory with anything he has created. He alone is to be worshipped and desired.

How kind of him to let you know how he feels about this and to be sure you understand this is poisonous and deadly for you to slip into such a practice. When God is generous with his leadership of you, listen. He is really saving you from hardship ahead. There are consequences to this chosen behavior. Do not be taken in by these erroneous folks who desire your destruction. Take heed, for fear of the disaster before you when you make that choice to worship these that God gave to all mankind to enjoy and to chart the heavens for a guide to travel, not to your life. Worship the Lord only all your days.

June 2

1 COR. 8:1; 13:1-3, 8-9

"...Yes, we know that 'we all have knowledge' about this issue. But while knowledge makes us feel important, it is love that strengthens the church... If I could speak all the languages of earth and of angels, but didn't love others, I would only be a noisy gong or a clanging cymbal. If I had the gift of prophecy, and if I understood all of God's secret plans and possessed all knowledge, and if I had such faith that I could move mountains, but didn't love others, I would be nothing. If I gave everything I have to the poor, and even sacrificed my body...but didn't love others, I would have gained nothing...Prophecy...and special knowledge will become useless, but love will last forever. Now our knowledge is partial and incomplete, and even the gift of prophecy reveals only part of the whole picture." NLT

How well this reveals that it isn't about doing great things for God. It is about loving others with a genuine, whole love that embraces those around us whom God has given us to care for and touch with his Good News and great love. It is about real life, because love is where life is! Our life came from God's great love for us that he gave his son to be our Redeemer, our Savior. As I said, love is where life is!

June 3

AMOS 3:3

"Can two walk together, except they be agreed" KJV

When I was young, growing up on the farm where my family grew tomatoes and other vegetables, it was my job to learn to hoe those little plants well so they had no competition for the fertilizer they were given. The teacher for me was my daddy. I was about twelve years-old at the time. Here's how he did it, teaching me so much more than just how to hoe. He taught me to hoe standing up straight, so as not to kill my back as I did a whole row. He gave me a slender hoe with a very thin blade that was sharpened to a razor edge. Those three things showed me a whole lot about working with people. He gave me the right size for me. He gave the right weight so I wouldn't get tired too soon and give up. He made certain the hoe was ready for the job. It was very sharp, able to cut the weeds quickly and with less effort from me. And he said to approach the job face-on, standing tall.

When you are working with folks, make sure you do the same. Give them the right equipment for them to fit their God-given abilities, well prepared so they don't get too tired too soon and give up. Encourage them with how to approach the job, to face it and stand tall to meet it. The last thing he did was to walk beside me as I started my "row to hoe." A good teacher is there with you to draw you on to the finish. Thank you, daddy, for walking with me down my personal "row to hoe" in life.

June 4

DEUTERONOMY 4:9

"Only take heed to yourself, and diligently keep yourself,
lest you forget the thing your eyes have seen, and lest they
depart from your heart all the days of your life. And teach
them to your children and your grandchildren." NKJV

Take heed to yourself are words of great wisdom to each of us. We would do well to pay attention to our choices that are slipping slightly away from God's way laid out for us in his Word. They don't move a lot to begin with; they move ever so slightly, inching along until we are a long way from his desire for us.

That same is true for our opportunities to teach right choices to our children. One day we will realize they are all grown and have slipped the nest to another place where they have a tendency to no longer listen to us if we've not made a strong relationship with them, one of trust and encouragement. It is important to share our experiences with the Lord earlier in their lives when they hang on our every word.

As grandparents, we also have the blessing from the Lord to share those ways of the Lord with the young ones that belong to our children. How sad if we never use that chance to share. They need to know of God's faithfulness to us, of his blessings, and of his trustworthiness in all things. We can both share his wonders and warn them of his hand of correction when failing to obey. We have experienced both! Don't miss this in their lives, even if you missed it with your own children. Share you God's word every opportunity you have. Leave the balance with the Holy Spirit to flesh it out in their memories in years to come.

June 5

1 SAMUEL 16:11-12

"Then Samuel said to Jesse, 'Are all your sons here?' And he
said, 'There remains yet the youngest, but, behold, he is
keeping the sheep.' And Samuel said to Jesse, 'Send and
get him...And he sent and brought him in. Now he was
ruddy and had beautiful eyes, and was handsome. And
the Lord said, 'Arise, anoint him, for this is he.'" ESV

The great part of this story told here is what each thought about
Jesse's youngest son, David. His father thought of him only as the
youngest who just kept the sheep for the family, sort of the last job
on the family list of chores. Even Samuel was surprised that none of
the older sons were considered the "one" that God had chosen. None
of the older brothers even thought of the baby brother either!

We do not see as God sees when we cast a look toward the folks
around us. We would not always choose wisely, would we? We are
impressed with the same things Samuel was as he checked out those
older boys, their appearance and their height. God even tells Samuel
in verse seven that he does not see as man does; he sees the heart of
the one being selected for his service. And when God saw David, the
youngest, the keeper of the sheep, he said this was his man!

So, when others don't see the value God has placed on you, do
not fret, God is not finished with you yet! You may be only a keeper
of the sheep, the bottom of the pile, so to speak, but God has plans
for you. Even your family may not see you as God does. That matters
not either. It is what God says about you that is important! Look to
him to see yourself with the calling of God upon you.

June 6

1 PETER 2:2A

"As newborn babes..." NKJV

When a new great-grandbaby enters our lives and households, that day is circled on our life calendars. It will be celebrated. It will be a day of joy and happiness. We hope to bless the new one with our love for all the days of life we have left, praying that will be many. I always remember back to the birth of our children and the joy and amazement we felt as each of those days unfolded.

Oh, yes, we gave God many chances to bring children to us. But it is only he who can bring life to bear. He is the one who chooses the time, the exact, the particular genes from each side of the family to place into the exact, particular child that makes each a one-of-a-kind, unique individual who can never be repeated or redrawn. Each is the only "one" that is that child. How incredible is that? They are each a blessing to us from God's own hand.

I also think about the freshness of "new birth" that comes from our Lord in our salvation. We too need to be fed at our Lord's table from his words that grow us, mature us and encourage us. It is words of blessing to us as he prepares us to live in the present time with each other. He has marked us with divine DNA that makes us uniquely set in his Kingdom. There is no other who has all the same markings as we each do. He has a plan for the individual that spans all of time. No one else can fill our place, do our job of praising him and serving him. It is ours alone. He has called us from before he set time in place.

Perhaps you have grown jaded in your appetite for the Lord in these rushing years. You are no longer a newborn babe in his Kingdom. Draw near to him. He will draw near to you and nurture you into maturity. Put a circle around today. Choose to make this day a day to be remembered as the one you let him teach, direct, sustain and encourage you to become all he created you to be.

June 7

1 PETER 2:2-5

"…as newborn babes, desire the pure milk of the word, that you may grow thereby, if indeed you have tasted that the Lord is gracious. Coming to him as to a living stone, rejected indeed by men, but chosen by God and precious, you also, as living stones, are being built up a spiritual house, a holy priesthood, to offer spiritual sacrifices acceptable to God through Jesus Christ." NKJV

Once we had the occasion to be with our ten -year-old grandson, along with his nine -year-old friend, in a "gem" mine store to sift through a bucket of dirt and rocks they give you, at thirty dollars a bucket, to see if there are any precious "stones" in there. I thought about the stones of God's word, those of us who know the "corner-stone," Jesus, and who are being built into a spiritual house for his glory. When I helped the boys to sift, I saw what the gem people called rocks and what they called stones. I could not tell the difference. In some instances, the stones had a heavy coating of rust on them and looked more like a rusty marble. To my surprise, that rust was hiding a ruby! But the rub comes with the knowledge that to get to the ruby you must tumble those stones in a tumbler which turns them over and over, bumping them against each other to knock off the rusty mess on the outside. Somewhere in there is the beauty that is the shiny red ruby. The three emerald stones were the same story. To get them out of the mire on the outside you must find them underneath the ugly outside. Then, they must be "cut" into the shape you desire.

You think we are possibly the same? God must clean the rust and mire from our outside ugliness to find the precious rubies and emeralds that each of us are made to be, those who know Jesus as our living stone, the "cornerstone" of our lives. If the ugly stones could speak, I think they would cry out at the rough treatment that must be done to them if they are ever to have the beauty they were designed to radiate to this world. I don't know about you, but I want

God to pretty me up so I'll shine for him as he strings me into the jewels he designed me to be. The ruby and the emerald are there all the time. It just takes a master's hand to deliver them from all that is one the outside to reveal the inner beauty in the depths of their lives. Do I enjoy the "tumbling" of my life? No! But I want to be all he has designed for me to be and that takes some tumbling. Thank God, he gives grace for it. We are his living stones, prepared by our Master's hand for his glory.

June 8

1 KINGS 19:5-6

"And as he lay and slept under a juniper tree, behold,
an angel touched him, and said unto him, 'Arise and
eat'. And he looked, and behold, there was a cake baked
on the coals, and a cruse of water at his head. And he
did eat and drink, and lay down again." KJV

I have told all of you many times that there is instruction for all needs in the Word. Not long ago, when I was sick, an angel, actually two of them, knocked on our door, bringing in a ''cruse'' of chicken soup (it was a big one!) and a "cake" of cornbread to go with it. They said in unison, "Get off that couch, arise and eat!" And when I did, I looked and there was the cruse of soup and the cake of corn bread. I did get off that couch and eat! I even let Big Buck eat too. When we were satisfied in our tummies, I did lay down again. These two wonderful friends literally fulfilled this scripture for us.

Somewhere, sometime in your future there will be an opportunity for you to bless another person with such a simple and wonderful gift of life, literally. Just chicken soup and corn bread but it was just what the doctor ordered for us and restored us completely. It's true what is said about that soup! It's bad to be sick anytime, but the older I get, the worse I feel when ill. So, remembering you too will be old one day, touch one who seems to be lying under a "juniper tree," all worn out and ill, and lift the spirit of that one with heartfelt joy and food. They will be as grateful as we.

June 9

1 CHRONICLES 28:9A

"… know the God of your father, and serve him with a whole
heart and a willing mind, for the Lord searches every heart
and understands the intention of every thought." HCSB

That you might know my father as I knew him, I will start with
the first letter of Father to explain as we celebrate Father's Day. My
Daddy was a farmer, a Faithful farmer. He knew the farm was his
way of providing for all of us and farms do not grow by themselves.
He worked each crop with all his heart whether he was tired or not.
That's the way farming was, always has been, always will be. Farming
is daily business!

I'm not sure whether he wanted a girl after those three sons or not,
but that is what God delivered to him. He never treated me as though
there were things a girl could not do and never discouraged me from
stretching myself to learn new things. He was way ahead of his time
with his attitude toward girls becoming all they could be. I found
Favor in him for believing in me and my heart's desires. He wanted
me to serve his God as he did. He wanted me to know the Lord even
closer and to love him with a whole heart. There was to be no divided
heart for God. After all, God knew the heart of every thought!

He was not one to share beautiful words of love. He said words
were cheap. Real love was expressed in actions for him. I never heard
those three little words, "I love you," but I knew! His delight was
ever on his face and in his eyes. Fathers are not perfect. They are just
Dads! What was your father like? Can you Forgive the hurt and cast
off the disappointments Dad sent your way, if that is your lot? Not
all dads are good, but they are always your dad, imperfect though
they be. God is the Faithful Father when your earthly one doesn't
meet the need. Look to him and rejoice that his love is not only
Faithful but also, perfect and unconditional. He loves you for his
word says so in many places. Search the Bible to find his expression
of that love.

June 10

HEBREWS 12:9

"… we have had human fathers who corrected us, and we paid them respect. Shall we not much more readily be in subjection to the Father of spirits and live?" NKJV

The letter "A" from the word father is my focus today. We all have fathers. Some are very good at doing the job. Some have difficulty and a few are very hard and painful as they try to fill the job. But they are always the man who gave us life, no matter their ability to be a good father or not.

My father was my first Accountability partner. I did not realize for a long time we were in partnership, but he did. When we were young, my three older brothers and I, they would send me to daddy to ask if we could do something or go somewhere that they wanted. I took that as quite a compliment from them. Or they thought daddy would be more favorable to his only daughter! I do not believe he was favoring me, but evidently, they did!

He was a man of very few words, but when he spoke, they carried importance. He was the first person I began to realize that language had so much ability to get what needed to be done, done! I would "practice" on him to see how speech made sense or brought favorability to the speaker. He was a willing partner there too.

Best of all, he was my first accounting of what God, my heavenly father, was like. Was he perfect as God is? No, of course not! But he was Always there for me, early morning and late at night. I learned to trust God as I learned to trust daddy, one step at a time. His words were mostly accepted by me. There were a few times I had to test him, of course. There were even a few I challenged, especially as an adult. Yes, I did the same with my heavenly Father! But each of them forgave and kept loving me. That's the first place I learned unconditional love, at my father's feet.

God is now my accountability partner. Thank you, daddy, for showing me how God works in our lives by the way you worked in mine. Can you see your father now with forgiveness for his mistakes and acceptance for the gift of life with which he brought you into this world? Forgiveness is a beautiful thing! It relieves the pain from having had a difficult daddy and sets you free from the chains that an unforgiving spirit binds around you. Choose forgiveness and freedom!

June 11

PSALM 119:30A, PROVERBS 4:1A, 2A, 4A

"Listen, my sons, to a father's discipline...for I am giving
you good instruction...he taught me and said, 'Your
heart must hold on to my words...'" HCSB

First, understand these truths are for daughters as well! How important it is to have a teachable spirit as a child. It doesn't hurt as an adult too. When I think about all those long- ago years under daddy's roof, I realize I had to "listen" through observation of him more than through formal sit-down type instruction. Mother taught more at her knee with words than he did. But he was my Teacher just the same. Here are the other "T's" for daddy:

He walked his talked in being Truthful, no matter the cost to him. He carried the load jointly with mother, for she worked in the fields with him. But together they showed me continually that one must learn to carry your own load. Be strong. Be Trustworthy, as he was, with working as long as was needed to succeed. It was very important in his heart for me to be True to myself.

The best and funniest way he ever expressed that was in a very short note he included in mother's weekly letter to me while in college in Atlanta, Georgia. It was the only note he ever wrote to me. It simply said: "Dear Vera Jo, Keep your chin up and your dress down!" I knew he cared that I enter life true to my upbringing!

Fathers, listen to what you are teaching your children whether you realize it or not. They see you. They hear you. They know you well. A lot better than you'd like them to know you! What are your actions saying so much louder than your words? It's not too late. Make a mindful change if you're being slack in life. They have a strong chance of being another you!

June 12

DEUTERONOMY 5:16

"Honor your father and your mother, as the Lord your God has
commanded you, so that you may live long and so that you may
prosper in the land the Lord your God is giving you." HCSB

My father was an Honorable man. But not all fathers are so.
Unfortunately, in this fallen world there are many who are abusive
and absent when needed by his children. But I am talking just about
mine. Since we are looking at the letter "H" in father today, I am so
grateful mine was an honest and caring one.

Daddy looked for the best in me. He walked beside me as I grew
and as I progressed into a young woman. He never told me there was
anything I couldn't do just because I was born a girl. I was free to
choose to learn what I was created to be. He took me to the packing
houses with him to watch what he did as he sold the vegetables he
had harvested that day. As he talked to the buyers, he would squat
down on the big platform where the end of his truck displayed his
goods, and would hold me next to him with his hand on my calf to
keep me steady so I wouldn't fall from that high floor. His hand was
my security. My sight of the Lord my God as Father was from the
care he gave. My God's Hand was as secure as his I thought. I learned
later it was even more so!

I also know Daddy was a Hopeful man. How? Because he always
planted another crop each fall and the next spring. He looked for the
reward from the labor of his own Hands. Those Hands were gnarled
from the physical work. I see that my hands and feet are much like
his. His were small for a man but they held all the strength I needed
as I grew up. I pray I walk in the footprints he left behind for me.
May I be as Honest as he. May I be as Hopeful as well. Look at the
man who gave life to you. Honor him whether he is as Honorable
as he should have been or not. It is good for you, even bringing the
possibility of a long life. The kind of character it takes to Honor one
not always honorable is the kind it takes to be wise here on earth.
That can give you a much longer life when you choose to be wise!

June 13

1 CHRONICLES 28:9

"…my son, know the God of your father, and serve him with
a whole heart and a willing mind, for the Lord searches every
heart and understands the intention of every thought." HCSB

I think of the letter "E" as I look at his life of teaching this little girl. One very strong reason my father was able to teach by his actions that he Embraced the God of his preacher father was in his regularly going to worship, being involved with church activities and needs. He had Eternity planted in his own heart and he became my big Example of following God his Father. He was chosen as a deacon when young while serving at the little local church in the farming area where we lived until I was grown.

He touched me with his strength of hope Every year when he planted a crop never really knowing what the weather or price would be for that crop. He was faithful in his Expectations of his God's provision for his little family. He gave all his Energy to his plan and trusted the God of his father to do what he had promised. When weather was harmful to the crop, he would be an overcomer by continuing his part of the job, never giving up. I don't remember ever having a failed crop where we did not have Enough for the coming days. It didn't always make much money but it was Enough.

When you consider you parenting days, did you give your full Energy to that important opportunity to teach your household to keep on Expecting the best for their future, full of Energy and Expectations with a heart full of God's Eternity, no matter what was before them? Pray for your children, grown or little, that they may see your heavenly Father in your own life and that they can know him because you were a good Example of him before them. If you weren't all you could have been, it's not too late to change by the power God gives in his Holy Spirit. Look up!

June 14

1 CORINTHIANS 4:7B

"…What do you have that you didn't receive?" HCSB

For the letter "R" in the word father: There are so many stories that I would like to share but there is not room enough for them all. But there is one that I must share. It is about the time when I went away to college in Atlanta, Georgia. I believe Daddy was a little concerned that his only daughter, his little country girl might not know how to be safe and secure in a big city.

I Received a very small note tucked in an envelope of normal length. There was room enough for a whole letter in there too, but the little note was all there was. I still have that tiny scrap of paper in a book of treasures that cannot be bought. It is priceless! Here is what the few words said: "Dear Vera Jo, keep your chin up and your dress down!"

It was some of the best, wisest advice a lonely girl a long way from home ever Received. That's what Daddy was to me, the giver of good things that I simply reached out and Received from his loving hand. So much the way my heavenly Father does with me still. He is my giver of the good life and I am the Receiver from his loving hand. My Daddy redeemed me from a life of want and fear while my heavenly Father Redeemed my soul. Thank you, Daddy. Thank you, Father.

Whether your earthly father was a good one or not, you can know the heavenly Father for a life well lived on this earth. Choose to know him. Be wise, receive his Redemption from his loving hand as you would from a loving father here.

June 15

2 SAMUEL 9:11B, 13

"'As for Mephibosheth, he shall eat at my table like one of the king's sons.' So Mephibosheth dwelt in Jerusalem, for he ate at the king's table. And he was lame in both feet." NKJV

Of course, Mephibosheth was Jonathan's son, and Jonathan was David's dearest friend in all the land. He was also King Saul's grandson, the king who had hunted David for years to kill him. After the death of both King Saul and Jonathan, David desired to do kindness to any remaining of Saul's family for Jonathan's sake! This was a pure love for Jonathan no matter what his father, Saul, had done to David.

This brought an observation to my brain. This is the way our God treats us. When we belong to him because of his Son, Jesus, we are allowed to eat at the King's table with his Son, for we are sons too. This is a pure love he has for us because of his love for his only Son. We are treated as a child of the King every day, able to eat his food, to receive his blessings with grace forever ours though we be lame in both feet! Our lives are not perfect. No, we are troubled with lameness all of our lives, but his mercy attends us, his grace restores us to a place at the table. We think Mephibosheth was eternally grateful for his position with the King.

We are eternally grateful for his mercy and grace toward us. Share this Good News with your world. Others, who are lame too can know this Son who gave us a relationship with the King, the One and Only King of the Universe. They can eat at his table daily. Share Jesus today.

June 16

DEUTERONOMY 8:2A,3

"And you shall remember that the Lord your God led you
all the way…He humbled you, allowed you to hunger, and
fed you with manna…that he might make you know that
man shall not live by bread alone; but man lives by every
word that proceeds from the mouth of the Lord." NKJV

How often our God reminds us to remember! In this case, we are to remember that God has already led us in this life to have nourishment when we hunger. In fact, he allowed us to be hungry so that we would understand it is by his hand we are fed and that we don't live on that kind of bread alone. We must eat the bread of Life that he supplies in full measure, his Living Word that came and dwelt among us, God as man.

We really do have a problem with grasping the thought that we need God, that we need to fulfill his commandments by the power of his Holy Spirit in us. We cannot eat the bread that the world offers in the place of God's words that fill us with his desire and obedience to him. We would rather believe that we are the ones deciding what is right, what is holy, what is obedience to his words. But he laid those words out already. You cannot change, add to or delete from them to suit yourself. They will stand in eternity and never fade nor go away.

Turn from your own way, let him lead you from the world's way to the right way by his own hand of love. He will not mislead you. He is trustworthy and cares about your life as it is right now. He can feed you with his heavenly manna that is sufficient for your every need. Feast on him today.

June 17

DEUTERONOMY 6:7

"And you shall teach them diligently to your children, and shall talk of them when you sit in your house, when you walk by the way, when you lie down and when you rise up." NKJV

A preschool teacher would call this finding the "teachable moment" in a child's life. Our God is telling us, parents of our children, to use the everyday places of life to share God's commandments, the statutes and his ordinances with each child. More life-changing moments are spent at a parent's knee than in any formal school setting. As we move through each day with our families, let us make certain that our mouths are engaged in conversation with them. And please, remember that conversation is a two- way thing. It means we spend at least as much time listening as we do talking, maybe more.

We can share the times that God has lifted our spirits, our energy and our love toward others to make us a greater help to those around us. We can let them know of times when God has met our need, relieved our pain. We have the opportunity to let them see our God through our behavior, our words and our interaction with our world. But to do this, we must also know what his word teaches. Choose today to begin with reading your Bible more closely, studying his word to be able to hide it in our hearts that we might not sin against him. They will learn just how important God's commandments are to us as they see and hear us each day. Today is a good day to begin.

June 18

"When I was a child, I spoke as a child, I understood
as a child, I thought as a child; but when I became
a man, I put away childish things." NKJV

Since I was going to meet with a grandchild who was about to turn twenty-three, I began thinking about this verse. This child had just entered adulthood. College was over; degree was earned. Was she ready? Prepared? Eager to move into the big world? At that, I began asking what is needed for a child to be ready, prepared, eager? Here are my conclusions.

A child needs parents who will allow that child be a child during childish years. Oh, to be a child while it is a child! For this young one not to have to take on adult behavior before becoming an adult. To be able to explore a child's world. To be allowed to speak as a child while still being one. To learn, in time, that everything you believed and thought you understood was not always correct. About being allowed to run new thoughts and new ideas through your mind, to examine them and to learn how to separate fact from fiction, truth from lies. Oh, to be equipped along the way to push words through the sieve of God's Word that moves only truth through the tight holes.

But oh, what a difficulty this so often is for parents to let go of what a child thinks, instead to give that child the ability to think! To give the grace to turn a rock or an idea over in the small hands and mind to decide what it is, what its meaning is or what it is good for, so they can accept or reject it on the rock's or idea's value only. Not because you said it had none, but because they can see it has none. You will not always be with your child. They need to be a child, to grow under your wings, to develop in time beside you into the person God created them to be.

Lead them, not in a commanding and demanding tone, but with leadership of words and examples of behavior. Use strong love and deep compassion for their youth and inexperience while you speak and behave as a grownup. Remember, your grownup-ness came at a price. You made mistakes. They will too. Make it easier for them to let go of childish things and to embrace adulthood by encouraging them to keep trying. Teach them the principles of living by God's truths. That's not always approval of their choices. It is about approval of them regardless of their choices. It is about unconditional love. Lord, make us as parents and grandparents, to be instruments of your peace in their lives, a channel of blessings from you to them through us. Remind us of your love and approval for us in spite of our childish ways displayed. Thank you for your steadfast love for us. May we give it on to our children that they may become adults when it is time.

June 19

1 CORINTHIANS 8:5-6

"For even if there are so-called gods, whether in heaven or on earth—as there are many "gods" and many "lords"—yet for us there is one God, the Father. All things are from Him, and we exist for Him. And there is one Lord, Jesus Christ. All things are through Him, and we exist through Him." HCSB

What a perfect message for those who are caught in the "knowledge" that the world offers! Humans have created with their own hands, from materials found in or on the earth "gods" for themselves. They have given them personalities and attributes, but when it is all said and done, they are non-realities. They are the figment of their own thoughts and creativity. They speak not, see not, nor hear. They have no power except the power their worshipers give them in their minds.

The end of the matter is that there is but one God and He is the Father. There is but one Lord and He is Jesus Christ. They see all humans, they can speak and hear, giving rise to all even our own existence. Whatever the world has to say that leads you away from these truths will take you away from the knowledge of our Father God and our Lord Jesus.

Yes, men like having gods and lords with no power, not able to interact with them. They don't think about what they can or cannot do or believe. They can make it up as they go along! But the Word tells us the truth about the one and only God and His Son, Jesus, who have all the power of creation and existence of that creation.

Do not be confused by these lies from the Enemy, Satan. There will be an accountability day for all mankind. Are you ready to give account? Or do you have the Lord Jesus to stand for your accounting? Choose today. Choose wisely!

June 20

2 CORINTHIANS 1:3-4

"Blessed be the God and Father of our Lord Jesus Christ, the
Father of mercies and God of all comfort, who comforts
us in all our tribulation that we may be able to comfort
those who are in any trouble, with the comfort with which
we have ourselves are comforted by God." NKJV

Ever wonder why you are strengthened by the Lord when you are in any trial or difficulty? Besides taking care to let you know he loves you and cares about you despite the circumstance you are living through, he desires you to be strengthened enough to be able to reach out to those around you in your world that you can become a channel of that same comfort with which you have been lifted and strengthened.

When you, by God's grace and mercy, overcome a battle in your life, he gives you opportunity to be his blessing and comfort to those who are experiencing the same kinds of struggles. He knows the world is hurting. He sees and cares. He wants you to be a part of the comfort he sends to those who are there with you. You become his hands and his feet, traveling between you and his other child in pain.

You can be a star of light to the one in the darkness of sorrow. You can be the one whom the Spirit of God uses to open the heart of another to realize they too can be an overcomer; they too can be victorious. The question is though, are you willing to be the light in the darkness that another feels in your realm of influence? Don't let your friend or family member drown in his plight of waves that desire to destroy. Touch them with the comfort with which God himself has comforted you.

June 21

1 CORINTHIANS 13:13

"And now abides faith, hope and love, these three…" NKJV

Faith is much like the beginning of life. It has to be nurtured by reading the Word, by my prayer life and by my heart listening to my Lord. I learn from these ways of hearing what God would have to direct me in this day, each one as it comes. I can gain strength and understanding with these disciplines. I can know that he has a hope for me that is beyond human wisdom. His hope is a sure thing, not seen, but well defined for me in his Word. God's great love for us gives the greatest of hopes for our future here on earth and for our future in heaven with him.

In these three words, I can stretch to become all God has created me to be, complete in his power to go forth in trust. There will be a knowing that I can step where I cannot see when he says to press on, to continue forward. Each day comes, moment by moment, with new opportunities to learn obedience to him in faith, realizing that some will be easy, some hard, some hurtful, some exciting, but all in his plan.

When you read these words about faith, hope and love, let the Holy Spirit interpret for you his message for you, just you. He has tailor-made his heart to your need. He will strengthen your faith, teach you about his hope and will love you forever.

June 22

1 CORINTHIANS 10:13

"No temptation has overtaken you except such as is common to man; but God is faithful, who will not allow you to be tempted beyond what you are able, but with the temptation will also make the way of escape that you may be able to bear it." NKJV

Oh, my, when we find we have fallen and have slipped into sin, whether a big thing or a small thing (sin is sin!), we try our best to make excuse for our behavior, don't we? We can dream up all kinds of reasons why we faltered so easily. We can talk of misunderstanding or not recognizing the opportunity to get it right, but the bottom line is still that we chose to do that thing! We really don't stop to examine the real reason for our choices, do we?

It hurts to grasp the truth that God made a way for us to be overcomers in that thing and we decided we knew best. Or we just went ahead and did it, regardless of any consequences that might happen in response to our choice. We act as children wanting what we want, the way we want it, when we want it, where we want it and don't care if there are any repercussions from it.

Sad, isn't it, when we do this even after God has instructed us that he made a way around that choice to sin? After all is said and done, God gave us the way of obedience, not the way of sin. Choose this day to follow his word, to hear his encouragement to stay true to him and benefit from obeying him. He is there all the time. He is ready to uplift you from the pit and to plant your feet higher than you've ever been. Stand firm, dear friend. Clasp this truth of the "way out" he's provided.

June 23

1 CORINTHIANS 1:8-9

"He will also strengthen you to the end, so that you will
be blameless in the day of our Lord Jesus Christ. God
is faithful; you were called by Him into fellowship
with His Son, Jesus Christ our Lord." HCSB

We will have no fear of the coming day of our Lord because God
has equipped us to finish the race all the way to the end. He is the
keeper of that end for us. We will need no special knowledge or
unheard speech to fulfill his calling into that fellowship with Jesus.
His enrichment completes our time here on the earth when He will
then present us faultless to His Father; we are able in Him to be who
He has called us to be.

He has given the spiritual gifts to share with the fellowship. He
has brought us the heart of a servant, that of Jesus's love for the life
he has delivered us into each day. We need not cower in unbelief but
to stand firm in our faith of daily trust in the Father. He is able and
because He is able, we are also.

Answer the call from the Father to walk in this fellowship of the
believers. Accept this particular free, but costly, gift. God loves you
and desires you to trust Him for each day's steps. Salvation is yours if
you want it. Come, walk with us in this glorious way of life. It does
not exempt you from pain here but it gives you the Spirit of God to
make it to the end and then eternal life with our Lord. It doesn't get
any better than that!

June 24

1 SAMUEL 10:27

"But some rebels said, 'How can this man save us?' So they despised
him, and brought him no presents. But he held his peace." NKJV

Saul has been anointed king over God's people by God's prophet,
Samuel. It's true he was a reluctant king, but nevertheless, he was
the chosen king for this time. While many thought he was perfect
for the job, there were some who didn't agree with the people. These
God's word calls rebels in this version. In the Holman Christian
Standard Bible, they are called wicked!

Notice friends, there will always be those who do not see the
hand of God in the circumstances of life for whatever reason. Many
times, these will be just thinking their own thoughts that seem the
wisest to them. But Saul doesn't get too upset by their behavior. He
doesn't get too riled about their hatred of him regardless of God's
anointing him as king. They refuse to do the least that was done for
a new king, the bringing of presents. He does a very wise thing. He
holds his peace!

Saul was not always so wise. Just read the rest of his story in these
chapters. But today, he is wise and keeps quiet rather than creating
a bigger problem. There will always be the rebels, the wicked, that
want to bring you down, who will not be a part of God's plan when
you choose to be obedient to his choice for you. Do not worry about
them. If you are following God to your personal destination from
his plan, stick to it. Keep your eyes on his goal, and walk toward that
point. He will bring you to it, all the way. Trust him every step you
take in obeying.

June 25

1 SAMUEL 10:9

"And so it was, when he had turned his back to go
from Samuel, that God gave him another heart; and
all those signs came to pass that day." NKJV

God made certain that the man who would become the king of Israel shortly would be at the right place at the right time with the right man, his prophet, Samuel to be anointed according to the Lord's perfect plan and purpose. Saul's father's donkeys had been lost, they had wandered off and could not be found. Saul went looking for them, taking a servant with him. When they could not locate those donkeys, the servant suggested they seek God's man to learn about them. They did so.

God made certain Saul was where he needed to be on time to meet with Samuel. He used the donkey search to do this. After Samuel anoints Saul, Saul turns to leave the prophet and God also gives this reluctant future king a new heart to do the job. This is all before the people have chosen him as king! This new heart does not mean that Saul will never sin again. Read the rest of the story of Saul! What it means is that God equips Saul for the kingdom and begins his work in Saul to do his calling, God's purpose for him.

God may be calling you to a specific purpose for you, only you, to do. He is not finished with you yet! He will equip you to do what needs to be done. He wants you to cooperate with him in this endeavor. Surrender to his calling. Obey what you already know from his Word. And he will give you greater understanding from the Scriptures you are learning daily. He will give you light for the next step when your foot hits the first one. Obedience is better than formal sacrifices any day. God will do his part. Will you do yours?

June 26

1 KINGS 18: 43-45A

"…(Elijah) said to his servant, 'Go up now, look toward the sea.' So he went up and looked, and said, 'There is nothing.' And seven times he said, 'Go again.' Then it came to pass the seventh time that he said, 'There is a cloud, as small as a man's hand, rising out of the sea.' So he said, Go up, say to Ahab, 'Prepare your chariot, and go down before the rain stops you.'" NKJV

Elijah had just told evil King Ahab that he needed to go eat and drink, for there is the sound of abundance of rain. Elijah could hear it even though it had not rained in three years! I suppose Ahab believed Elijah. He went up to eat dinner while Elijah went up to prayer. Six times Elijah sends the servant to look for rain toward the sea. Six times there was nothing in sight!

But on the seventh sending, the servant brings back news of a simple, small, stinking, unimposing, tiny little "size of a man's hand" cloud on the horizon coming out of the sea! Then he sends the servant to warn Ahab of the coming storm. He needed to hurry or he wouldn't make it down ahead of the rain.

The "In the meantime," phrase is one I really like. So many times, we expect God's answer in the "front and center" of our lives. We are not told how long Elijah prayed. We are told that he bowed himself before the Lord on the ground, put his head between his knees and after, sent his servant to see about the results! He continued to check for those six times. And then, he sent a seventh time. He sent until he saw God's answer. He was praying for that rain continually!

When you have deep need, pray. Elijah had just reported to Ahab he could hear the sound of abundance of rain before it came! It's not about the size or the length of your prayers. It's about the size of your God. Pray until God gives you peace about that need. Note: I did not say to pray until you got your way! Pray for God's way in that thing first though you also pray for your heart's desire. Pray, child of God. Pray. It may be a short time. It may be years. But pray for that peace that God's way brings. It will surpass anything you ever imagined.

June 27

1 KINGS 17:13-15

"And Elijah said to her, 'Do not fear; go and do as you have said, but make me a small cake from it first, and bring it to me; and afterward, make some for yourself and your son. For thus says the Lord God of Israel: the bin of flour shall not be used up, nor shall the jar of oil run dry, until the day that the Lord sends rain on the earth.'" NKJV

This woman thought she was going to bake her meager portion of meal and oil for her own and her son's needs into a cake and then die! But this man was daring to ask her to bake his cake of meal first and then bake for herself and the son. He wanted her to share her small last meal with him. True, Elijah did promise that God said the barrel of meal and the cruse of oil would not fail until God sent life to the earth in rain. For some reason the woman did just that. She believed Elijah I suppose. And, just as Elijah said, the two did not fail just as God had promised.

My mother was a great believer that the hand of the Lord failed not and that he always wanted our first of anything to go to him. She lived that truth with all the crops we ever grew. God's came first and then we got the balance. He was faithful all those years. I suppose that's one reason she never turned anyone away from her table. She offered her first fruits to him and then counted on him to divide her food as was needed among those around that table. I think she probably enjoyed this story of Elijah being fed from the hand of those in need. God saw that her sufficiency was equal to her need.

June 28

1 KINGS 3:3

"And Solomon loved the Lord, walking in the statutes
of his father David, except that he sacrificed and
burned incense at the high places." NKJV

Solomon was a great king with more wealth and riches than any other. He was given the privilege of building a temple for the Name of the Lord. He was given great wisdom by the Lord God. But… but he kept one practice that was not good. In those days the heathen worshiped on the hillsides & mountain sides where they had built altars to other gods than Jehovah God. Solomon continued this practice.

In his eyes, it was but a small thing. Everybody was doing it, it seemed. There was so much good he did. This one small thing just couldn't make a big difference to him. Could it? But it did. Small things can be such big things when seen from God's point of view.

What are the little things that you hold on to even when you know they are not really right? We put so many little things before our God in our lives, don't we? We waste our time with those small things. We step over the good and cross the street to get to the little things we want. We try to convince ourselves they are not such a big deal. We often convince ourselves we are right!

But the last word is that one God recorded about Solomon: He did good, EXCEPT that he sacrificed and burned incense at those high places. Solomon just mixed his worship just a little bit with the world's worship. Consider your ways, believers. Sit down long enough to take those little things that are not of the Lord from your lives. It's not too late to get it right.

June 29

1 KINGS 19:7-8A

"Then the angel of the Lord came back again the second time and touched him, and said, 'Arise and eat, because the journey is too great for you.' And he arose and did ate and drank, and went in the strength of that food forty days and forty nights..." NKJV

Elijah had just finished one of his great moments in the service of the Lord. But he was exhausted, depressed and a day's journey into the wilderness. He was running from the wicked queen Jezebel. He really was in a wilderness experience to the point of wanting to die! But the Lord answers him at his point of need, not at his request to die!

We all have those times in life when we know our strength is depleted. God knows when those happen. He is not ignorant of our weaknesses. He knows when the journey is too great. He has heavenly baked bread and water available for us. It is simple fare but completely sufficient for our day. It is the grace he has promised to each of his children. He will even supply it in abundance. In Elijah's case, he provided it twice. What strength there was in his provision. What sufficiency. We can go to our Lord's provision for us too. It is his Word. He has sent heavenly messages to us, to each of us who belong to his Kingdom. It is everything we need in this life to live victoriously in spite of our circumstances. Read his love letter to you today.

June 30

"Does the Lord take pleasure in burnt offering and sacrifices
as much as in obeying the Lord? Look: to obey is better than
sacrifice, to pay attention is better than the fat of rams." HCSB

As human beings, we like to do the rituals we call worship. They make us feel good and that we have done something special when we go through them regularly. But God is not so impressed with our "worship" when it is not accompanied by obedience to his words of instruction.

Sometimes we excuse ourselves by saying we didn't know about that part of his word and we gloss over the disobedience. There are other times when we say we couldn't because we were tired, or worried, even too busy to notice we were slipping into sin. We have more excuses for our disobeying than you could ever imagine! Some even sound to be reasonable to our ears.

But the bottom line is always called disobedience when God calls it out. Don't go to worship or try to worship anywhere else when you realize you have sinned against him. Get it right wherever you are so that your heart is not held back from true worship; do not just go through those rituals that cover our idea of being righteous. God wants you to obey! Period!

Samuel tells King Saul that his disobedience has cost him the kingdom over the nation Israel. God does not trifle with Saul. Neither will he play with us about this. Choose today to learn more of his words of instruction, to listen when God speaks your name for correction in love. He does not lightly apply that correction to us. It is for our benefit every time.

July 1

1 PETER 5:8-9

"Be serious! Be alert! Your adversary the Devil is prowling around like a roaring lion, looking for anyone he can devour. Resist him and be firm in the faith, knowing that the same sufferings are being experienced by fellow believers throughout the world." HCSB

When we are struggling in our lives and often feel that others are unfair in their dealing with us, even cruel or deliberate in aiming to hurt us, we can stop, think and remember that the word says we will have days and times like these. The Apostle Peter clearly speaks to us that we will have sufferings this side of heaven. But he also says that believers all around the world are having the same experiences too. We will not be kept from these attacks from the Enemy, the Devil, also called Satan. He is roaring around trying to drive us away from our faith.

We are to resist this one. We must not listen to and believe the lies, the deceptions he is so skilled at telling us. We can resist by listening to the Holy Spirit instead as we read the word of God and ask the Spirit to interpret the message to us that we might not sin against our God. The Spirit is our bringer of truth. He enlightens our minds when we take time to set our minds and hearts on eternal things, on heavenly things. The things of this world have a strong pull on us. Do not weaken, but hear the word of the Father and choose to obey it rather than to turn to the desires of the flesh. Pray for the other followers of Christ in other lands who are struggling too.

Keep the faith as you stay in communion with your Lord. It is he who holds you to himself. Lean on him and look to him to finish the good work he has started in you. He will not fail. Our job is to resist the Enemy. Resist, believer!

July 2

1 PETER 5:7

"Casting all your anxieties on him, because he cares for you." ESV

Once our family celebrated four birthdays at one Sunday dinner. It is my practice to give each birthday person their choice of their favorite menu. So, we had tacos for the twenty-four- year-old, roasted chicken breasts for the one turning fifty-three, shrimp and grits for the forty-nine- year-old and chicken alfredo for the one getting all the way to twelve.

Now think a minute, if I being a human mother and grandmother with frailties and a sinful nature know and love to do for my loved ones a simple thing like a favorite meal, how much more our heavenly Father knows his children so well and cares for us so much; he asks us to throw our care onto his Being and leave it there.

He knows what we need to "eat" to provide us with the strength to exist in a fallen world every day. He has given us his Word, preserved complete for us to feed on each day just as we eat daily for sustenance to meet the day's tasks. The food must be equal to the physical tasks. The nourishment from his Word must also be equal to the spiritual tasks that face us. Have you had your breakfast, lunch and dinner from the Word yet? If not, stop and read that you may be equal to your daily needs. You cannot store up food intake for long, neither can you go without your daily portion of the Word.

Admit you are not able to do it all by yourself. God loves a humble heart. Lift up your arms with all your strength and cast your care onto your God that you may walk away strong in your trust and faith in him. He is able. Then shout your thanksgivings to him.

July 3

"Righteousness exalteth a nation, but sin is
a reproach to any people." NKJV

When we celebrate our nation's birth, let us lift our eyes to the heavenly things and set our minds on them. When we look horizontally, to those things around us, it is too easy to be distracted from eternal things that lift us above the mundane to a better way of responding to what's important. We are readily drawn to getting more toys, more money, more power and prestige for ourselves.

We have been so blessed by our God in this country. We have been led down streets of mercy toward others across the world. We have been taken to heights of glory among the nations. But there has been tremendous cost to this. So many have paid the ultimate cost with the loss of limbs, sight, peace of mind and life, both men and women, to give others that wonderful opportunity we call freedom. Do not glory in these facts, believers. Instead, be grateful that your names are written in the Lamb's Book of Life! That's the best gift of all from your God.

Set your mind and heart on those eternal sights that teach you the giving of yourself to help those standing by you, whether they believe the way you do or not. Take a few moments to thank your gracious Lord for his kindnesses to us, this United States of America. He owes us nothing. We owe him everything.

The world's people need us to be righteous in this unrighteous world, to give grace where needed, mercy to the unmerciful and forgiveness to the harmful folks who would destroy us. That doesn't mean we are not to defend ourselves as a nation. But we must always remember that it is the Lord who gives the victory!

Take today and choose, yes, there's that word, to be the righteous one in your group that the world you exist in can see the face of the Lord on yours. You are his light around you. Be bright. You are his breath of kindness with those you walk among. Be sweet. You are his platter on which he serves up his bread of life to others. Be tasty, instead of sour! Why? Because Jesus calls us to be righteousness and because this mama said so!

July 4

GENESIS 1:14A, 15,16A

"And God said, 'Let lights appear in the sky to separate the day from the night… Let these lights in the sky shine down on the earth.' And that is what happened. God made two great lights- the larger one to govern the day, and the smaller one to govern the night. He also made the stars." NLT

Once we took four of our grandchildren to the Kennedy Space Center on Florida's east coast. We spent the night in a hotel by the Atlantic Ocean. Of course, everyone wanted to swim, that is, except me. Well, Big Buck and the four kids did, for I sat on the sand watching them horse around with each other. I did not trust anyone of them! I knew what they would have done to me.

When the tour started the next day, I think the two oldies were the most excited. We remembered living through this evolution of space travel. The kids thought it was all great. But none of them saw it the way we did. When we went through the room where all the stars, the constellations, the light, new stars, the colors, the shapes, the beauty beyond our language to describe were displayed, it was more than the two of us could bear without tears. I thought of Paul's words, "No eye has seen, nor ear heard, and no mind has (even) imagined what God has prepared for those who love him." (1Cor.2:9)

It is July the fourth all over America today. There will be fireworks breaking in the sky or over waters and land. But nothing will compare with what God has already done. We are still on the edge of learning how vast his creation is! There are stars and creatures, planets even, being discovered today. We know so little. Much of what was once taught to me in college is now known to be untrue or obsolete. What we believe now may be decided to be wrong tomorrow as we gain more knowledge. But this we know, God has had the correct answers since before he laid that time line! We so often rule him out of the equation. But that is a mistake. So, tonight when you watch the "lights" over you, whether man made for the show, or God made for us to enjoy continually, decide whose are the greatest and rejoice with me over our God's wonder-filled creation.

July 5

2 KINGS 15:2A, 3-4

"Azariah ... the king of Judah, became king... he was sixteen-years-old ... and he did what was right in the sight of the Lord ... EXCEPT that the high places were not removed; the people still sacrificed and burned incense on the high places." NKJV

The high places were where idolatry was performed. It had been so a long time. Although the young king did well in the sight of the Lord, he still had an "except" in his reign, his leadership. Except is another word for the "how-ever," the "but" in one's life. We all have them. You know, those places where we do well, but we stop just short of the goal, the best that we needed to do. It wasn't that Azariah didn't know about those high places. He just tolerated them. He just halted his movement toward complete obedience. If you read on into his life story and reign, you'll learn there were big consequences to this "except."

Today would be a great time to ask the Lord where the "but," the "however' is for us. Where have we stopped short of his goal for us, our complete obedience to his word? Where have we compromised with our world? Let's not be content with less than our best, with doing well but not finished with reaching our goal. Ask the Holy Spirit for his light to be turned to our hearts to know where we fall below the end mark. And, remember, when we know, we are responsible to do something about what we know! Ask, as well, for the wisdom and strength to deal with what the Spirit reveals to you. Our God is able beyond our wildest dreams or imaginings to aid in our growth. Look for your best to give to him. And, he will go all the way with you to the finish.

July 6

1 THESSALONIANS 5:23-25A

"Now may the God of peace Himself sanctify you completely.
And may your spirit, soul and body be kept sound and blameless
for the coming of our Lord Jesus Christ. He who calls you is
faithful, who also will do it. Brothers, pray for us also." HCSB

It is God who sanctifies us, that is, sets us apart for his Glory and purposes. He has called us and we have accepted his offer of eternal life. He desires to perfect us and he is able to do it. He is faithful to his calling of us and our response. But we must surrender our lives into his loving hand to do his job of this perfecting.

Those who are our spiritual leaders need our prayers as well for them. We must not neglect them as though they have no struggle in surrendering to the Lord. We are all fallen creatures who need to uphold one another and love each other. That loving includes praying diligently for both our leaders and the fellowship of believers sitting in the pew next to us.

Yield to his plans for you and watch him draw you into the paths he knows is best. There will be times when it may hurt. There will be occasions when we don't understand the way he leads. But trust is about surrendering in spite of our feelings about the course we have been placed on for this day. Ask your Lord for whatever it takes to complete this way you are traveling and look for his face above the fray. He is doing his job. Let him carve out your way before you because he has traveled that path ahead of you. He is faithful to finish that good work he has started in you.

July 7

2 KINGS 3:15B, 16-18

"… the hand of the Lord came upon him. And he said, 'Thus says the Lord: Make this valley full of ditches. For you shall not see wind, nor shall you see rain; yet this valley shall be filled with water, so that you, your cattle, and your animals may drink.' And this is but a trivial thing in the sight of the Lord; He will also deliver the Moabites into your hand.'" NKJV

This is Elisha talking to the three kings: the king of Israel, the king of Judah and the king of Edom. The land of God's people was divided at this time into Israel and Judah. The king of Judah was Jehoshaphat. There was much sin among God's people in both halves. The king of Israel had called for help from the other two kings for a rebelling conquered nation, Moab.

When confronted with difficulty on their way to fight, fear decides that God has decided to bring them to destroy them all! One man, Jehoshaphat, asks to find a man of God to inquire about their circumstance. Just one man! They had all been preparing to fight without consulting God at all.

These are God's words given through the prophet Elisha to them because Elisha saw this one man among the group! Elisha regarded the presence of that one man. Jehoshaphat was not the greatest, nor sinless at all. But he did have enough sense to seek God's direction for them! This one sinful, unworthy man calls for God to give instruction to the group! Read all of the third chapter here for the whole story. It is an exciting part of God's grace shown to his people.

And best of all, God gives them a whole valley of water to fill their need. They had only to put the ditches in to hold it! But notice, God doesn't just fill their immediate need. He also fights the battle for them too in advance of the battle. One man made the difference. You can be that one man or woman in your group too. It isn't about being worthy of God's help. We are all sinful folks. It is about seeking God's face before we face our circumstance, our battle, our need of the power of God to withstand or to become an overcomer. God is your strength. Trust him with your life and then stand and wait for God's instructions to follow. It will be good for you. It will be very good for those around you!

July 8

LUKE 10:33

"But a Samaritan, as he traveled, came where the man was;
and when he saw him, he took pity on him." NIV

"How does pity rank as it concerns love? It shows a great concern for the one being pitied. But pity can also show contempt for the one as well. So, let's examine that thought."

Pity is a feeling we give to those who are in situations of life that we feel sympathetic towards. We have to watch the definition of pity as it relates to contempt. It is easy to look down on one in such distress & to be glad it is not we who are experiencing that life. Remember to give grace where it is needed, just as God did for us. That will help us to watch for contempt rising in us. Sympathy is good. Empathy is better. That allows us to see ourselves as though we are experiencing that life. Empathy often compels us to reach out to help where we can. Pity, sympathy & empathy are some of the feelings that lead us to be kind and generous with our grace. Compassion leads from sympathetic consciousness of their distress to a desire to alleviate it. That's how Jesus looked over Jerusalem: with compassion. He was broken hearted toward his people. That's love! And then he died to show that love, to alleviate their distress.

It has been said often that pity walks on after taking note of another's plight while compassion drives us to help as possible. Read the story of the Good Samaritan in Luke ten. The priest who should have had compassion on the man, walked on, and the Levite actually went over to see him. He appeared to pity him, but still walked on by. But the Samaritan had compassion on the man and was moved to help. Let us become like the lowly Samaritan with deep compassion for others. Reach out and touch!

July 9

LUKE 12:22-24

"Then he said to His disciples: 'Therefore, I tell you, don't
worry about your life, what you will eat; or about the
body, what you will wear. For life is more than food and
clothing. Consider the ravens: They don't sow or reap;
they don't have a storeroom or barn; yet God feeds them.
Aren't you worth much more than the birds?'" HCSB

Jesus puts this so simply and so quickly to the point for us to be
absolutely sure of our value to our Father. We worry about so many
things in this world that we think we must have in the abundance
that we consider "enough." Jesus comes to the main issue in a few
words. Our life is so much more that what we eat or wear in everyday
existence. But we spend so much money and time on both!

You will notice he did not say we would never be hungry or in
need of clothing. We are just not to worry about that because our
stewing over these will not change a thing. We need to work when it
is available, be careful with what we have but be willing to share the
small amount we do have. It is attitude that is important on these
items. Instead, we are to think long and hard about the ravens, that
is, birds! He counts his human creation to be of far more value than
the birds and he feeds them too. Your basic needs are simple; some
food, some clothing and some shelter. The number or the expense
of these is not what matters! I used to tell our teenagers that clothes
were meant to cover their nakedness! Your body is not a billboard!
God cares about his creation. You are his workmanship!

July 10

LUKE 10:38

"Now as they went on their way, Jesus entered a village.
And a woman named Martha welcomed him into her
house. And she had a sister called Mary, who sat at the
Lord's feet and listened to his teaching." ESV

"As they went on their way" is the way life is lived. We move into our day with the normal road before us, doing the normal things we do every day of our lives. But the one going on his way that day was Jesus. The woman that day was Martha. A normal, everyday woman with a sister named Mary, two common, normal names even today.

But the blessing here is that Martha invited our Jesus into her home that day as he came to her village. What an opportunity for her! Wonder if she even thought twice about the invitation? Wonder how many times we miss the opportunity to invite Jesus into our homes when we miss the chance to invite an everyday, normal kind of person there? Try it today.

Find a normal, everyday kind of person or two and include them with your family so you can pour your love for Jesus over them as they go on their way into their life. Jesus cannot sit with you right now. But those around you can. Who knows? You can be like Mary and sit at the feet of Jesus and hear his teachings as you share.

July 11

"Even a fool, when he holdeth his peace, is counted wise; and he
that shuteth his lips is esteemed a man of understanding." KJV

Oh my, how I wish I had learned this in my early years. Too often we
think we must speak up and tell our thoughts to anyone and everyone around on any subject or event. We speak that we may show
our smartness, or our brightness. If only, we could understand that
we aren't quite as smart and bright as we think before we raise our
voice and prove it. How many arguments, how many hurt feelings,
how many sleepless nights could be avoided if we simply kept our
mouths shut. When we give ourselves a little time to mull over the
options available to us in a situation, we often realize we don't have
all the answers to every life occurrence. So often it is better just to let
a thing go for a while and wait for a more opportune time to address
it when our brain is in gear and our hearts are in tune with another's
heart. If I wait on the Lord to kick me into gear with a right attitude,
my words are usually better received. And sometimes, I realize it is
not my job to correct everyone. In other words, I try to listen to the
Holy Spirit before I speak. I did not take the world on to raise. That's
God's job. I can be an instrument of his peace in the Holy Spirit's
hand when I listen first, then speak.

It's always a sound idea to keep mouths closed while God puts
our brains into a functioning mode. There are so many things I simply do not know. And the list is growing daily! May my Father open
my mouth after he has my tongue in hand to be used for his glory
and other's good. Until then may I hold it in silence.

July 12

PROVERBS 15:1A

"A soft answer turns away wrath…" ESV

When I was very young, (no, I was not always white haired), I had a sharp tongue, I was what I called "quick witted." Amazing how we can justify anything, isn't it? I was impulsive and head strong, fast to voice my opinion about anything, whether I knew much about the subject or not. I must have thought it was my job in life to correct other folks. I had not learned yet, that others have the right to be wrong!

But when I became aware of my failings, the Lord began to teach me and to help me with both. He gave me a constant reminder to stop, shut and shine instead of start, speak and shame. I began learning to simply stop the normal process and to think before I spoke. God began blessing with the ability to give grace, to be kind. But that was not my nature! It is a process, this learning to follow his love into obedience.

My advice to you today is to begin this process that shows you how to give the soft answer when provoked. The need for the soft answer shows there have been words spoken that gave you opportunity to speak back harshly. But the softness can squelch the pain that can flow from harsh words. There can be no offence intended if there is none taken. Choose (there's that word again) not to take offence from other's words or actions. Simply be kind and give grace, then press on. It quiets the heart of the other's wrath. So, stop, shut and shine for the Lord today!

July 13

SONG OF SOLOMON 2:15

"Catch all the foxes, those little foxes, before they ruin the
vineyard of love, for the grapevines are blossoming," NLT

In the garden, right now it is not foxes that are the problem...it is
the coons who love our beautiful white corn we grow each spring.
We can always tell when the corn is maturing and getting close to
being ready to pull because the coons come into the rows at night
when we're asleep to check the corn cobs themselves. They know that,
when the silk rising out of the ear starts to turn dark brown, and the
ear begins to stand away from the stalk in a proud way, that the ear
is good to eat. They know so well, they don't bother with the ones
not ready yet. They can tell the difference! They can even tip the ear
closer to the ground and peek in to look in the shucks as they tear
them away from the ear of corn. In other words, they know how to
shuck corn! They have no problem eating what is yours!

That's the way it is with our lives as married folks. The Enemy
and his evil ones come in under the dark of your life while you aren't
paying close attention, knowing there is about to be some maturing
between you and your love. They often let the ones stuck in their
immaturity alone because there is no danger of those doing anything
to glorify our Lord. They rise up on your "stalk" of daily living and
pull your ear down to whisper lies to you and lay you as close to the
ground as possible. They will eat up the good of your life, discour-
aging you and making you believe that God no longer cares for you
and your marriage relationship.

But you must catch the little foxes, or as in our case, the big ole
coons, to stop them from destroying your peace of mind and trust
in your heavenly Father. Recognize that they are bad, and have only
bad desires toward you and yours. Keep growing in the Lord. Stay in
the Word. Hide it in your heart that you might not sin against God
or your love. Carry on a conversation with God daily. Don't just

do all the talking either. Listen too with all of the energy you have, remembering that conversation is a two-way street. And you must catch all the foxes, because just one can do a lot of damage to your personal vineyard. Blossoms are the evidence of fruit to come in the future. Take special care of them, nurture them with tenderness and passion. They are the beginning of each new day with your love and your God. As you see them emerge from the vine, encourage them and rejoice at their strength. Make a little love every day so that you both know where your heart lies.

July 14

PROVERBS 16:24

"Pleasant words are like an honeycomb, sweet to
the soul, and heath to the bones." NKJV

How our world needs to have people who bring words of pleasant-ness to a relationship. Not only our world, but the specific places of Gods people too. We use harsh word to our fellow believers far too often and push them over the edge of the life in which they feel caught. We need gentle words too, even though we are believers. We need a soft tone with a hand of tenderness as we live in a world that is hard outside. Those kinds of words are health to our very bones, our deepest core of who we are. May He who made us for them give us a desire to use our tongues, our thoughts, our mouths to lift a heart up rather than push that one down. Step out this week into the places where God has put you and raise up those with whom your lives touch.

Use the strength of your lips, the desire of your heart for fulfill-ment of their deep needs. God is giving each of us the opportunity to respond to his call to be a deliverer to someone who has a need for the honeycomb of the words only you can share. We will realize that we are getting a step up along with the ones we speak to in kindness. Kindness has a way of returning to us. Open your arms to share and open them wider to receive back God's kindness. And remember to thank the Lord for his mercies to you.

July 15

"Grandchildren are the crown of the aged, and the
glory of children is their fathers." ESV

Grandchildren are a joy beyond measure and a delight to be around. We love to see them, visit with them, take them places, feed them and send them home when they are tired. They truly are the blessings you get for not killing your teenagers! It is a shame we didn't get to have them first, but then, we couldn't send them home when we're tired! But it is the second part of this proverb that I really like.

I believe that fathers are incredibly important to children and grandchildren. Their influence is a crown for them to wear all of their lives or it can be a cross they must bear up under if that one is a bad example. No one can take a father's place, but many a man has filled the shoes of a father for a child and they are to be praised for doing so. The genes will never be theirs, but the jeans can be filled as you live as a father to another. It is a place of honor to be a father figure to a young one.

My own father was called to heaven many years ago. But his influence over me is still in place. There are few days I do not think of him and the things he taught me, the ways he demonstrated a godly life. Was he perfect? Of course not! But he was real, he was there and he was faithful to me and our family. That is the key. It's not about being perfect, or even close. It is about being there, all the time that you can. It is an opportunity that you have to be a great influencer of the coming world.

July 16

PROVERBS 15:17A

"A bowl of vegetables with someone you love is better
that a steak with someone you hate." NLT

Now think about this and consider which you think is netter? I have a list of the vegetables we grew on the farm that would make a marvelous dinner. How does this sound as a menu? Begin with a very large salad bowl. Let's put some broken up leaves of Iceberg lettuce with four leaves from a Romaine lettuce and add some spinach leaves and radishes, sliced very thin. On top of that we'll put a few sliced cucumbers with the fresh skin left on, bright and green, because they won't have wax on them to preserve them for market. We can add some thin slices of celery, including the inside white leaves too. Top those all with a wad of julienned carrots and a few shaved purple cabbage threads.

We can even place two or three very, very thin slices of young, pale yellow crook-neck squash around the side of the bowl. If we've had time to cook a few gorgeous red beets and slip their skins, we'll slice them; they would look wonderful on the sides between the squash. To top it all off, we can scatter a few spears of broccoli and cauliflower across the top in the middle of the bowl. A little salt and pepper with a small amount of olive oil and salad vinegar mixed together and we'd have a beautiful and fresh salad for two. We could have two forks, two glasses of water with a wedge of lemon or lime and two chairs overlooking each side of a round table with our love seated across from us. What more could anyone want? Where love is, there is peace. What joy! No steak, without my love, could touch such a wonderful evening.

July 17

"A wise woman builds her house but a foolish woman
tears it down with her own hands." NLT

Many years ago, a young woman came to me about her 'house"; that
is, mainly about her husband. There was no abuse, no addiction or
adultery. It was the "normal" things most wives complain about with
their fellows. So, we sat down more than once and talked about what
it means to be a wife from Scripture. This was the verse we spent
most of the time on each occasion we met.

After many words and many prayers, this girl decided she wanted
to know why it should be herself who should make the first move in
their relationship, since the husband was seemingly unaware of any
problem. Now, we talked about getting to the place where she could
talk to him in honesty and openness. But we had to get to that place.
It wasn't happening! I confessed to her it wasn't necessary that she be
the one to try first. She could sit and wait for him to see, understand
and change, but, if he wasn't even aware of a problem, he probably
wasn't going to start changing on his own.   Or she could ask
God to help her to be what He wanted her to be in the relationship
and work there first. She had the right to ask God to start developing
her into the woman he had created her to be. That way, she would
learn how to begin to reveal herself to the husband without losing
who she was in that process or without damaging her man. Wouldn't
you know it...she chose to stay mad at him without dealing with
anything God would have had for her. Down the road, a very few
years later the couple divorced. She still wanted God to change him
without any thought about God changing her.

Marriage is not about who does things first, but about doing
those things that will build the relationship, making it stronger and
more caring of each other. It's not about "you." It is about the "we"
and learning daily how to serve each other. It is about the 100% from

each person, not a "50-50%, an equality of effort. A lot of pride got in this woman's way and she lost the relationship completely, even though they had several children.

Women, build your house each day with the heavenly arms of love, mercy and grace. There is no more beautiful woman than one who gives grace! And pray that the Lord opens your man's eyes to see how to do the same. Be wise and ask for help. God can help. He can break down strongholds in another's heart. He has told us He doesn't even mind giving us wisdom when we ask. It may take a while, but it is worth waiting on the Lord instead of tearing down your own house with your own hands.

Note: Abuse, addiction and adultery often take the intervention of outside professional help here on earth. God has no problem using humans to help us sort out our lives & our problems Don't hesitate to get it.

July 18

PROVERBS 27:1

"Do not boast about tomorrow; For you know
not what a day may bring forth." NKJV

I had a job to do today.
I worried o'er it with sorrow.
I thought and thought,
I know what…
I'll do that job tomorrow!
But tomorrow never came
And my head hangs in shame.
Now I know and I can say,
I should have done that job THAT DAY!!
Message sent…
Message received??
Your mama loves you!

July 19

PROVERBS 21:31

"The horse is made ready for the day of battle, but
the victory belongs to the Lord." ESV

We are all supposed to make ready for the days ahead. We are to be wise and think through our circumstances before us, to plan what we believe is the best source for materials and the best counsel as to how to proceed. We are not to be careless and lazy as we begin a project in our lives. We are to consider the options, the opportunities and the consequences of the choices we make.

But we are always to remember that the only victory we experience comes from the Lord. He is the orchestrator of our future. He is the one to seek counsel from first. Then follow through with others whom you trust in this undertaking. Gather all the information you can before beginning the first step. When our children were young, I would remind them to do their homework before it was too late. That is still good advice as adults. When contemplating your next move, do your "homework" on the job to be ready for the law of unintended consequences. Because that law will kick in and you will be surprised! There are always those unforeseen things that come up that you are not ready to overcome.

When all of this is completed, go over the plans, lay out the project and commit your way to the Lord. You have done your "homework" well. The victory is definitely his!

July 20

PROVERBS 27:9

"Oil and perfume make the heart glad, and the sweetness
of a friend comes from his earnest counsel." ESV

When saying goodbye to a friend, whether at an airport or a grave-side, it is good to remember the times spent with that one. Those times were and are a part of who you are, who you became because of that interaction with that one alone. That's what good friends do. We sharpen each other as the fellowship moves through the years.

Once, many years ago, I had such a friend. She was an artist and a fisherman. Both she did with all her heart and energy. That's the way she was, full of both. Her skills at each were amazing and exciting to watch as she developed them faithfully over her entire life. She shared her thoughts with me, a young bride with very little sense. It was about bringing up children and dealing with husbands. It was about cooking and laughing together at mistakes we each made. It was tears at things that couldn't be changed, like death. It was about going on when everything you experienced was painful.

She was a real friend who told you the way it was without fear of losing your friendship. She loved that much! I look back at the years that slipped by; we often didn't get to see each other in those later ones. But when we did, it seemed we just took over where we left off the last time. Be a friend to someone today. Your friendship is a gift only you can give to another. Its value is priceless!

July 21

PROVERBS 22:1A

"A good name is to be chosen rather than great riches..." ESV

It is fun to watch how many folks treat rich people in this life. They pay deference to them. They choose to be with them and enjoy the rich paying attention to them, as well. It excites them when a rich person enters the room and they will migrate toward that one. The rich receive honors easily from regular folks.

But as I think about this, I remember how wonderful it was when a close, poor friend came to my aid when I was in need, regardless of their poorness. It didn't seem to cross that one's mind that there would not be enough for their household if they helped me. They just did it! I remember how often I sat with a poor family at dinner when it appeared there was not sufficient food on the table for them, much less for me and they still shared. They did not count noses before they included me for supper.

These people are remembered by me as having a good name, a name that called them generous, kind, sweet. Their "middle name," as old folks would have said, was Generous! They were rich with spiritual gifts that elevated them above the richest people I knew. When you are seeking those good things in life, remember to choose to have a good name. It cannot be bought. It cannot be stolen. It must be earned. And only you can do that! Mama' just saying!

July 22

PROVERBS 15:17A

"A bowl of vegetables with someone you love is better
than steak with someone you hate." NLT

All these years that I spent growing up on a farm, learning about crops and harvest, then, marrying a farmer too, I have found this to be true. A plate of veggies just can't be beat. Think how many restaurants now serve veggie plates. When I am sitting across from the man God gave me to love and share life with, it really doesn't matter what is on the plate. Where there is peace there is love. It is a quiet strength that has given us our place at the table. The table itself has given us joy as family and friends gather around it to share in what God has gifted us with each day. It doesn't matter who the others are at the table when Big Buck is there too.

God gives the food as he gives the rain for the crops that flourish to harvest. He gives the strength to work the crops all the way to picking. Every time we sit down to eat, it is a reminder of his goodness and our dependence on him for everything. Our table is a big one, twelve feet long that holds twelve to fourteen folks. He has given food for us, for the family, for extended family, for friends and for the stranger near. He has worked with us each day in the fields and the harvest. He has granted peace with the one I love, even if the only food on our plates is the very vegetables we grew. I am glad with what is and do not yearn for what might have been. I am content at my Father's bounty.

July 23

PROVERBS 24:3A

"By wisdom a house is built…" ESV

Of course, we all know what it takes to build a house. Right? There are no physical materials gathered here for this building. There is no architect laying the plans out on paper. There are no carpenters picking up nails or lumber. There are just two people joined together to start a home…together!

God shares a mighty truth in these few words. It takes wisdom to build a house that will sustain you through many years of growing and changing. It takes standing before the Lord with questions in mind, with answers needed before starting the process. You will need to take your time. Time is always your friend. Sit still and wait for the Lord's wisdom to be yours.

You will need the mercy of God to aid you in forgiving the inhabitants of this house. You will need love that exceeds the biggest love you've ever experienced. You will have to have grace that you're willing to pass out to those in that house who will need it. And they will need it. Just as you have needed it from the Lord repeatedly. You must have a heart that is for those sitting across the table from you. You will want them to succeed, to become all that God created them to be.

Search the word of God for clues on how to build your house together. There are many words of comfort when you make a mistake, and you will make them. There are strong words of growth for leading the family closer to the Lord. You will need them as you both change over the years and learn to grow together instead of apart. It is an art form you both will need. But God wants you to be victorious. He is all for you. Work at the way the heart moves that it not grows stale. Love as he has loved, unconditionally. It works, my friend. Trust me!

July 24

PROVERBS 25:24

"It is better to live in a corner of the housetop than in
a house shared with a quarrelsome wife." ESV

Oh, girls, listen to these wise words if you would have a house filled with peace and joy. It is a dangerous thing to let our emotions get the best of us at home. We strive to keep our balance out in the world and drop all pretense when we enter the door of our own house. We save the smiles for those who really don't love us but only use us to profit themselves. But we keep doing it anyway.

It is so easy to let the mouth take over our minds and pour out words that harm those we love and who love us. The bottom line is a life lived in carelessness. While we build up a false life elsewhere, we destroy the base of our lives at home. Before you see your home beaten down by your own hands, stop long enough to take stock in what is really important to you. Do you value those outside your door more than those inside? Do you think they will come to your aid sooner than your loved ones? I doubt you do. It just goes back to a life style of carelessness toward those who are the center of your heart.

Learn to choose not to be a quarrelsome woman. Don't look for the offence in everything and instead, choose to give room to those with whom you live every day, not just those with whom you work or play. To be able to go home at night to a room full of those you love and who love you is a treasure that cannot be bought. Value it and make a place in your heart for them above all others.

July 25

PROVERBS 11:16

"A gracious woman retains honor." NKJV

What is a gracious woman? I went to the dictionary for what the world defines as gracious and to the Bible for God's thoughts. Webster's New Collegiate dictionary* says to be gracious is to be: godly, pleasing, agreeable, acceptable, marked by kindness and courtesy, graceful, marked by tact and delicacy, characterized by charm, good taste, and generosity of spirit, merciful, compassionate, cordial and marked by pleasant and easy in social contacts.

The Bible describes this woman as virtuous, a crown to her husband, wise, building her own house, a good thing, the man who finds her obtains favor from the Lord, prudent and from the Lord also, full of faith that brings healing to others, one whose acts preach the Gospel and becomes a memorial to her, is full of good works and giving to the poor, trustworthy because the heart of her husband trusts in her, she does him good, she works, does business, is strong, has a good self -image, aids the poor and needy, tends to her household and herself, her works raise her husband in other's eyes, speaks in kindness and wisdom, does not eat the bread of idleness and most of all, fears the Lord! And last of all, her value is priceless!

The world has a dozen descriptive sayings for her. But you can read Proverbs and add Matthew 15:28, and Acts 9:36b to find the descriptions from the Word and know for yourself what it means to be a woman of grace. There is no more beautiful woman around!

---

*   Webster's New Collegiate Dictionary. A Merriam Company (G.C. Merriam Company Springfield, Massachusetts, U.S.A.

July 26

PROVERBS 3:5

"Trust in the Lord with all your heart, and lean
not on your own understanding." NKJV

Oh, my, how smart we so often believe we are. We trust that our knowledge of the way things work, is something we know already and are in good condition to make wise choices that will enable us to do well. We really think this way! There are so many subjects we know so very little about that it would surprise us to understand how deep our ignorance is. We usually wait until we have goofed up on an important choice we need to make before we take a moment to check anything out.

But how wise it would be if we understood the importance of going to the Lord first before we make those important movements with our lives and the lives of our family. How many times have you gone to the Word when choosing a way of progressing? Or do you more often look to friends, or people you think may know what's good in the choice that's before you? Do you know how to search the Word for an answer to your problem? Friends can mislead you. Those who seem to know your situation can mislead you.

But when you look into the Word of God for a clear understanding on the subject of the difficulty facing you, you could be surprised how much the Lord has to say on what your behavior needs to be. Your own way may seem right, but wisdom seeks for a second opinion! A godly friend may steer you right by knowing some Scriptures to save you time in seeking God's plan and timing on your options. Take a moment and see what the Word has for you. That's wisdom; trust Him, not your own way of thinking.

July 27

PROVERBS 3:6

"In all your ways acknowledge Him, and He
shall direct your paths." NKJV

How wise we would be indeed if we sought God's will in everything
we chose to do. When we are in the process of making these choices,
we are already too far in to seek His plan for us. It would be much
better to go to Him before we even know what all of our options are
in a particular circumstance.

If we want His wisdom and blessings on this event, we must look
for His will first. Too many times I have gone about deciding what I
could do, or might do, far in front of the actual choice. I find myself
looking for all the possibilities before I look for what the Lord has to
say on any part of the decision. I wonder out loud, I think what I call
"through it," and I try out many ideas in my mind.

What do you do in like situations? Can you identify with me
or do you always seek God's way first? If you are wise, you would
do the latter, but too often, I imagine, you too, run ahead of Him.
So, what can I do to rectify this problem? The Word says to seek
the Kingdom of God first to have all the other things added to you,
things of necessity, clothing, food, shelter. Our God knows we need
those things already. But the Kingdom of God in our lives is to be
the rule of God there. Make a mind change. Start with the request
to your Lord for your needs and for the way you can proceed to have
them met. He has promised to direct your paths when you do.

July 28

PHILIPPIANS 2:5, 7B

"Let this mind be in you, which was also in Christ Jesus,
(who)… took upon him the form of a servant…" KJV

Oh my, what does he mean, the form of a servant? My Jesus took upon himself the shape of a servant, that is, one who serves others! I think I have a good test for determining if I have that form of a servant in my heart. You try it sometime too.

If I find myself being angry or even just irritated, when others treat me as if I am at their beck and call, as they say, a servant, I might not have it! When others ask me to hand that book to them, even if they add please, it is not a request. It is a command instead. It may have been asked with a sweet voice, it may have had please added, but it is still not a request. I cannot choose to do it or not without offending them. They are treating me as their personal servant…maybe a servant who is sort of their friend too, but still a servant. How do I respond? Do I feel a little short down deep, especially if they have often used that type of "requests"? I can check my "Servanthood" easily by being honest about my feelings. Even when I do hand the book over, there can still be a sense of being put-out, of being used. And we have a tendency to resent such.

I am not advocating that we not respond cheerfully, giving the book willingly. But then, that would mean being willing to be treated as a servant, wouldn't it? I am suggesting that we remember how Christ gave willingly to us when we didn't even ask at all. He has served us in this life. May we in turn serve others as willingly as he did.

July 29

PROVERBS 3:11-12

"My son, do not despise the chastening of the Lord, nor
detest His corrections; for whom the Lord loves He corrects.
Just as a father the son in whom he delights." NKJV

When our children were young, they did not appreciate the mild
hand of correction they received from their father or from me. But it
was necessary that we both loved them and corrected them daily that
they not grow up thinking they were the center of the universe. That
attitude comes about rather easily to children, doesn't it?

Well our heavenly Father does the same with each of His children as well. Those whom he loves, really loves, he does correct. And
thank God, he does! To not chasten us would prove his lack of love
for us. It is the hand of love that moves a child from the dangers
before the little one. It is a proof of deep love and care for that one
when a small child wants to touch the snake who looks so neat and
pretty running across the sidewalk. That father delights in the child
that he runs to save from heartache.

Your God is also that Father who corrects the much-loved child
who desires those things that will hurt him. He proves his great love
every time he lifts us away from the pain we would receive if we kept
on the same path toward it. Trust that his discipline is meant to be
healthful to you, not to harm you in any way. But it can be very painful when we insist on having our way as a child does. Correction is
the very sight of infinite love shown your way. Choose not to despise
this chastening from him. Accept it as from the hand of great love.

July 30

PROVERBS 4:18

"The way of the righteous is like the first gleam of dawn, which shines ever brighter until the full light of day." NLT

Most mornings I rise early enough to see the sunlight of dawn sliding over the tree tops across the pasture from our front porch. It is a sight to see as the darkness gives way to the ever-increasing light. The pasture is still and the cows are resting nestled beside one another. You can hardly make out their humps of bodies from the mounds of hay that rise behind them to give shelter from the light breeze blowing.

One of the joys of choosing to live the life of following Jesus is that, though the light is small, it is growing moment by moment as the time advances into the rising of the sun. The steps of those making this choice is outlined, one step at a time over a lifetime. The way may seem dark at the beginning, but the light increases with each movement of obedience to his command to follow. They are seldom seen more than one at a time. As we reach out with our feet in preparation to step, the light reveals the next one and the next one, until we can look back to be surprised and delighted at our progress.

His love enlightens our way faithfully. His mercy shows us that we are accepted in Jesus and gives the go ahead to move. His grace is outstretched to us that we might respond to His call to go up higher, to keep advancing. He has given light that is sufficient for the next step. Over the years of walking in faith with him, you trust more easily that the light is enough for the day even as the grace is for each day, more and more, until he takes us to be in his full light of home with him.

July 31

NUMBERS 6:24-26

"May the Lord bless you and protect you. May the Lord
smile on you and be gracious to you. May the Lord
show you his favor and give you peace." NLT

What more could I ask of the Lord for you today? He is the avenue to blessing, protection, delight in you, grace, favor and peace. Walk in his way today that you may have all of these. There will be choices to make (it's always about choices, isn't it?), feelings to overcome, desires to be put off, tasks to do, but it will be worth it all.

Resolve to be obedient in the way you know. Don't worry about what you don't know yet. Just obey the things you do know. Your hands will be full with that! Then, resolve to learn more of your God each day as it moves into another. He will be faithful to teach you as you desire to know more. His Word is full of the knowledge of the Lord. Be one with a teachable spirit that you may move more easily to follow him all the way. As I said, it will be worth it all. Mama's just saying!

August 1

PROVERBS 3:9

"Honor the Lord with your wealth and with the
first fruits of all your produce." ESV

Every farmer understands this literally. As we brought in the crop,
no matter what variety it was, we shared it with our pastor at the
time, and with others around us so that all enjoyed the bounty that
God had provided for us. He was generous and gracious, so we were
generous and gracious too. It was easy to see the relationship of the
honoring him with the "first fruits" of each one.

When we work in other careers, it is not always as easy. But it
still applies to us, no matter your kind of job. As you are paid, you
bring a portion of your increase to the Lord's house to be used by
him. That way, his house is able to stay open and functioning. It still
is pretty easy. You just need to make up your mind that it all is what
he enabled you to do to earn a living for you and your home. When
he gives much, it is easier to give back. But when it is a small amount,
it may seem harder to do in the same way. Again, it is a choice you
make.

Over the years, many of them, there has been much and there has
been little. But we made the choice to return according to his giving.
We have never been sorry. We have never been without our necessities, though there have been times when it was close. We learned
there was a difference between our necessities and our desires!

Trust the Lord with all you have and honor him with your portion. He is faithful to you. Be faithful to him.

August 2

PROVERBS 12:4

"An excellent wife is the crown of her husband…" NKJV

To excel, is admirable indeed. To be considered the crown of my husband would be a delight also. To be thought of in his mind with joy and excitement would be wonderful as well. I will have to explore this thought a little farther!

The idea of excelling is one that is sought by many and often, but found by far fewer than those who seek. I believe that to be considered excellent as a wife might mean that I would rise above the call of duty. That call is to meet the need of my husband for food prep, clothes clean and bed covered in clean sheets. That is duty for me! In no way is this for everybody. That would be the least I could do and feel I had met my duty in this marriage.

In our household, it is love that calls him when the food is on the table and then pulls out the chair for him to be seated. When he is finished, the table is cleaned and he is returned to his comfort chair by the television. It is love expressed to sit beside him as he scrolls through all the channels available on that screen! When getting up in the morning, the clothes are ready in his closet to be chosen by him. And when retiring at night, the sheets are pulled back and turned down for his arrival.

But duty could do all this. So, what is the rising above? Here's the thoughts of a wife of sixty-one years. I believe in him, I trust him completely, I extend my arm of comfort when he is weary and I lie beside him every night with joy from his heart to me. I go the extra mile when working beside him in any endeavor he undertakes. I talk about him as he moves among our friends because we can laugh with and at each other. Whether in his arms or in his face, I tell him the truth of our lives. We walk together whether happy or angry. I am cupbearer to the King of this household. After all, the Word said I am his crown! Once in a while I want to crown him! He even occasionally lets me wear the crown! PS This has been written in fun. So, laugh my friends! Laughter is good for the soul.

August 3

NEHEMIAH 1:11B

"…In those days, I was the king's cupbearer." HCSB

Now I realize that Big Buck, the big man around this house, is not the KING around here, but I have always used this verse to remind myself to serve that one whom God gave me so very long ago to walk the road that He had laid out for me. Not because I have to, but because I choose to do that. There's that word again: to "choose." You see, when I choose to do a thing, everything about the situation changes. It is not duty. It is love expressed in the way that I perceive Buck's need to be at that time. If I felt that I had to do that given thing, it would rub me the wrong way and cause me to become a little angry or irritated. When anger or irritation is left unattended for long, it becomes a deep - seated resentment in my heart. The longer it remains under my skin, the stronger the feelings become, giving rise to being expressed at odd times, helping no one, dealing with nothing and leaving a rift between us. Also, if Big Buck demanded the thing be done, commanding and demanding, that too would bring a smoldering of ashes in my mouth that would burst into flames in places that have nothing to do with the original problem. Again, nothing would be gained, dealt with, or settled. Believe me, my mouth can be caustic, painful and destroying of anything in its path! My, how God has had to work on that in my life!

Though I did not know this many years ago, service is Big Buck's "love language" … who ever heard such words back then? When I learned what "love language" meant, I realized how much more he would hear of what I was trying to say when I would say, "I love you," if it were couched in service to him. Saying those three words didn't ring deep in his heart because that's not the way he perceived love. What a revelation! I don't mind being the cupbearer to this king now because I know he hears my words when I do things for him. Am I saying you should be doing as I do for him? Of course, not! What I am saying is find your spouse's language of love and show your love in those ways. It is not about your saying love your way. In fact, it is not about you, at all!

Big Buck's small motor skills are not overly developed as years have gone. Have you ever looked at the size of his hands? But his big motor skills are unbelievably developed. I watched him last week take the tractor with the big blade on the front of it, plant a big tree, cover it with dirt, smooth it off and drive away as though it were nothing! But when I hand him a bowl or glass, (any glass!), he has been known to drop it. I've heard him tell friends it was easier for me to wait on him than to clean up after him! We have laughed so many times over the things he has broken. It helps to take a good look at ourselves, to laugh with good humor and to accept the things we aren't good at doing. Each of us has limitations!

But the best part of being cupbearer to the king is the fact that he trusts me with his life. What an honor for me. Just as the king trusted Nehemiah and knew Nehemiah would never do him harm, Buck receives my service as love expressed. Find your love's way of receiving love and try it. You might find you'll receive love back.

August 4

PROVERBS 3:7-8

"Do not be wise in your own eyes; fear the Lord
and depart from evil. It will be health to your
flesh, and strength to your bones." NKJV

Oh my, how God hates pride and how often I see it in my life! My eyes fool me. My thoughts give away my senses. My desires get in the way of my smarts. My heart gets divided between good and evil, meaning anything that is opposed to his perfect plan for me. I trot off on my foolish journey to get what I want, when I want it, and so often, regardless of the impending consequences. I look neither to the right nor the left as I step into what my desire is at the moment.

But the warning here is to fear the Lord instead of thinking you are the wise one. To fear him is to be amazed at his wonder as the Creator of all that is. To fear him is to stand in awe of the way he has splashed all heaven with his firmament that falters not, that runs as he made it to flow together in complete control from his hand. To fear God is to realize in the minutest way the story of his redemption available to all mankind. To fear God is to stand in humble adoration of his love and grace that is everlasting to everlasting. To fear him is to bend the knee to him in honor of him with everything you are and all that you have.

He is above you in all things. He is worthy of your fear because he cares for you through all of your life. You cannot imagine what he has made for you in your future with him when you are his child. Stand in awe of your God!

August 5

PROVERBS 4:26A

"Ponder the path of your feet..." NKJV

My feet are what take me from place to place. They carry my weight. They are strong enough to lift me over thresholds that I might go into most areas without any question. These two feet are meant to be a blessing to me and to walk me on to bigger and better things in life. They are small but adequate for the job.

But sometimes I find myself in places where it is not good for me. At those times, I need to reconsider my feet and how I got just where I am. Did they take me away by themselves? Did they think and start off in another direction? Did these two little feet devise a path of their own? Or, did I begin to think about those other things and people I wanted to see, to just catch a glimpse of what the rest of the world lives like? Did my heart gather together pictures of what I was missing by living for my Lord? Wherever the path became a wrong one, I need to go back there to examine what steered me away from the straight and narrow. It is so easy to slip away from the circle of obedience to my God.

I must consider my feet and the choices I made that smoothed the way to the wide road that leads to destruction. I must establish my ways before the Lord God that I do not turn to the right or to the left to see evil. I must keep my eyes on the goal that my feet will follow my Jesus. May I remove my feet from temptation to do wrong. May I ponder, that is, think deeply about where my feet are treading. They do not act on their own. They follow the thoughts in my mind and heart. Think about where your feet are going too. Keep your heart and soul in love with God that you will walk in righteousness.

August 6

PROVERBS 12:10A

"A righteous man regards the life of his beast…" KJV

As a young girl before tractors and modern equipment, my Uncle Boy, who worked for my daddy, drove a mule to do the hard labor of laying off rows for the crops. Daddy would be driving the other mule for cultivating the young plants in an adjacent crop. When the end of the day came and the mules were "put up" in the barn, my uncle would feed and water those big sturdy and strong mules, caring for them with honor and respect. When I asked why he did this with such tenderness, he replied, "The mule gets no pay, no reward, nothing special for his labor. The only thing he gets is food, the honor of a thanks and respect for a job well done." I learned years later about this verse that declares a man as righteous who cares well for his beasts.

It shows me that even a lowly animal's care under my hand is important to our Lord. I am to respect those who work for me or with me in this world though they be just an animal. So, we no longer use mules on the modern farm. But all lowly beasts are still valuable in God's plan for us. We enjoy them as we feed them with tenderness and rub their ears in pleasure when they come beside us, whether a horse for riding, or a dog and cat for walking in companionship. Never abuse one of God's creatures. They are a part of his world and deserve to be appreciated. He took such care in making them to fill our lives with joy and love. And the Lord regards how you treat his world with its creatures here. Be kind.

August 7

PROVERBS 15:3

"The eyes of the Lord are in every place, keeping
watch on the evil and the good." ESV

It amazes me to no end that the world thinks that God is ignorant of the goings on and the actions of humans here. We are the ignorant ones. His eyes are everywhere and on all things at all times in every generation that has ever lived. He has missed nothing and he keeps perfect records. He sees both the evil and the good. He is aware, not only, of the words spoken or the actions taken, but also, of the motives for doing either.

How wise we would all be if we stopped long enough to take stock of our behavior and our motives for even wanting to say and do such things. We have in our power the ability to send blessings on others or to slap a curse on them. It is always about our choices that we make in each single day as it comes. The mouth has great power in itself. But we carelessly put it in motion quickly and passionately without ever considering the consequences. Our hands can bless those around us or hurt them. It is a choice we make. Our feet can bring good to others or carry pain to them without a single thought about it.

We must ultimately take charge of our feelings, our behavior and our speech. Be wise and realize that God is seeing it all. He is completely aware of your days and all your ways. Today is a good day to begin to seek his way and his plan for you so that you do not even think of displeasing him. He loves you and wants you to share his love with his world. He sees the evil and the good. Choose wisely which yours will be.

August 8

MICAH 7:8B

"…when I fall, I shall rise; when I sit in darkness,
the Lord will be a light to me." ESV

In everyone's life there are times when we fall. It may be from health issues. It may be from financial troubles. It can be because friends and family disappoint and we waver with the burden that we feel we must carry alone. There will be those times! There are also the times where we can't see even our hand in front of our faces for the darkness there. We know not how to move one or where to step for our next step as we struggle to find the right path. There will be those times too.

But our God has told us not to fear the enemies behind nor the unknown before us. We can know that we can rise again. We can walk in the light of his face regardless of the apparent dark that is staggering, waiting at our door. He has promised us light, his light. He cares what is happening to us and though he does not always choose to remove the circumstance we are experiencing, he will help us to rise to face it. He will give enough light for us to keep being obedient to his word.

Walk on, dear friend. Keep putting one foot in front of the other, knowing that you can trust what you cannot see, that you can have faith when all seems to be a struggle. He is there, whether you see or feel him or not. His word just told you so. Your God is able to lift you, to shed light on that next step. Walk on!

August 9

MATTHEW 17:1

"And after six days Jesus took with him Peter and James, and John
his brother and led them up a high mountain by themselves." ESV

It is interesting to note that Jesus had a few select friends out of
his group of disciples that were closer to him and who were given
opportunities to experience more of the road that Jesus was to trod.
Everyone needs those who are closer, for whatever reason to us, those
who will go the extra mile with us and for us.

There have been those for me. And I imagine you have had them
too. They will stay when others have determined that what you are
feeling is too hard to handle. They will come when others decline for
many reasons, all without a second thought about you. These friends
will talk with and listen to you when you need a sounding board for
your fears or dreams. Friends such as these will take time from an
already busy life to stand by you when you are right or wrong in any
given situation. They do not even mind. They may be weary themselves, but they will be there when you call.

Start looking for a friend like this. Or better yet, start asking
God to show you one or to teach you how to be that kind of real true
friend. We can begin by paying more attention to those around us
who need this kind of friend too. God wants us to be willing to be a
real friend to his children who need one. Today is a good day to really
listen to those around us to what they are saying with their hearts if
not with their words. Jesus had them. You need them. Others need
them as well!

August 10

MATTHEW 26:41A

"Watch and pray, that ye enter not into temptation..." KJV

What strong words of wisdom to us, the followers of Jesus from his own mouth. To guard, to protect or attend are all words describing the term "watch." They are strong and yet, simple words. We all know what each of them means. A dog guards his yard or his home. A parent protects the family. An employee attends to his duties. A Christian must do each of these if that one is going to be able to stay away from temptation.

But how often we are as the dog who is sleeping in the sun, completely overcome with the warmth that induces the deep sleep. We snooze on looking at nothing but the backside of our eyelids. We are capable of standing guard. We are equipped to do just that. We are strong...but asleep! And the Enemy slips on by, taking advantage of our slumber, to take advantage of our weakness in deep sleep.

The parent is busy, so busy! There are so many things to do, so little time to get it all done. The child is oblivious to danger because he is young and the parent is "on duty." Or is supposed to be! And the Enemy moves into the area of protection, or lack thereof, and the child is harmed.

The employee is standing at the gate, attending to the door. But he is seeing only the passers-by carrying large bags of goodies. That employee is wondering how they afford so much stuff. And the Enemy waltzes right out the door with unbought items in his bag.

Be aware, friends, that it is way too easy to enter into the temptation to sleep, to be too busy, and to be way too careless. WATCH AND PRAY.

August 11

MATTHEW 18:10

"See that you don't look down on one of these little ones,
because I tell you that in heaven their angels continually
view the face of My Father in heaven." HCSB

How important the children are to our Father! He lifts them from
the street of simple existence to raise them to the level of giving their
angels access to the Father of the Son of God continually. What a
blessing to each little one!

We must not deliberately entice or cause one of the little ones
who believe in him to sin. He cares about their growth in the life of
following Jesus. The smallest believer is as important as those we look
to for great sermons and grands songs. It is not about the idea of who
is the greatest, but about lifting one another up to aid each other in
becoming all we can, in becoming all God created each to be. Pride
will get in the way of obeying this call to us to help and not hinder
the little ones, be they children who believe or brand new believer
adults, babies in Christ.

Be careful how you treat those younger in the faith than you. Be
very careful how you behave toward the little children who look to
you for encouragement and strength in this walk. Do not lead any
astray. He is watching. He cares about the least. Choose to walk worthy of our Christ that those who follow in your footsteps can read a
clear path to the Savior's plan for each.

August 12

MATTHEW 26:41

"Watch and pray, lest you enter into temptation; the
spirit indeed is willing, but the flesh is weak." KJV

In our Lord's hour of need, he finds his disciples, his closest of followers, asleep. These are his words to them. How often over these
years of following my Lord I have found myself asleep when the
temptation came. I was neither watching nor praying. And when I
realized that I had fallen, my heart was broken for my carelessness.

But, oh, how delighted I was when I remembered my Lord loves
me, gives mercy and grace when I tell him of my sin. He is ever there
to restore, to lift me up, to set me on a higher plain to walk again in
victory. He knows my frailties. He knows my flesh is weak and I am
prone to stumble. Praise him for his forgiveness to me!

His love, mercy and grace is yours too when you find you have
slipped and are on the road to defeat. He is ever there to restore, to
forgive and to lift. When you fall, look to Jesus, the Author and
Finisher of your faith.

August 13

"Now when Jesus heard this, he withdrew from there
in a boat to a desolate place by himself." ESV

Jesus had just learned about the evil Herod having John the Baptist's head cut off and served on a platter to a dancing girl! What depravity! The news was painful, I'm certain. Our Lord often went away to be by himself and to pray. He saw the "hand-writing-on-the-wall" from the terrible tetrarch Herod. He knew the love of John for himself and the Father. He needed time alone. The crowds pressed him repeatedly no matter where he went. Their need was so great they clung to any hope of healing from Jesus.

But Jesus knew that he would have what he needed from the Father when he took time to be with him all alone. We must realize that God is always waiting for us around our bend of disappointment or pain, sorrow or fear. He is there before us every time. But we must meet with him to be able to go down that road that leads to our bend beyond which we cannot see, that place that instills fear of the unknown in us.

Jesus found that the crowds followed him soon. There was no place he could go for long to get away. We can be assured also that the bend in the road is still there ahead for us too. But before we approach that curve there, we need that alone time with the One who understands us, who sees our slow walk toward the future. We can go to him anywhere, anytime, to let him walk by our side so that we can go on into the curve, banking on his strength to get us through what we cannot see just now. It may be a desolate place, but our God is with us beyond the way of darkness ahead. He is our Light for each single step. So, take one step at the time, believing him for the next one. His strength is yours. His way is sure. His heart loves you more than any other. Trust him completely, friend. He is able to be your overcomer. Obey his call to come to him.

August 14

MATTHEW 11:28

"Come to me, all who labor and are heavy
laden, and I will give you rest." ESV

In my heart's eye, I see my Jesus standing at my door reminding me of his invitation to come to him. It seems such a simple thing for him to do. But I hesitate and I wait a moment or two. Then I talk to myself about the questions that I have no answer for in this life. I go to the door to see him holding out his hand for me to open that door. I hesitate again. I stand there debating about the sincerity of his desire for me to come to him. Why would he be willing to do this for me?

I change my mind a dozen times while halting there between the door and my desire to reach out to the latch. I walk back to the other room and wallow in my self- pity for a little. I return to the door to see he is still there, waiting for me. I must be strong myself, I think. I must do this by myself I reason. I decide he is really there. He really does care. But I keep thinking inside my head that this is my mess. I must tend it myself!

But from somewhere deep in the back side of my thoughts is the memory of times when he has called before for me to come to him. And I hear again the call I have heard him make before when I have created a mess for myself. And I rush to my door to throw it open to my Lord, crying out with each step. And he is still there! He is still saying, Come to me!" I surrender to his waiting hand. I have labored alone for too long. I have been bent down with the load of my mess. He reaches out that offered hand and I sit at his feet in relief. He is at your heart's door as well. Open it quickly. Do not hesitate, but surrender to his will. Thank you, Lord, for such love!

August 15

MICAH 7:18-19

"Who is a God like you, pardoning iniquity and passing over
transgression for the remnant of his inheritance? He does not retain
his anger forever, because he delights in steadfast love. He will
again have compassion on us; he will tread our iniquities underfoot.
You will cast all our sins into the depths of the sea." ESV

Oh, the joy of knowing how gracious my God is. When he deals
with me and my sins, when I have faithfully confessed them to him,
he pardons and passes over them. He does not stay angry with me or
pout about how disappointing I have been to him. He forgives completely and then pitches them far into the sea away from me never to
remember them anymore.

His forgiveness leaves nothing else to be attended to at all. Jesus
has finished that work of the cross! He has been brought back into
full life that gives us the assurance of our own salvation and resurrection. Those sins can never come back to condemn me again. My
Jesus took care of that forever. When Satan, the Enemy, arises to
remind me of them, I must call out the name of Jesus who forgave
and restored me. I don't have to be fearful of that Enemy. Thank you,
Lord, for your steadfast love that has done all of this for me!

Stand on the cross of Christ for your forgiveness too. It is available for all, but you must accept this free gift. It is free, but it was so
costly for him. Reach out today. Wait no longer. His love is for you
too and it waivers not.

August 16

MATTHEW 13:1

"That same day Jesus went out of the house
and sat beside the sea." ESV

When your days are busier than usual for too many days in a row, it is good to realize that our Lord of all the universe needed rest too. He simply walked out of the usual and into the outside where his creation was waiting to be enjoyed. Of course, the people found him soon, but he just plain went outside and sat down first. I too, need that. You need that as well!

When life is not necessarily bad, but just too busy, take a few minutes to go out into the surrounding area for a rest, to rethink and to be refreshed by the Lord's hand as he lets the beauty he created revolve around you. Stand in awe of him and all that his hand made for you to let you see him in it all. I have a big two- person swing in a big oak tree on our patio where I go to find this rest. There is a joy that I find there when it is nowhere else to be found. I am alone in that swing and that is alright. Everyone needs a little down time once in a while. It is good to be alone long enough for the Lord to be able to crack that exterior that we build over our lives to keep our sanity!

When you have had time to unload the cares that mount up into more than you can carry, you are ready and able to hear the still small voice of our God whispering in your ear. He doesn't shout to be heard. We must clear the way for his sweet words to be laid into our hearts. He is there all the time. We just can't hear or see because the way is cluttered with too much life. Find a small place for his rest to open your mind to be able to rethink your days, and for him to refresh your energy with his lifting hand. He wants you to be filled with joy from his heart to yours.

August 17

MICAH 4:5B

"…But we will walk in the name of the Lord
our God forever and ever." ESV

Every day I must arise and begin to make choices. I look in my closet to pick out clothes and shoes. I look in my dresser to find under garments for those clothes. I decide what to eat for breakfast from the many choices in the pantry or refrigerator. I choose to go where my schedule takes me, or not. I decide with whom I will ride. Choices all throughout the day, from directions from my boss, or which thing to do in my own business. It is always about choices.

My spiritual life is the same. I must make choices all through the day there as well. It needs to start at the beginning of the day before I have set all these other actions in motion. Far too often it is an add on to my list of other items that fill each day. But I have learned over the years to make that first one before my feet hit the floor. That way I am ahead of the game of choices.

I have "put on" my day with my Lord at the head. He is to be first, foremost and number one for me to have my day in any order that works best. When I choose to walk that one day in the name of my God, it doesn't matter what anyone or the Enemy of God pitches at me. I can stand in his name alone.

Today is the first day of the rest of your life. Start with your God and line up with his words before you start any other part of your list of to do's. Put on your garment of righteousness that God has given you in the name of Jesus our Savior. It fits you perfectly. Wear it that others may see his face in you and come to desire him too. You are his best or worse witness. Choose to be his best by choosing to walk in obedience to him. Choose each moment as they fly by to honor your God.

August 18

MATTHEW 15:35-37A

"And directing the crowd to sit down on the ground, he took
the seven loaves and the fish, and having given thanks he broke
them and gave them to the disciples, and the disciples gave them
to the crowds. And they all ate and were satisfied..." ESV

This is a wonderful report of Jesus feeding the crowds with so very
few food items: seven loaves of bread with a few fish. It wasn't about
the amount that he took into his hands. It wasn't about the number
of folks he fed with so little. It wasn't about the disciples doing anything grand. It was about what was had that was given into the hands
of Jesus. Jesus made an orderly sitting down on the ground at his feet.
There a several thoughts I have when reading this.

The first is the fact that what they had they gave to Jesus willingly.
It was little, true. It wasn't fancy either. It wasn't special in any way. It
was given as it was to the hands of the one who reached out to take
the food from the disciples, that is, Jesus. When it was in his hands,
he made it work for them all.

The second fact is that, when he took them, he gave thanks for
what was in his possession. He didn't lament the fact that there was
not more or its simplicity. He was thankful for what he had at that
moment. In his acceptance of the food, he took his hands and broke
it up into pieces to be handled as was necessary to be shared by all.
The disciples reasonably set out among the crowd sharing it with
them. But it had to be broken before it could be eaten by so many.
We don't enjoy being broken so that others may share in the joy that
Jesus gives us. But it is necessary. Trust him when you are broken.

And the last fact is that all the folks ate and were satisfied. Their
tummies were filled but there was more to be had from this man
Jesus. Through him they could have a filling that would give new
meaning to life. In fact, it could be new life! Never fear to give Jesus
all you have. In his hands it is much, it is worthy of thanks and it
will be broken so that others may see your Lord in you. But in that
breaking, there is multiplication, not division. Your life may be simple, but it is grand when given freely to him.

August 19

MATTHEW 26:35

"Peter said unto him (Jesus), 'Though I should die with thee, yet will I not deny thee. Likewise also said all the disciples.'" KJV

Oh, how brave and strong we answer our Lord's calling us on to the life of follow-ship. We speak so swiftly, so surely, so over the top when we see not what that really means to us. We do not count the cost to follow him, to willingly take up our cross to do so. We think we know, but then reality sets in as the hardship reaches us with pain and loss of the things we believe are so important. We turn and look back never seeming to understand that the way of loss is really back there. It is not things that are important. It is obedience to his command to love God with all I have and am, and to love my neighbor as I love myself.

We might want to give poor Peter a hard time about such rash words, except that every one of the other disciples said the same words to Jesus too. Which gives me an insight into what we are all like. It is too easy to say the right words, but so difficult to live them. We are brave as long as there is no real threat to our status quo, our life as it is. How much better to count the cost of following him with all that we are and all that we have. And then, choosing to follow his lead to die to this life and to live for him, knowing we are willing to pay that price, as he paid the price for us to have this salvation. He gives the strength to obey as we move in the first step to follow all the way. Life takes on new meaning at this point.

What wonderful words of forgiveness to have Jesus touch us when we have denied him and to restore us as he did these disciples. Choose you this day to follow, to obey, to deny yourself and to take up your cross to live where Jesus places you in his "choice" place. It is the perfect place for you to live for him.

August 20

MATTHEW 14:23

"And after he had dismissed the crowds, he went
up into the mountain by himself to pray. When
evening came, he was there alone." ESV

When was the last time you went "up a mountain" to pray? Perhaps you don't live close to the mountains you say. But we all have "mountains" that rise before us as we live in this fallen world. They are more than we can manage, we think. They don't belong in our lives, we argue with ourselves. We shy away from dealing with those mountains for fear of being totally overcome by the enormity of our "mountains" that fill us with dread.

It might be a better idea to climb those personal mountains with firm feet and a heart ready to be poured out to our Father about them. It might be more advantageous to our growth toward a vital faith to stretch out those tired and weary limbs reaching for those stars just beyond the mountains. If our Lord Jesus wanted to go up the mountain before him to be ALONE with his Father to lay his thoughts, his needs, his life out there, how much more do we need times alone with our Father?

Dread not the storm, nor the path that seems dark in front of your eyes. Instead, look beyond them to the Father who is on top of the mountain that blocks your forward progress. He is there to aid you going to the top, not to evade the pain or the weariness, but to lift you above each stress that looms higher than you are. He is aware of your weakness, your tiredness, your fears that draw you down. He is there to raise your heart to meet the mountain from where he is above you. Look to him. Trust him. Today is not your enemy. He is there already in your every day! Rise up and go to the Father, up your mountain.

August 21

MATTHEW 24:13

"… he that shall endure unto the end, the same shall be saved." KJV

For the last few mornings I have been in the yard hoeing weeds, and pulling thcm too, from my magnolia garden that also has roses in it. Some I have to get down under to pull to keep from hoeing up the roots of the roses. I started last week but found it too big a job to do in one day, so I applied my personal rule: "You can empty your ocean with a bucket if you just keep at it." I managed to get about one-fourth of the way around the edge of stones that encircle it. That took two days by starting at seven each morning, after all, it is a big area. Then came the weekend. Monday came before I was finished with the weekend. But I started over anyway; early again. I can work only until about nine-thirty or ten o'clock because of the heat in Florida's summer. And because of just plain being old! I can return in the late afternoon when it is cooler. But until then, I must head for the AC and iced tea with the sofa close. While there, I do the everyday things of household items. Started me to thinking about the perseverance of the saints.

It seems to me, an aging one of those saints, that living the Christian life is much like pulling or hoeing weeds that are always growing in our lives. Some days they are easy to get out with the hoe, but some take more effort that requires getting down on that situation and being pulled out by the roots with my hands. They are very resistant. They grow in hard-to-reach places. A few are easier, just growing in the shade where it isn't even hot to get them. Obstacles (weeds) are a part of every life. I realize that by the time I get them all clean it will be time to start over again. But I can handle that because God gives me my day that way…one moment at the time.

God gives grace for the moment. Watch an hour glass. The sands fall from the top into the bottom one grain of sand at the time, singly. I can do that. If it all fell at once, I could not live life with its

difficulties. How kind of Him. Therefore, I remind myself throughout the day that I can empty my personal ocean with my bucket if
I just keep at it. Daily routine is what it takes. Pressing on is what it
needs. Walking by faith is where I learn to be faithful. Keep on shoving that bucket into your personal ocean. It is done one moment
at the time. Moment by moment I can persevere. You can do this.
Perseverance, child, all the way to the end. And then, there is rest.

August 22

EXODUS 33:14

"Then He replied, 'My presence will go with
you, and I will give you rest.'" HCSB

Every year we are blessed with a couple of hawks having one or two babies in the big oak at our front door. We can sit on our porch and watch them interact with each other. It is so much fun to see how the parents take good care of those babies.

This year there is only one. We named him "Big Bird"" because that baby is huge! But big or not, he is still a baby. He has been programed by God to do everything the grown-ups do, to catch his food, to fly, event to soar high as he matures. Yes, he has been programed, but he must still go through the process of learning to fly. These last two weeks he has been hobbling, fluttering and flapping from limb to limb in his effort to fly. His mama still brings him food too. She is careful to be certain he is able to fly with strength.

For the last three or four days she flutters just as he does, from limb to limb, even going to the tree next to his nest to encourage him, to call him on to do what he already "knows" how to do! She reveals the way to do it, slowly and surely, patiently and repeatedly. As we sat there to peek in on the two of them, I remembered this verse from Moses' cry to his God to be with him as God had promised. God had called Moses to a grand job, that of leading his people out of slavery in Egypt. And God gave him a reminder that his very presence will go with Moses.

As mama hawk flies with Big Bird, she is sometimes leading the way, but there are other times when she stays behind him for a short distance. Occasionally, she flies across to the adjacent tree to draw him on to bigger and better things, a way to being who he was created to be, a big, grand winged creature that can soar in the heavens. Other times she will even go off to a far tree, always pulling him onward, sure of his safety with her.

That's the way God's presence is with us. He often leads out in secure ways. But he also stays behind watching us hobble, flutter and flap as we grow. But he is always there! He encourages, he patiently moves in tandem with us or he draws us on to bigger and better things. He shows us how to live as the New Creature in Christ he intends us to be. He has equipped us to fly. We are created to go forth into our world, to show Jesus to our own personal part of his world. He still feeds us with his Word, his Living Word, that we might be able, as he has programed us, to be and do with the strength of his Holy Spirit. And his rest is assured as he provides for his child and shares his presence with us all.

His birth is an opportunity to reveal his love to your realm of influence with a bountiful heart. Share his coming, his salvation available through the cross and his truth that will endure for all generations. It is time for you to fly. So fly!

August 23

MATTHEW 5:16

"In the same way, let your light shine before others,
so that they may see your good works and give
glory to your Father who is in heaven." ESV

Today is the day you have, the only day you have, for you to make changes in your life. Why? Because you don't live in tomorrow yet. It is not here and it will never come. You cannot back up for yesterday either, my friend. It will never come around again. We have been given directions for our lives and the light that shines forth from our days lived. We must go forward into today with the light of his love keeping us full to the overflowing toward others who walk in the darkness of this world.

How can we do this light shining brightly thing? It is shining when we give kindness in the face of unkindness. It is giving a light worthy of the Lord's Light when we love as others hate. It is amazing how bright that light is when we turn the other cheek when we've been wounded by the words or actions of another. We can shine when someone else needs the Light of unselfishness carried into that life. Our lives shed light over our workplace when we help our coworkers with a strong hand of mercy, when we share our goods with others willingly and when we take upon ourselves to do what's righteous not what the world thinks is "right." The choice is always ours to make. Choose wisely. Shine for Jesus today.

August 24

PSALM 111:10A

"The fear of the Lord is the beginning of wisdom…" ESV

We all need wisdom in every day we experience as we pass through this day to day existence that leads us home to the Lord. If we are to have the wisdom that is needed on this earth, we must begin at the beginning. The number one exercise that must be the start of this great endeavor is to stand in awe of our Creator, our God, the Lord of all the Universe over which he stands guard.

When we have that down, or think we do, we must move on to the learning process of just how we can be amazed at our God. We will learn from his word that he is, not only the Creator of our world and all that is in it, but he also is the One who keeps it rolling as it was meant to do. He selected each person who has ever lived to be in this world. He has placed each one in a particular place, family and life. After all, he is the One with the knowledge of how to grow every person into all he created each to be. We will learn life is not fair. It is just fact! We can "get on the bus," so to speak and start making life into what it should be or just stand back and complain.

We can be patient with ourselves as we do learn a little more all the time. Give yourself a little extra time to grasp that God is good and really does have a plan for you. There are those who will make it harder if they can. But we must not be sidetracked by them. Keep pressing on, gathering the understanding of standing in awe of God. That attitude will bring wisdom into your life and you won't fear life; you will be wise enough to accept it as it comes. Make it better while it is in your hands. Live it to its fullest while you can. Today is the day to grow and learn!

August 25

MARK 1:40-42

"A man with leprosy came and knelt in front of Jesus, begging
to be healed. 'If you are willing, you can heal me and make
me clean.' Moved with compassion, Jesus reached out and
touched him. 'I am willing,' he said. 'Be healed!' Instantly
the leprosy disappeared, and the man was healed." NLT

When we come to Jesus with everything open and presented to him, our hearts broken with our uncleanness in true humility, trusting that Jesus both can and will want to heal us, we find his heart is moved by our plight. His answer to this man is compassionate and kind. He is moved to reach out and even touch the untouchable. The heart of Jesus is open to those desiring to be made clean. There is no one who is not in need of being made whole and clean. But not all want to be clean.

We are like the leprosy covered one. We are undone and only Jesus is willing to move in our direction, much less touch us. How beautiful was our Savior as he looked at his much- loved child and saw the brokenness of sin that marked his creation with ugliness!

Oh, to have the love of our Savior for those who are strapped in sin's ugly state. Just to be willing to touch that one who craves the acceptance of another person. We bow before our Lord asking him to create in us a deeper love for his Kingdom and his children. Choose to touch someone with your compassion today. Watch that one come alive before your eyes. Fill them with hope and care. Jesus has told us to love one another as he has loved us. Just do it!

August 26

MATTHEW 5:14-15

"You are the light of the world. A city set on a hill cannot be
hidden. Nor do people light a lamp and put it under a basket,
but on a stand, and it gives light to all in the house." ESV

Another of Jesus' wise words to us are these. We have the ability
to be a light to everyone around us, especially to those of our own
household. When I was a child, we did not have electricity. We had
kerosene lamps that gave very little light. But what did we know? We
had never had anything else! Homework was done after dark by the
light of those small and weak lamps on our dining room table. But
they were sufficient for the day.

My mother never brought those lamps to life and then stuck
them under any bushel basket that we had in the yard for crating
up our veggies after picking them. The lamp went in all its simple
glory on that small table for the four of us to sit around doing that
homework. It was hard to keep our pencils held so that the shade of
our hand did not cover the writing. Too often we cover our present
light of the Lord in us with our hands being in the way. Our words
hang in between us and others so that it is difficult for them to see
by our light. Our behavior keeps the world around us from knowing
our Lord and his perfect Light that he has brightened our lives with
each day.

Be careful little hands with what you do, little eyes with what
you see, little mouth with what you say, we used to sing as children.
Today is a good day to choose, yes, there's that word, to choose, to
be a light unhidden, uncovered for all to see the Light of Jesus in us.

August 27

MATTHEW 9:36-37

"But when he saw the multitudes, he was moved with compassion
on them, because they were faint, and were scattered abroad, as
sheep having no shepherd. The he said unto his disciples, the
harvest truly is plenteous, but the laborers are few." NKJV

Late one Sunday afternoon, I was picking the beans from the bean
rows that I had complained so strongly about hoeing the grass from
a few days earlier. I repeated the procedure the next day. I picked
about two bushels all together. I was so glad the grass was gone from
my hoeing them so it was easier to do the job. It was amazing the
difference in the plant's production of beans.

Soon after the bean seed sprouted we had a spring storm that
went through the crop. Many were hurt when the wind blew them
around and the rain pelted hard on them. The first seed to come up
were the ones hurt. The later sprouting seed were protected by the
dirt. These grew into beautiful bushes, while the damaged plants
were a little scraggly. Now, in the plant world, when a bush is hurt
really badly, it has a tendency to try to reproduce itself fast. So, these
plants bloomed quickly and began developing little beans. The
undamaged plants just kept growing bigger and bloomed later. They
were so pretty. But when I turned the plants up to look under them
for beans, it was the bedraggled plants that were loaded with the
crop hanging everywhere. When the big, lush ones were turned over,
there would be two or three beans, since they had spent their energy
on growing pretty. Made me think.

The plants could not be judged by their outward appearance.
The beautiful ones reminded me of those in the body of Christ who
would not miss a church service or function, but never think about
going across their back fence to minister or witness to a neighbor.
Or those who would never give anything to the mission fund to
send others to witness. While the ones who were worn out, tired

of holding up their little leaves, having trouble just covering those whom they were glad to minister or witness to, had a multitude under their covering. Which one are you and I? One thing to think about on the beautiful plants. In time, they grew and finished maturing, so they too, had a bountiful crop under their leaves. I pray that means that in time, immature believers can keep growing and begin to grasp the idea of ministering and witnessing. May we check our hearts to see where we are in God's plan. Are we maturing early or late? Are we maturing at all?

August 28

MATTHEW 10:29

"What is the price of two sparrows----one copper
coin? But not a single sparrow can fall to the ground
without your Father knowing it." NLT

What a wondrous thought to hear. Our Father cares about the seemingly "worthless" creature that sells two for one copper coin. Actually, I understand, if you bought two for the one price, you could buy four for two coins and they would throw in a fifth one free! So, what man thought was completely worthless, one little sparrow, has the attention of God the Father. Amazing! In his sight, that worthless creature was worth noticing. How much more you are worth to him! He notices when you are in need too.

God still has a plan for your life. He hasn't written you off, not ever. He will touch you with his hand of mercy and grace. His love is everlasting; it is forever. No matter what is going on in your day, he still cares. Take those cares to him and be honest with him. After all, he already knows what is in your heart! He can lift you above your circumstances even when he chooses not to remove them. He gives sustaining power to be an overcomer in each day. You are worth so much more than a little sparrow that he notices as it is in difficulty. He is already aware of your struggles. Talk with him about them. And above all, listen to him as he speaks to you from his word. He has covered all of human experiences in that word.

August 29

MATTHEW 10:30 NKJV

"…The very hairs of your head are all numbered." NKJV

Can you imagine the awesomeness of this fact: God has numbered each hair on your head! He knows you so intimately that he even knows how many you have there. There is nothing he does not know about you. You are precious in his sight. You may misbehave, you may become prideful, you may talk unkindly or with trashy thoughts, but the you there is, is precious to him. He will put things or events in your way to turn you from the paths you have chosen. He will speak to you in the recesses of you mind to alter your thinking. He will show you where you are missing the mark. He will correct your ways to move you toward obedience to his way. But he still loves you completely.

When the correction, the turning, the events or the soft words of wisdom he speaks to you come, that is a really good time to stop and turn around to head in the right direction. That is the time to ask yourself where you are losing sight of your Lord. Then is the time to listen to his words and to move toward him, toward his way. If you choose to be stubborn and demand your own way, you will regret it. After a while, the Lord will allow you to have your own way and it will be troublesome to you in the long run.

No one else knows you so well. He has checked you out, as a new mother looks over her newborn to see if all parts are there and working. He took the time when he created you to number the very hairs on that head of yours. Trust him because his way is the way to victory in this life, to joy immeasurable and to sustained strength.

August 30

MATTHEW 6:28-29

"And why worry about your clothing? Look at the
lilies of the field and how they grow. They don't work
or make their clothing. Yet, Solomon in all his glory
was not dressed as beautifully as they are." NLT

My cactus that hangs in my big oak tree in the front yard all year blooms only once each year. It's always in early June. It bloomed as it always does at night. After all, it is a night blooming cereus. There were close to seventy or eighty blooms hanging from different limbs at carrying heights. Quite a show from the ground. Little Brooke, my grand-daughter of eight years old, came to see the show. Each of the blooms are ten to fifteen inches across, looking so much like a star burst with each petal a long thin strip of white to amber and spread in every direction just as a star's light is. That bloom lasts only the one night but it does its thing so perfectly you would think it was going to be there forever.

I thought about that for a while and decided we need to do our thing, our calling, so perfectly that we wouldn't be worrying about how long we were to be here. Just that we were to do that one thing on our one night to perfection. We should remember that Solomon in all his glory was not as we were on our one night though it be for one day, one hour, one moment. God made us to shine forth as the stars as we share his story of Jesus and his love for us. No one else can do our moment of shining…just us. Shine, my friend. Shine.

August 31

PSALM 116:15

"Precious in the sight of the Lord is the death of his saints." ESV

Each time the Lord has called one of my family or dear friends to come home to himself, it is with pained heart and broken spirit that I have stood by that grave to say the human goodbye to the one I loved. There is pain that you cannot imagine until you have stood there watching the mourners file past you with loneliness already being experienced by all. We each know what is ahead as we adjust to being without that one. We each know it will not be easy, but that it must be done. It is one place where no one else can take your place. It is a road that you walk into wondering how you will survive.

When you enter that lane, and start walking forward, there are so many times you will want to turn back and start again with the one gone ahead. There are times when you desire to race on and meet that one early, rather than late. It is empty where you stand…alone. Others can't understand what you feel or think. The mind can play cruel jokes on your heart.

With each step you take on that road though, you can see that the Lord meets you, drawing you on to the completion of his plan for you, but you must walk it. That plan is not dependent on the one who left you at the grave. That plan is with you and the Lord. Rejoice that he has not left you at that grave site, nor has he left you alone. He does not take lightly the calling away of that one you loved. He calls you forward to the race you must finish now. He accepts your hand as you move in answer to his call.

September 1

PSALM 130:3-5

"If You, Lord, should mark (that is, take note of my)
iniquities, O Lord, who could stand? But there is forgiveness
with You, that You may be feared. I wait for the Lord,
my soul waits, and in His word I do hope." NKJV

The joy that the Lord gives is part of his forgiveness. Oh, what joy there is found in that wonderful grace that affords us his mercy. To be forgiven is one of the greatest gifts he delivers to us from his full and loving hand. Not to have my sins, my iniquities, all of them, laid at my door, is joy unspeakable. It lays beauty over my ugliness. It surrounds my weaknesses with strength. It delivers all my sins to my Lord Jesus to be marked, "Paid in full!"

I do stand in awe of you for the forgiveness that came to me at your expense. There is none left over from my long list of sins. Jesus paid it all. I owe it all to him. Though my sins have left a terrible stain, you removed it all.

Friend, where are your sins laid? At your own door of life or on the person of Jesus? There is forgiveness there and in no other. Choose life today. It is always about a choice, isn't it? He has offered it long ago to you and to all mankind. Accept it now.

September 2

PSALM 119:105; JOHN 15:12

"Your word is a lamp to my feet, and a light to my path."

"This is my commandment, that you love one
another, as I have loved you." ESV

My children, my friends, this is my prayer for you this day:

May you walk the path of obedience all the way, whether it is
straight or has bends in it.

Make your steps firm as you trust Him for your footing, never
looking down, always forward.

Hold your head high in adoration of the One who made you to
walk upright.

Keep your eyes on the goal and your ears attentive to the Holy
Spirit's voice.

Look at the creation all around you: the roses, the blossoms of
trees and shrubs,

The bees, the birds, the bright clouds.

Miss nothing that your Father has planned for you this one day.

Prepare for his divine appointments that will be scattered along
the way.

Make music in your heart and share it with your world, whether
in notes to be sung or in pleasantness,

For you will never pass this particular way again with everything
the same.

May your voice have a strong lilt in it and your smile spring forth as easily as the trees sway.

May your heart move in love and encouragement toward those around you.

May your hands reach out to those whom you meet as you pass through this day.

May you communicate with Him and, just as easily, communicate with family and friends.

May you be concerned with your Lord and know completeness in Him as you obey.

Today is the first day of the rest of your life.

Be glad in it and rejoice.

Use it wisely, redeeming the time.

It is the day the Lord has made for you. It is the only day you have!

Your Mama loves you.

Love,
"Mama"

September 3

PSALM 118:14

"The Lord is my strength and my song; he
has become my salvation." ESV

Many years ago, when my mother heard me sing, she decided that I should learn to play the piano! I will forever be grateful for the way she attended to my lessons and training on that instrument. She did not let me quit taking those lessons! And she saw to it that I did as much practice as I could what with school lessons, church and helping out at home with girly things.

Because she was faithful, I have had an outlet for my faith, even though I was not a very good singer. I have been able to play at churches, weddings, funerals and able to teach piano for sixty plus years. Mainly because of her!

Because she showed her strength in overcoming my childish protest, she also taught me to see the strength of the Lord in my life and upbringing. Every time she did what was right for me in my development, she revealed a little more of how the Father does what is right and best for me as he develops my faith in my heart. I learned early that both of them were right and both of them loved me enough to say, "No!" when needed.

Through all of this I have been given a way of singing with my fingers and creativity of music. His salvation gave me eternal and new life and my music gave me the chorus of songs that I play every day in honor of this salvation. Don't you know already that mothers and God are always right? Sing to him on any instrument that you have, whether your voice or other. Sing in his honor every day as you light your little part of the world with songs of his strength and salvation.

September 4

PSALM 103:15-16

*"As for man, his days are like grass; he flourishes like
a flower of the field; for the wind passes over it, and
it is gone, and its place knows it no more." ESV*

The death of a loved one or a dear friend is a time for realizing how fragile the golden thread of our life is. It is so thin, but it is good to know that only God can cut it to end it. But still it hurts as we experience the finality of such loss. There is no going back and starting over with that particular one. What has happened is forever. And we think to ourselves, it was not enough time. But the word says time here on this earth is very short. It is like grass, vibrant today, wilted tomorrow and gone the day after. It even says the place where it was doesn't even remember it being there!

But God also says that we can know the God who created us and follow him into eternity. What a blessing beyond measure. Forever with him. The beauty of such words to the ones left behind in the place where emptiness dwells now is also forever. We remember and we think of better times. But the best of all is the knowing we can join that one by knowing our Savior, our Redeemer and Lord. There is a place with him where we falter no more. We will never wilt, for the streams of living water will fill us with life. Mourn not as the world does, believer, for your saved love one. Mourn only for your loss, not theirs, for they live in the presence of the Living God. Praise him from whom all blessings flow!

September 5

PSALM 103:8-9

"The Lord is merciful and gracious, slow to anger
and abounding in steadfast love. He will not always
chide, nor will he keep his anger forever." ESV

It is so wonderful to know that our God is so gracious, so merciful to us even when we have sinned grievously. How I rejoice at this knowledge and run to him when I have missed his mark for me. I am so glad to see that he is slow to anger. How I am grateful and how I count on his never-ending love that he holds out to me every day. That love is forever and always.

But I must be wise and realize that there is a time when he will call me to account for what I am choosing to do or be. He does not want his much-loved child being careless with my life and desires or actions. He wants the best for me not just a good, but best.

I am also happy that he does not deal with us according to our sins or we would never be able to go forward. We would flounder and not be what he has planned for us. He deals with us in that mercy and grace, but we must not test his patience with foolish choices. This word says clearly that he will not always just keep chiding us about our life. Make better choices, starting today. You can and you will be glad. You can and you will rejoice again at his feet of kindness and restoration.

September 6

ISAIAH 26:3

"You will keep in perfect peace all who trust in you,
all whose thoughts are fixed on you." NLT

The peace that God speaks of here is not an absence of concern or of thinking on a subject. We are told to live carefully in this life, thoughtfully taking care of our family. It is much deeper than the idea of willy-nilly going about our days oblivious of what is going on around us.

The key to this kind of peace rests in the second part of the verse. I am to "fix" my thoughts on him, completely, on my Lord, my God, keeping all other avenues of rescue closed to my mind when experiencing any difficulty that happens here. There is only one God who has the ability to overcome the hardships in life. It is he that I must set my eyes on, keep my heart centered upon and live with my trust in as I go through every day. There is room for no other in my line of vision.

Today I will make the choice to believe what his word says to me about trust. I will depend on his word for strength, for wisdom, for energy to make the day before me. I will entertain no other who tries to tell me to lift my own self up by my bootstraps to make myself better. I will say to them that I am trusting in my God to give me this peace while I work through this pain, sorrow or difficulty. I will do what I can, for whom I can, wherever I can, and I will trust him to do what I cannot. He is able. He has overcome this world.

It is a good Southern saying to "fix" your eyes on something. So, "fix" your thoughts, the place where your behavior originates, on him. And walk on in peace, the kind only he can give.

September 7

SONG OF SOLOMON 5:10-16

"My lover is dark and dazzling, better than ten thousand others. His head is finest gold, his hair is black as a raven. His eyes sparkle like doves beside the springs of water; they are set like jewels washed in milk. His cheeks are like gardens of spices giving off fragrance. His lips are like lilies, perfumed with myrrh. His arms are like rounded bars of gold, set with beryl. His body is like bright ivory, glowing with lapis lazuli. His legs are like marble pillars set in sockets of finest gold. His posture is stately, like the noble cedars of Lebanon. His mouth is sweetness itself; he is desirable in every way. Such … is my lover, my friend." NLT

This is a day to be celebrated, my lover's birthday. I can think of no other Scripture that says my love any better for the one God gave to me to have and to hold for all these many years. It matters not that we don't look this way anymore! It matters that we are still here, together. We walk today where we have not tread before. The eighties are upon us. Where did the years all go so quickly? We want to stand together in these late days, upholding one another, basking in the beautiful memories we have drawn in each other's lives, the canvases we have painted on deep in our hearts. The days we have left, appointed to us from the Father, are numbered. Each one is accounted for already.

You would do well to learn from our experience of being the old folks that each day is what you are given. Treasure it with all your strength. Paint and draw while you are able. Only you can pull from your own hearts the beauty that has been yours alone. Remorse makes sorrow even deeper if you miss this opportunity. Be Jesus to your own lover! Love with all your being. Redeem the time while it is yet today.

September 8

PSALM 103:8

"The Lord is merciful and gracious, slow to
anger, and abounding in mercy." NKJV

When my mouth is full of ugliness, when my thoughts have been there ahead of my mouth's harshness, my heart is heavy with unuttered horrors that surprise even myself. It is beyond my understanding how quickly my mouth, my thoughts and my heart can become so enraged with anger and outrage at others. I am an easy person. I think… I wonder at how easy it is to slip into another whole person.

Those are the times I hear my God calling me to turn around. I hear the voice of love reasoning with me to rethink my attitude, the who I am in Christ Jesus. I cannot be both. I must choose every day to follow him or to do my own thing with only myself at the top of my desires. Either Jesus is at the top of my heart, seated firmly on its throne, or I am. There is room for only one. I must confess how often it is the wrong one there. I have sinned, O Lord. Thank you for your mercy and grace. Please, be seated at the very top of my heart's desire.

You don't just give plain mercy, Lord, you give an abounding mercy, over and above all that I need. You cover me with it. Thank you for being slow to anger. Otherwise you would have destroyed me so long ago. But your love corrects me and pulls me close to you as a child that has made terrible choices. Thank you for turning me around to hear your call every morning to come to you for your love, shown to me in great mercy and grace.

September 9

PSALM 94:14A

"For the Lord will not forsake his people..." ESV

When disaster strikes, as it does in all lives in a fallen world, take heart. God will not abandon you. When the pain of losing one so dear to you knocks at your door, insisting on coming in, fear not. Your God will not forsake you. When disease is stretching its arms over your body or strength is forgotten as age comes upon you, do not panic. Your God will never leave you without hope.

One of God's great gifts to his people is his word, preserved for you to know. Go to him with his very own words and call on his name for him to fulfill his promises to you, for him to explain his thoughts to you as you wait on him to teach you more. Take his word deep into your heart and settle it into your thought process that, when troubled, you can recall it for strength for the day.

And as you read his words aloud to him, know that he hears and cares for you. He knows you are frail and weak in the hard things of everyday life. He understands your tiredness at the struggles you experience. He wants you to trust him in each pain you feel, in every problem you face and in every broken relationship that tears at your heart. Memorize these words for today and praise him for his mercies new for every day. And when the hard facts of life happen, say them aloud that your own ears may hear them and rejoice, knowing that your God will not forsake you, ever!

September 10

PSALM 103:1-2

"Bless the Lord, O my soul, and all that is within
me bless his holy name. Bless the Lord, O my
soul, and forget not all his benefits." ESV

To bend my knee to my Lord is to bless him, to bless his holy name.
I will bend my knee in devotion, in praise, in thanksgiving and in joy
at the benefits he has blessed me with every day. I can never tell him
enough that I love him, and that I know of his love for me because
he has told me so repeatedly from his wonderful word.

King David was a man of many sins. Just as I am. He had many
reasons to need the Lord. Just as I do. He came to the place where
he understood his weaknesses and presented them before the Lord
for mercy and forgiveness regularly. Even as I must. And because his
God is faithful to deliver him from all sin, he blesses the holy name
of his God. He holds nothing back from his God. His entire soul is
laid bare and he bends his knee, giving honor to the Lord.

When you have sinned, go to the Lord with an open heart. Hold
nothing back. His forgiveness is available to you. The verses following in this chapter lay before us all the benefits of belonging to the
Lord. Some of them are forgiveness, healing, redemption, crowning
of you with his steadfast love and mercy. Read the whole chapter.
You will learn many reasons to bless the Lord with all your soul.

September 11

PSALM 139:3

"You observe my travels and my rest; You
are aware of all my ways." HCSB

Oh my, when I went to a dictionary* for a better understanding of God's "observation" of me, I learned so much more that just the idea of looking at me! To observe means to guard, to watch, keep and inspect. It means to "see" through paying careful analytical attention.

We have already learned that it means to know, which is through consideration of the facts, even to our sitting or standing. But the definition I like best from the entire list is to "celebrate." What a joy to know that our Lord celebrates us! The idea of "ways" means more than our walk; it is our behavior.

When he sees us falter, he knows his Holy Spirit will convict us of our sin and draw with arms of love toward himself. When we do well in our journey, he knows the fellowship of his people will encourage us to keep pressing on. When he observes our pain, he hears our cry to him and sends his peace and love to lift us upward and onward. He is ever "there" wherever we go, whether we feel him or not. We cannot escape his observation! Even when our weariness drives us to rest, he sees and guards even the rest we need to take. The Word says so. He "celebrates" us! Thank you, Lord. Take time today to praise the Lord for his close "observation" of you.

---

*   Webster's New Collegiate Dictionary. G.& C. Merriam Company. Springfield, Massachusetts, U.S.A. Page:793

September 12

PSALM 104:19

"He made the moon to mark the seasons; the
sun to know its time of setting." ESV

The day is coming to a close. The sun is sinking and the angle of its rays are breaking behind the old oaks in the west making its way toward the north a tiny bit more every day as it brings summer with it. It is comforting to know that the seasons continue as they have, occasionally a little early or late with the heat or cold, but always coming and going as they should, as God set them in motion and charged them to do.

It is a joy to see the seasons unfold, often silently slipping through almost unnoticed until I realize spring is here! Or one morning I wake to a cool breeze mounting over the rooftop to signal that fall is upon us. But it does move from season to season letting me know that God is still in control. I can count on his caring about me as well. I am certain he is aware of the seasons of my life as they are passing from one to another. He is totally aware of the setting of my sun too. I can be assured it will not catch him by surprise at all. I may be a bit surprised, but not my Lord!

He is watching over you, my friend. He is seeing your seasons progressing too. He knows the setting of your sun. He is blessedly in control. Trust him and thank him for every day he gives. Each one is a treasure for you with your name only on it. Open each gift of each day with joy.

September 13

PSALM 119:66

"Teach me good judgment and knowledge. For I
believe Your commandments." NKJV

When I think about this verse from God's Word, I learn several things. It says much to me before it ever starts to help me to understand anything. Let's look at those few items for thought.

First, I realize I need teaching. I do not know most things, much less everything. Before I get to the judgment and knowledge that I need to know, I must have someone to be teacher to me. It may be a parent, a grandparent or a Sunday School teacher. It may a friend who had another teacher spend many hours teaching that one. It may be a preacher or pastor that I have learned from over the years. But I must have a teacher that the Lord will use to open the Word to me.

Second, if I need to learn judgment and knowledge, that means I don't already possess those. Perhaps, I would be wise to accept that ignorance on my part. If I do not develop a teachable spirit, I will never learn anything worthwhile knowing. Ignorance is a terrible thing, but I don't have to stay in my ignorance! Ignorance is not a sin. Staying there is when you have opportunity to learn!

Third, the primary teacher that I have is God's Word. When I am willing to believe His Word, willing to listen with an open heart to it, He is able to teach me, using those we've listed already, or using simply that Word of His by the power of His Holy Spirit alone. He knows what will help me learn the best. His teaching is tailor-made to me. Then, he opens the ability to receive good judgment and knowledge at his hand. Thank you, Lord for the power to learn. Choose to believe his commandments and learn of him. It's always about a choice.

September 14

PSALM 103:17

"But the mercy of the Lord is from everlasting
to everlasting on those who fear Him, and His
righteousness to children's children." NKJV

To stand in awe of God is the definition of fearing our God. It is beyond my earthly and limited understanding to comprehend such awesomeness as is His. My mind is incapable of grasping such perfection and holiness except in a small part. But I do understand enough to know how far beyond anything I know, or think I know, he is.

His beauty surpasses everything I know as beauty. There are no words in any language that are capable of describing his beauty, his loveliness. His power is greater than any military or enormous army ever amassed by any nation in any generation. His power can establish or destroy any government or crown.

But the joy of this verse to me is that his mercy and righteousness are established forever to every generation ever to come who fear him. Every person can know of him. His very heavens reveal his existence to all mankind. And I stand in awe of him because of that, dear friend. Though he gives many reasons to fear him, I need no other. Do you? Mama's just saying again…

September 15

PSALM 91:1-2

He who dwells in the shelter of the Most High will abide in the shadow of the Almighty. I will say to the Lord, 'My refuge and my fortress, my God, in whom I trust.'" ESV

There are days when I feel bare before a world that does not like me. I feel uncovered by my life circumstances in which I am struggling. I am at a loss for my next step and have a tendency to wander around without purpose or plan. And then, the words that I have hidden in my heart from the Lord will creep back into the backside of memory and come tumbling out to bring purpose and plan back into focus.

I have a Savior who has made a way for me to press on into the world that I occupy. I have a God who has made a shelter to run into when the storm is too great. I have a Redeemer who has been my refuge in the past and he has not moved! I have a Fortress greater than all the enemies in my world. I can completely trust that One.

Why wander when he is there all the time? Why be overwhelmed at the door opening in front of me, when he has been my shelter, my fortress for all of my life? He leads me through the wilderness which I fear. He has been and will continue to be for me and will walk every step I must make with me. I can stay in, dwell in, the shelter he alone provides. I can live in his fortress in the cover he provides. Trust in the Lord with all your strength and dwell with the Almighty. He has overcome the world.

September 16

PSALM 94:18-19

"If I say, 'My foot slips,' Your mercy, O Lord, will
hold me up. In the multitude of my anxieties within
me, Your comforts delight my soul." NKJV

There are times when I feel overwhelmed with the day before me. There are times when I am overcome with the many tasks that are ahead. There are also too many times when the day is longer than my energy and I am afraid I am going to slip over the edge of my strength, not being able to rise again to finish. I become weary and discouraged in these trying times.

Then I remember that when I am afraid, I will trust in you, Lord. I will cry out that my foot is slipping too close to the fall that I dread. In your great mercy, you touch me with your strong arms of everlasting love, moving me back from that precipice. My anxieties are many, my strength is weakness, my mouth is dry and my heart is trembling over them all. And then, my voice is found as I speak to you from the smallness of my mind and my fear. And you hear! You are gracious, my Lord. You are kind, my King.

The deeper my doubts, the broader my trust in you becomes as you speak with your sweet Spirit to me. The weaker my limbs, the farther your love takes me into your place of refuge. The simpler my mind is, the wiser you are as you faithfully whisper in my heart that you have everything under control. Your comforts are many and they are there for me when I look to you to see. You renew a right spirit within me and give me sustained hope in you and you alone. I will trust you with my everything. Are you weary, friend? Trust the comforts of my Lord. He loves you and this mama does too!

September 17

PSALM 69:16

"Hear me, O Lord; for Your loving-kindness is good. Turn unto
me according to the multitude of Your tender mercies." KJV

It is good to know that God hears our heart cry when we bring our
needs to him. But even deeper in my joy is the thought, the knowledge, that my God turns himself toward me according to his tender
mercies, the multitude of his tender mercies, not my deserving character or behavior. What a cause for rejoicing! What a blessing to be
grateful for in this life. According to his tender mercies (plural!). It
all rests with him. My outcome is at his disposal. I trust you, Lord,
with it all, the sorrow, the pain, the disappointment, the discouragement, everything that has a strong tendency to hold me back from
full obedience to your word. Thank you for your loving-kindness
that is for me. You are forever loving this child! I will lift my heart
and voice in praise to you.

Aren't you forever grateful to him for this same living-kindness
that is toward you, his child, his much-loved child? Lift your heart
and voice in praise too. He gives according to his own love toward
you, not just according to your character or behavior. If he responded
to that only, that completely, with no mercy, you would be destroyed.
Thank him today, all day.

September 18

PSALM 93:3-4

"The floods have lifted up, O Lord, the floods have
lifted up their voice; the floods lift up their waves. The
Lord on high is mightier than the noise of many
waters, than the mighty waves of the sea." NKJV

In every person's life, there are times when the floods of sorrow, pain
and disappointment are risen above our abilities to ride those waves.
They are so far beyond our reach to overcome. We feel as if we will
drop into them at our peril and go down never to be able to come up
again. It is more than we can bear; we think. We turn, but at every
turn there is more of the sorrow, pain and disappointment. At each
avenue, there is a road that we are unsure of, that we hesitate to take
for fear it will lead to more of the same. The fear in our heart drowns
out the voice of our Lord. It is lost in the voice of the waves.

And then, His call rises above our flood waters. It is faint to
begin with, but with each bobble on the wave, we rise higher to hear
it better, stronger and more clearly. It is his love that we hear. It is his
grace and mercy that we see above the rising waters. It is his Spirit
calling to us to reach out and accept his hand of redemption from
these waves of sorrow, pain and disappointment. He never promised
to remove all the waves as they came. But he has promised to lift us
above those circumstances that overwhelm us, that come as floods
into our lives. He will walk with us, ride every wave as it comes
toward us and stand above each so that we may trust his plan to be
Overcomers in this life. He will not be thwarted in his desire for us.
Look to Jesus when you feel the waves. Listen for his voice above the
noise they make. He is the Lord All Mighty! Mama knows; mama's
been there!

September 19

PSALMS 93:1A

"The Lord reigns. He is clothed with majesty; …" NKJV

What a glorious thought. To be able to say our God reigns over all, through everything, before anything ever was; we can say with assurance that he reigns. He rules all his creation, including mankind. He knows it all intimately, better than anyone or anything else. There is nothing he has missed or overlooked. He is, he was and he is to come!

My heart will wait for him in all that I face or experience in this journey we call life. I can quietly say to my trembling hand that he will be with me through this time. I can know that nothing comes to me without passing through the hand of my Savior. I can walk surely into the desert before me that I dread with confidence of his love and compassion for me. When the road is dark and the trails are many, I can ask for his guidance to the right path stretched out though there be no light there. He is my Light, my Source of Strength.

When you are wavering, look to Jesus, the Author and Finisher of your faith. He is the only One to trust. Go to his Word and find solace for your fears. He has addressed them all there and has repeatedly revealed to you his way of obedience. Do not turn to the left or the right as you follow his steps. Put your toes in his footsteps and walk on to his goal for you.

September 20

PSALM 86:11A

"Teach me your way, O Lord…" ESV

How easy to ask him to teach me his way, but oh, how hard to accept that teaching when it hurts the deepest places of my life. There are some things I have learned that were easy and soothing to my soul. But there have been pains from most of the lessons he sent that made the most productive life changes.

Those brought kindness out of anger, love from a boiling hatred and showed me how to wait for him, to trust no matter what events or occasions looked like at any point. These revealed his will was so often diametrically opposed to my will. There were times when he took my hand and filled it with goodness instead of revenge; filled my heart with joy in spite of the breaking it was experiencing in my night seasons as patience was taught, where gentleness was gleaned from a heart of harshness. These lessons picked me up and lifted me from the realms of this world's answers to walk in his grace by his Spirit's power. Have I arrived yet? No! But by his mercy and grace he will one day complete my lessons. Praise him!

He will finish the good work he has begun in you too. Trust whether you can see the end of the road or not. Walk in faith forward, forget the things that haunt you from the past. He holds your future. Don't stop when there appears a bend in your path. Bends often hold disappointments. But beyond the bend lies your future road. Press on! Mama has been around the bend.

September 21

PSALM 89:13

"You have a mighty arm; strong is your hand, high is your right hand. Righteousness and justice are the foundation of your throne; steadfast love and faithfulness go before you." ESV

There are days when you feel weak, too weak to go into the day before you. You know, the one that has more hard things ahead, things over which you have had no control, things that will bring tears or pain. And, as you look into that day, you fear what is before you. You know there is no way out, you must continue into that one day as it is.

That kind of day is just the right one to remember this verse about God's strength. His arm is mighty, not just simple strength. There is nothing it cannot stand up to in your day. Attached to that mighty arm is his strong hand with his right hand held high. The right hand is the hand of blessing and it is poised high to deliver. His strength is yours for the asking. We can reach up to him to lean on his breast and simply ask for that might as a much- loved child of the King. His joy is our strength.

Righteousness and justice are in front of him to be sent out at his bidding, in his timing, to make right out of wrongness. One day all will be righteousness; just not yet. But his throne is built on these and will one day be carried out completely. Again, at his bidding, in his timing.

But, best of all is his never-ending, forever love that is yours, faithfully delivered into your day. That is his free gift to you, moment by moment, equal to the day before you. No matter how hard, painful or fearful. His blessings can cover that one day with his joy. Do not fear. Your God is near, at your heart's door. Open that door to let his peace come into it's very depths. Accept his great love today

September 22

PSALM 77:11-12

"I will remember the deeds of the Lord; yes, I will remember your wonders of old. I will ponder all your work, and meditate on your mighty deeds." ESV

When I am lonely and seemingly forgotten, I stop long enough to start thinking about my God and the wondrous works he did, the mightiness of his hand in creation and I realize I am not alone, for he has made a wonderful world for me to enjoy at these times. It is when I am remembering only my own situation, my own desires that I begin to feel this loneliness. I turn inward and the view becomes very small!

I look up and am struck by the vastness of the heavens and those that occupy that vast expanse over me. The thought that he created it all overjoys me with the place little me has in his great plan. I am a part of his creation. I am unique and so are you. Everything about you is you! Only you! He has made the tiny flowers to sprinkle through the grass. If you don't stoop to see them, you miss them completely. He has crowned his creation with every human he has made throughout all time. Man is his joy and pride as every parent says over each offspring. He has made a way for erring humans to be forgiven and restored to the wholeness only he can do. He had a plan before he even laid the timeline and he will finish "on time" in his plan.

I look around at the lay of land as we ride by the flats of the plain, the rolling hills and the mountain tops of each area of this world. He is beyond my imagination when I see the differing animals, birds and sea creatures. His works declare his greatness. Thank you, Lord, for today, unique in itself, never to be repeated again. As I ponder his magnitude, I am thrilled at his loving me and you. Thank you for lifting my head above my plight and letting me know you are here with me and you care. I am not alone! I am not forgotten. I am a part of your world and you have a plan for me to carry out. Friend, you too are loved and are a part of God's plan. Reach out, open your mind to him. He's waiting for you.

September 23

PSALM 86:7

"In the day of my trouble I will call upon You;
for You will answer me." NKJV

We began life together, Buck and I, with a big helping of untried love, certainly immature love, and a huge portion of stupidity. Perhaps, I should have capitalized that word, stupidity! We were really long on that one. We had no idea how quickly our lives would be challenged by reality.

By the time we were married only a year and a half, our first baby girl was born and died the very next day. There were no words to say, not even thoughts to express the sense of our loss. In months to come we would re-walk that day in our youthfulness. The way to recovery from that and the days of waiting for me to heal from the traumatic birth were hard. The doctors all said I needed corrective surgery if I expected another pregnancy. Miss Smarty-pants (me), thought all we had to do was ask the Lord for another baby. Well, we asked and nothing happened. Finally, I had the surgery and six weeks later I was expecting! God was very plain; I gave you doctors to help and heal you. Listen to them! And nine months later another baby girl was ours…to keep.

Our faith was tested, our faith was growing, but then, I miscarried twice after this. It was a blow. It was four years before we delivered another live baby. Six weeks before this baby came though, Buck's dad died from cancer. God does not always say yes to our cries. We were twenty-five. The lessons were piling up but our God's grace was so sufficient for each day. We learned more of him and of his plan for us. There was more surgery for me and to be no more babies. But God's plan included two little ones directly from his hand into our hearts. We adopted a little girl and then a little boy. Our family was now complete as we had asked for four children in those first months of marriage. We had Deborah Hope (deceased), Alicia Love,

Elizabeth Helene, Sarah Yvonne and Daniel Leon. Perfect family of four! He had a plan from the beginning. He has a plan for you too! Start today to seek his plan through his word, his Holy Spirit and other believers who love you.

September 24

PSALM 75:3

"When the earth totters, and all its inhabitants, it
is I who keep steady its pillars." ESV

In every generation, there have been times when those who lived
then felt the earth tremble and shake with what was seen to be the
end of it. Here, though, we have God reminding us that it is he who
steadies the very pillars that hold it in place. It is he, and only he,
who can topple the earth. We are to live believing that he will see to
it that the earth is here until he decides it is time to crumble it and
to make it new again. We have a job to do until that day occurs. We
are to occupy until our Lord returns.

So, instead of worrying about the end of earth, we are to do as he
has already told us. He has commissioned each of his children to go
into all world sharing the Good News about Jesus' first coming.
We are to share with the people around us that Jesus saves and Jesus
forgives. We are to shout it to our realm of influence that Jesus alone
can restore our lives with his purpose and plan. We are to serve as he
served. We are to be kind, to be loving and helpful as he was. We are
to be his hands and feet right where we are.

It means I am to be kind to the unkind, generous to the stingy,
loving to the unlovely and a friend to the lonely. It is an opportunity
to know that we love as he loved, when we can be loving to those
who are unlovely. We can give value to those others would say have
no value. We can see his world as he sees it, with eyes of genuine
compassion that makes it the way of service for us. When confronted
by those wishing to harm you, give voice to your Jesus by opening
your mouth with words of grace. Let him provide for and protect
you as only he can. Be his servant. He has called, he has commissioned, and he has prepared your way.

September 25

PSALM 92:1-2

"It is good to give thanks to the Lord, to sing praises to the
Most High. It is good to proclaim your unfailing love in
the morning, your faithfulness in the evening." NLT

For many years, usually before we both get out of bed, we have
prayed for our day, for the Lord to order it for us, for our family and
extended family, the friends God has given to love and, last, for our
own needs. Buck leads this portion and then I, as mother to the clan,
dress the two of us in the armor of God for meeting this one day
before us. I have the opportunity to give thanks and praises that our
hearts are full with from the day before. God's grace is so complete to
us every day that we count on his mercy toward us with his strength
to finish the day he has set in front of us. He brings each one to our
eyes to look into before we even begin. We commit our families to
him to care for and to draw closer to himself as those hours slip by
them. As Job did, we pray for them by name every morning that
God would woo them with his strong arms of love. At the close of
each day we are so grateful we have both returned to each other, safe
and still able to be moving! How thankful we are for his unfailing
love that was equal to the challenges he orchestrated for us in that
one day. We met each head on with him and were able to succeed at
most, but were happy to admit where we were unable, for whatever
reason, to do as we had hoped. His love met us at both doors of our
life…the good and the bad. His mercy was unfailing and complete.
Thank you, Father, for each, for food and shelter, for the time you
allotted to us. May your Name be praised by our lips and those of
our families, for you have been faithful in all things. How important are your prayers for those with whom God has gifted you. Pray,
parents, pray!

September 26

PSALM 90:4

"For a thousand years in your sight are but as yesterday
when it is past, or as a watch in the night." ESV

There are times in life when the "things to do "list is overflowing
with items that seem you cannot change or remove. At the end of a
school year, for instance, there are graduation preparations and par-
ties, exams to take, end of the season ball team gatherings, weddings
and baby showers and the job that comes five to six days a week that
enables the family to do all of these. It seems that our days are flying
by at the speed of sound, that we are torn between the conflicting
events and each child who stand there looking at us wanting us to go
to their special occasion.

At times such as these, I think you, Lord, must look at us and
wonder at our sanity! We are tired but we cannot stop. We are weary,
but we press on to the next thing. This is when we experience the
sensation that we've just gone through a thousand days in one! But
alas, to us there are allotted no thousand days lived as one day, so we
cram it into our few days and when they are over, we look back and
wonder where they went.

Lord, when tomorrow arrives as today, order our day so that we
can see you in it before our feet hit the floor and we are off to the races.
Let us know that you are there with us to help us to choose wisely
so we don't miss the things you have planned for us, those divine
appointments that make life worth living. Let us know you love us as
we run here and there to accomplish what our family needs and what
you have for us too. Let us see your face in at least one thing we do
from the time our eyes open to the last glimmer of light we catch as
we self- destruct on the way to our pillow. Thank you, Lord.

September 27

PSALM 88:13

"But I, O Lord, cry to you ; in the morning
my prayer comes before you." ESV

How many times in my life have I wished as the day wore on that I had shared my heart with the Lord before I began my hectic day! But, because I thought I had too much to do, that my schedule was too stressed already, I had rushed through the morning routine and dashed out the door escaping the press of the list in my purse I thought. I had it. I would finish it somehow that day.

But when I have pushed my day out in front of the Lord, I have set up for my own destruction as I try to do what I did not prepare my heart to do by sharing it with my Lord. He could have put a better order to my day I am sure. He could have helped me to set my priorities better. He would have listened well and spoken to me with the quiet voice that I've come to know and trust. If I had made room in my morning for a little time with him, he could have helped with my crowded day. He could have seen that I set better priorities to accomplish what I set out to do.

It would be smart of you to do the same. Consult with your counselor before you dive into the streets to accomplish that long to do list. He waits for you every morning to sit a spell with him.

PSALM 86:11

"Teach me your way, O Lord, that I may walk in your
truth; unite my heart to fear your name." ESV

When I ask the Lord for his teaching and I look around at his creation
of the heavens and the earth, I see his name everywhere, sculpted in
every star and planet, in every creature before me, in every plant,
tree and flower. There is no place in anything that I do not see the
revelation of his existence displayed grandly. His way is forever in
direct line of my vision. I have to ignore what I see and hear to think
there is no God.

He teaches at every birth of a new star, animal or baby. He reveals
his glory in every sunrise or full moon as each makes its arch over the
earth to light the day or night. He continually shows his beauty in
shrubs that flower and flowers whose leaves are as brilliantly colored
as flower petals. Each reveals his truth to me. He is not bound by
the simple thoughts that occur to me. His are so much higher than
mine. And yet, he wants me to think beyond the simple to realize
how dependent I am on him, to stand in awe of his power and might,
his creativity and love for his creation.

Lord, bring my heart to understand that I need you and I need
your truth to guide me through this life you have given me. Your
name is before me to show your love to me. Thank you for pulling
back the curtain that I may see your creation as from your hand to
give me no excuse for not knowing you are, you have been and you
will forever be. You are the Great I Am! And you bend to touch
your children with an intimate relationship through Jesus. Thank
you, Lord.

September 29

PSALMS 1:1-2

"Blessed is the man who walks not in the counsel of the wicked, nor stands in the way of sinners, nor sits in the seat of scoffers, but his delight is in the law of the Lord, and on his law, he meditates day and night." ESV

For many, many years I have chosen to write notes to, first, each of my children, then each of my grand- children, in a Bible that is for that very one only. The notes are tailor-made to that particular personality. I just started a new one for my fourteen-year-old grandson. Where would you have chosen to begin for one of yours? I chose to make my first notes to this young teen on the first chapter of Psalm where the blessed man is compared to the wicked man.

Here is my note: "This is the man I want you to learn to be. It is a process. It will take time. But it all begins with a choice. You make a choice early in life, like right now; you must choose where not to walk, stand or sit. Second, you choose where to find your delight: God's Word. Third, you choose to think, to ponder deeply on his Word. When your thoughts are continually, day and night, on the Word, it leaves little space for the Enemy. Love, Mimi."

Grandson, choose not to walk in the way of the wicked. Oh, they will entice, plead and plan for you to be a part of them. It will sound good at the time. But don't be fooled. There are consequences to following their choices. Don't stand in the way of sinners nor sit in the way of scoffers. There too, are found hard consequences. There are both negative and positive choices to make every day. Be wise, young man. Be blessed. It's your choice to make. Mimi cannot make it for you.

September 30

PSALMS 19:1

"The heavens declare the glory of God, and the
firmament shows his handiwork." NKJV

What a storehouse of memories are contained in boxes of old pictures. I found some of my grandparent's generation in one recently.
There was one of two ladies, long ago relatives of mine, who were
riding in a carriage drawn by a stunning horse. They were arrayed
in beautiful long sleeved dresses with homemade lace, tatting and
ruffles on the cuffs. Hollywood would have had nothing on them
for their prettiness. I was so taken with their clothes I hardly looked
at their faces. I thought they must have been someone else. They
couldn't have been my relatives! But the names on the back said differently, so I'll claim them.

I began remembering how long in the past my parents lived.
They came from a world of walking, wagons, work horses or mules
and women in the fields with their husbands. They rode in a Model
A Ford truck with "sideboards" on each side to hold the vegetables inside the truck on the way to market. Eventually, they had
a Chevrolet Coupe with a trunk in its back, a real truck. No, my
brother who drove this car didn't make me or my brothers ride in
that trunk!

They plowed mules, eventually drove tractors, and in time,
learned to use computers. At least, my Mother did. She left the field
for the office and Daddy kept experimenting with more advanced
ways of growing crops. With that, came more profitable crops.

They lived to enter the "space age," exploring a world they had
only seen from afar; places they really only knew as the Bible had
described them until man walked on the moon. They loved it!
Therefore, I can only imagine what my great grand-children will see
and experience. And I'm sure they will love it too.

God had given them enough information to believe in him through his Word that said God made the heavens that totally glorified and revealed him. His "handiwork," that is, a personal work of creation, made with his hand at the command of his voice, shows forth his reality and greatness. We needed nothing more to know of God. It is wonderful that we have explored the creation he gave us. It is magnificent how we move to more knowledge. He desires us to care for and enjoy the creation of his hand. But look up! His very heavens tell you he is!

October 1

PSALMS 25:16

"Turn to me and be gracious to me, for I
am lonely and afflicted." ESV

There are times in every life when loneliness sets in for any number of reasons. It may be health. It could be the loss of a dear one. It may be any loss that occurs in everyone's life at one time or another. It can be financial reversals, or fellowship broken with a close friend. These are happenings in human affairs. They are part of the human condition of living in a fallen world. But what do we do when these happen in our lives? This Scripture gives us some very good insight into how we can progress to a wholeness again.

First, we can call out to our God to look at our plight. We have the right as a child of the King to ask the King to turn to us, to face us with his brightness and tenderhearted love that we may have hope again. Our hope is in him only. There is no other that we have with the power to lift our minds away from the circumstances of each day and to give us strength to go on when our hearts are weary.

Second, we can count on God's great grace toward us in each and every day that he has allotted to us. Here we learn to be willing to admit our weakness and to look to him to be gracious to us. Again, he is the only one with the power to shower us with grace when we are in times of affliction. He is willing and has promised grace to us equal to our day. He knows our affliction intimately. How wonderful to come to our God and lean on him!

October 2

PSALM 32:8

"I will instruct you and teach you in the way you should
go; I will counsel you with my eye upon you." ESV

Oh my, my God will personally instruct me and take time to teach
me exactly how I should proceed in my day. He will sit in my heart
long enough for me to hear his words of instruction and counsel for
my direction. He may use many instruments of his peace from my
world, whether people or things to give me clear understanding. But
he will be my teacher in these things. He will tailor make his instruction to fit the ways that I learn.

There have been many human teachers along the way who have
given good instruction, wise counsel and encouragement to me that
stretched me beyond anything I would have ever done on my own.
Those teachers were a plus in my life and I am eternally grateful for
their devotion to their profession. They have been instruments in
God's hand for my good. There have been faithful Sunday School
teachers who equipped me with the word that I might be able to
stand in a world of sin and go forward instead of backward. For
them too, I am grateful and will love them into eternity.

Thank you, Lord, for never taking your eye off this slow learner.
You have been trustworthy all the way and there has never been
a more wonderful, careful and loving teacher over all these years.
Thank you for giving me your word that is a map to my life that I
may stand secure in a fallen world. Thank you for the knowledge that
you are a forgiving God who knows all my frailties and failures and
still loves me steadfastly. Now that's a real teacher!!

October 3

PSALM 31:15A, 24

"My times are in Your hand…Be of good courage, And He shall strengthen your heart, all you who hope in the Lord." NKJV

Some of you are still bringing up young children, many of you are in the "sandwich generation," still with young kids, but caught between those young ones and aging parents to care for as they finish the race God has given them. A few of us are in the time of life when we watch our children become grand parents and their children giving us great grandchildren. How quickly life changes, doesn't it? You really didn't see it all coming, did you? Me neither. I've told you before that I went to bed one night a young woman and woke up an old one! That's how fast it moves.

Buck's dad died at fifty-seven when we were just twenty-four. His mom died at sixty-one. We were twenty-nine. His sister was only forty-nine when she was gone. My brother died at thirty-six. I was thirty. My parents did live to be older. But we really don't know about that timing of life being over. We really don't know why God chooses to take some so early and others are left to reach old age. We don't know why he chose to take our first-born baby girl at just ten hours old, why he let me have two miscarriages and to have only two biological daughters.

But the main thought to me is this: my times are in his hand and I can be of good courage because he does strengthen my heart. I do hope in him. No, I don't always understand, but I have learned (it is a process), to trust him. He has a track record with me. He has proved himself over and over that he is trustworthy. It is that record that I remember and dwell on when I can't understand. I "ponder" those remembrances in my heart so that I am quieted in my spirit. Your children learn to trust you by you being trustworthy with them.

It takes time, but then, my "times' are in his hand and I hope in him. My hope was not in vain either. God honored our trust by giving us two more children through adoption to round out the four we prayed for from the earliest days of our marriage. He supplied our family with another daughter and a son. What a blessing. What a joy. What love he shared with us!

There are those of us who are facing the "time" of life that closes our door here and opens the one in his presence. It is all in his hand. Even, then, we will trust in him for all we need.

October 4

PSALM 56:8,9B

"You have kept count of my tossings; put my tears in your bottle. Are they not in your book? … This I know, that God is for me." ESV

This acknowledges that God is aware even of the night "tossings" that occur for me some times. Yes, there are times when I just can't unload all of my thoughts before I lie down to sleep. It isn't often, I'm glad to say. But it does come at times. It delights me to know that God sees my flip-flopping and counts them! He takes the time to count every one. My, what love of his child is expressed in that one thing.

But wait, there is more. He saves my tears in a bottle. Wonder if it is labeled with my name? I am sure he knows who's those tears are! Everything God does with his children is so personalized, that I am certain it's mine alone. If he counts my uneasiness on my bed, I think he keeps my tears in their own bottle! That too, is not all. He has it all recorded in his own book! He keeps perfect account of my life. What joy for me.

And last of all, but certainly not least, is the fact that he is for me in every day that he has counted out for me! He wants me to grow, to be more in love with him as my Father in each one of those days. He encourages me with his words. He strengthens me with his Spirit. He talks to me constantly through his words, saved for me and you. You can know him too. Read his word. If you do not have his word, call upon his Name and look to those around you who know him. Ask them to tell you the joy of belonging to him. Today is the day for accepting his love expressed in his Son, Jesus. Choose him.

October 5

PSALMS 23:4 A

"…Though I walk through the valley of the shadow of
death, I will fear no evil, for You are with me…"

It was early in June of that year that our first daughter, Deborah
Hope, was born one night and died early the next morning. We were
devastated. I was asked by my mother to go to a big convention in
Miami for gladiolus growers, which we were then. Mother thought
it would help for me to have something to do away from home for
a weekend. I definitely need something to help me move beyond
my hurt.

The thing I remember most about that occasion was the dress
she made for me before going. Now, my mother was a seamstress,
not someone who just sewed. Money was tight, but she said we
could do it. So, we found one and a half yards of a remnant for fifty
cents. The zipper was another fifty cents and the thread a few cents
more. For less than a dollar and a half she made a beautiful sheath
style, sea green dress of a shimmering material that brought many
compliments to my weary heart. It was as if people poured out their
smiles on me when I needed it so much. Why did she spend her precious time and effort to do this? Because she cared that I was hurting.
Although there was nothing she could do to change my pain, she
did what she could with what she was very good at doing, sewing. I
had the dollar and a half. She had the knowhow and the desire. She
stood with me in my pain and shared something beautiful with me.
Did it stop the hurting? No, but it did help me to pass the days with
her doing interesting and fun things that required no hard thinking
or planning. After all, it was a flower show! She was willing to walk
beside me in that shadow of death that took my baby girl. Yes, God
was with me all the way. But how it helped to have a strong shoulder
here on earth to lean on beside me all the way too. She walked with
me through the process of healing. God loves it when we step in

with him to stand with another in dark hours of life. He may have one for you who needs that now. Look around and reach out to that one with a strong shoulder of your own. Can I now do less than she walking through this world?

October 6

PSALM 31:14-15A

"But I trusted in thee, O Lord; I said, 'You are my God. My times are in your hand …'"

There are times in this life when I am weary of what is and wish for what might be. I feel discouraged and overwhelmed with all that is in my day or looming on my horizon. I start looking toward what seems not to be doable with the strength I have. I play out the scenarios within my mind, over and over, coming to no conclusion. I wonder how I can ever live through this time of stress that covers me with darkness. I sit alone and talk to myself about it all. I separate from friends and family. I try to decide what I can do, what I must do or what can anyone do when overcome by circumstances.

And then, I read a little more from this same Psalm, in verse 24, "Be of good courage, and he shall strengthen your heart, all you that hope in the Lord." Where is my hope? Where is my strength? Where is my courage? I realize I made a choice (there's that word again!) a long time ago that you, Lord, would be my God forever.

Therefore, I will trust you because my times, my life, are in Your hand. When the sword hangs over me dwarfing my strength, when my hope is shaken, when my feelings spell discouragement in my mind, when I wish for what might have been, not wanting what is, and when I struggle with being totally overwhelmed, I will remember deep in my memory, my heart, that you are my Everything, my All, trusting you totally, not my feelings. You alone can fill me with good courage that strengthens my heart. Thank you, Lord.

October 7

PSALM 30:8, 10

"To you, O Lord, I cry, and to the Lord I plead for mercy …Here,
O Lord, and be merciful to me! O Lord, be my helper!" ESV

When the storms gather over us and we are overwhelmed with our
pain or sorrow, it is to our Lord that we cry for mercy and for relief.
When disease or the grave are before us, and we believe we can no
longer stand under such pressure, we lift our voices over the sounds
of the weeping in our hearts and plead with our God to hear.

There is no other who can give us the peace that is beyond understanding. There is no thing that will bring the same comfort that his
words can to our aching heart and the turmoil of our minds in these
circumstances. Only the Lord will do. He does not even mind our
cries to him. He feels our pain. He knows and is acquainted with our
grief. He has been there before us and has overcome even the grave!
And to us he gives that power of victory as well. Praise him today.
Raise your voice to him in thanks giving when he reaches down and
lifts you up to plant you on a firm foundation in spite of your situation or circumstances.

Look into your heart and rejoice at his coming to you in your
hour of need. He will meet you just where you are and will take you
to where you need to be in his plan. He knows you intimately, my
friend. He loves you with his deepest love. You are important to him
every day of your life. He has your days all numbered and he has
even bothered to count the very hairs of your head, much as a new
mother counts the fingers and toes of her newborn baby. He loves
you! Remember that every breath you pull into your body. Mama
knows. Mama's counted those fingers and toes!

October 8

PSALM 30:4-5

"Sing praises to the Lord, O you his saints, and give thanks
to his holy name. For his anger is but for a moment, and
his favor is for a lifetime. Weeping may tarry for the
night, but joy comes with the morning." ESV

When I arise in the morning, I can sing my praises to my God for his goodness, his mercy and his everlasting love. His name is altogether lovely every day as his heart is touched by my needs for that one day. He reaches me with his right hand to steady the moments as they fly by my eyes. I can rejoice at the beginning of each new morning.

But there are those times when the Lord brings correction to my house, to my heart and my mind. Thoughts are hatched in my brain that slip down to my heart where I entertain them too long and they become wrong deeds or words for which I am accountable to him. And he, so faithfully and surely opens the door of my wandering mind to reveal the hidden sins that are there. Correction is not pleasant but it is for my best and it does not last forever. His anger attends to my slippage and I am set on a higher way to walk in obedience to his words. Yes, I weep when I realize how I have saddened my Lord. But the weeping is for the night seasons and my joy returns in the morning of his light. What joy indeed!

Know, if you are in that time of loving correction, it is not forever. Listen and make changes to your thoughts that led to the wrong actions. Remember, the thought is the father to the deed! His joy is for the morning of a new beginning.

October 9

PSALMS 1:3

He is like a tree planted by steams of water that
yields its fruit in its season, and its leaf does not
wither. In all that he does, he prospers." ESV

Of whom does this Psalm speak? It speaks of the blessed man. The first two verses tell us that the blessed man walks not in the counsel of the wicked, nor stands in the way of sinners, nor sits in the seat of the scoffers. This blessed man is one who finds his delight in the law of the Lord.

Oh, my friend, man or woman, believe me, the wicked, the sinner and the scoffers will try to entice you, they will plead with you to listen to them. They have a better way of doing things. They think their way is a more prosperous way. But do not listen. Their way leads to death and destruction.

But the man who delights in the law of the Lord is planted by the Lord himself by streams of water that feeds that one with everything needed to sustain life fully. That man will be able to bring forth fruit in the right timing. That one will be a blessing to others who can partake of that wonderful fruit. The leaf of his life will not wither no matter what comes his way. The water he receives from the Word will keep refreshing the soul. He can count on that refreshment each day, though he be walking through a desert in his way. His prosperity comes at the hand of his Lord, not dependent on his circumstances. His feet are firmly planted by that stream that never dries.

All of these wonderful words apply to women as well. God can plant ladies by those waters too! Delight yourselves in the law of the Lord today!

October 10

PSALMS 23: 1-2

"The Lord is my shepherd; I shall not want. He makes me to lie
down in green pastures. He leads me beside still waters." ESV

As I was looking out over the pastures where my grand-daughter,
Claire's, cows were grazing, I thought about these verses where God
is described as my shepherd, the one who is, who guides, who leads.
It is comforting to have a shepherd when you are a sheep!! Sheep
have difficulty not wandering around to nowhere.

But this reminds me that my Shepherd is mine and I know his
voice. I know whom I am to follow. I respond to his voice as he calls
my name. And because of that, I shall not want, that is, be without
my necessities for life. Following him is the very best that I can do.

The Good Shepherd takes me from brown pasture to green pasture, from rough waters to still waters. It is deep waters that run
smoothly, for rapids are made by shallow ones. It is deep that I need,
that I am not to fear because they will supply enough for me to draw
life from those waters. There is plenty for others to drink as well.
When they follow my Shepherd, he lifts them over the mountains
to the valley where the waters are not rough but are deep and still,
where they can breathe and take rest beside them. The waterfalls and
rapids have been done. The patience of following has paid off and we
lie down beside our Shepherd in peace. Choose today to follow my
Shepherd, friend. Be wise.

October 11

PSALMS 16:7-9

"I will bless the Lord who has given me counsel; my heart also instructs me in the night seasons. I have set the Lord always before me; because he is at my right hand I shall not be moved." NKJV

Believe it, or not, there are night - seasons for all of us. We had one of those the other night and it was very late before we stopped remembering all the events the Lord has taken us through in this life time. Why spend time remembering? Because we needed the encouragement from him of his strong right hand, the hand of blessing, and a reminder of his never- ending love, his continuous mercy and his ability to do what we need at the right time, showing us again his perfect, promised grace for every day. And knowing that his timing is not our timing, keeps us humble and trusting of him as we wait upon that right hand.

It isn't always that something is terribly wrong. Sometimes it's just an uneasiness that the human body goes through, especially in older age. You'll know one day when you, too, are old! But, in this case, the most strengthening part was the remembering of his Word, like these verses. Because we have made a choice, (there's that word again!) to set the Lord always before us, we know he is right there beside us giving us what we need in order to put out the hand and foot to step in faith into the next place in our lives. And the ninth verse says it all best: "No wonder my heart is glad, and I rejoice. My body rests in safety." This does not mean we just smile, walking on. It is not stoicism. It is not a grin-and-bear-it attitude. It does mean we shout for joy as we drift into sleep in the middle of the night, safe and secure with each other and our Lord, regardless of tomorrow's happenings. What peace to know we will not be shaken no matter what we awake to in the morning.

You, too, can have that peace in him. Learn his Word and use it to quiet your heart in your night seasons. They will come. Be ready.

October 12

PSALMS 27:1A

'The Lord is my light and my salvation; Whom shall I fear?" NKJV

A few evenings ago, I was at a friend's home for dinner and Bible study. At the close, I went toward the car to put things away and leave. As I rounded the sidewalk curving in the dark, I realized I could not see where I was going at all. The porch light was behind me; the car a good distance from me. There was no extra light from their garage door yet. I had run ahead of the hosts turning it on. There was only darkness ahead of me. For just a moment I almost panicked with fear of the unknown steps. I actually had my foot in the air but was fearful of placing it down on the edge of the cement and tipping over. Talk about "cow-tipping!"! I did remember there was a hedge along the sidewalk and reached out to touch it with my hand to judge the distance that I had to put that foot down safely. And then there was the touch of another's hand on my shoulder, slightly behind me, from one of the guests who had followed close behind me. I had not seen or heard them. You can never imagine my relief unless you too are close to the eighties and a little unsteady. How grateful I was.

Which brings me to my thought about God being my light. Yes, he is that and my salvation, as well. But he used a hand right beside me to steady my faltering step. He used a fellow believer on this earth to give me the strength and direction I needed at that very moment. How I praise him and the sojourner there with me who didn't mind touching an old person with a strong hand of love and respect. There are many opportunities for all of us to be that steadying hand for another. It's always about choosing to be there for that need. There have been many times in many years that God gave me that opportunity and I chose to reach out and touch. God gave me that same from the loving hands of another.

October 13

PSALM 138:8

"The Lord will fulfill his purpose for me; your steadfast love O Lord,
endure forever. Do not forsake the work of your hands." ESV

When I read these words, I remember that I am the workmanship of
the Lord's hands. He has a purpose for me. He did not make me for
no reason or without planning to fulfill his exact purpose. I can rest
assured he will lead me in that plan and purpose. His word says so
and I believe his word.

Where are you today, my friend? Are you wondering why you
are here and what you should be doing? God didn't make a mistake
when he fashioned you and placed you exactly where you are right
now. Look around and see what the Lord has already done in you to
prepare you for his plan. Do you enjoy people? Do you find work a
pleasure? Do you look for a reason in things and hunt for the goodness in others? Do you have an inquiring mind that needs closure?
Look hard and see! You are made with the right stuff for fulfilling his
purpose and plan. Don't stop looking for it. Reach out as long as it
takes to see his hand in your makeup. It is there for sure. Life may
be short now; you may already be getting older. Makes no difference.
You still have a purpose for being or you would be gone already! Find
it and do it. He has equipped you to succeed in it. Look to him and
praise him for creating you. His love is forever and his plan is perfect.

October 14

PSALM 31:14

"But I trust in you, O Lord; I say,' You are my
God.' My times are in your hand." ESV

The "but" is so important in these few words. What is on the other side of it is an answer to how this one has been feeling. This writer has been feeling with strong deepness that his life is too hard, that he is broken and dead. It was difficult to keep going up the hill that had come to feel as if it were a mountain.

To be under the bench, hiding from the morning in fear of the night, is a bad place to have to spend much time. When your friends and family are not there and your pain is weighing you down to the bottom of the barrel, and you feel all alone, to say, "I will trust you, O Lord!" That is the key to keeping on when all seems lost, when all others are gone and you are fighting by yourself, you think. Instead of thinking about your fear, draw on his word to press on into your battle with him at your side.

And grasp this idea as well: All of your "times" are in his hand. He is in control of it all. He knows when you are weak and brings renewal. He understands your feelings and he stands with you as you press on toward his calling to you. He is there all the time and desires for you to keep walking in faith. Trust with all your heart. He is the only one who can bring to a close your "times." They are safe in his hand!

October 15

PSALM 103:12

"As far as the east is from the west, so far has He
removed our transgressions from us." ESV

When I am remembering some of the terrible sins that have been chosen by me over a lifetime, I remember with shame. If I dwell there too
long, my shame brings back those feelings of guilt that I had when
the Lord corrected me for them. But, glory to him, I also remember
this wonderful thought from his word. He has forgiven me.

The joy of remembering that forgiveness is more than I can
know on any other thing in my life. He reminds me that the sin
from my past does not exist anymore. If I were to ask him about any
one of them, his answer would be what sin? He has forgiven and he
remembers them no more! He has removed them from me. Glory to
his name!

When the Devil would want to bring to your mind the sins from
your past that you have confessed to your Lord, send him packing.
He has no right to bring a false guilt to your heart. The Holy Spirit
has already attended to that guilt. And your loving and forgiving
Lord has removed it from your life. Praise him today for the forgiveness only he can give.

October 16

PSALM 127:3-5A

"Behold, children are a heritage from the Lord, the
fruit of the womb a reward. Like arrows in the hand
of a warrior are the children of one's youth. Blessed is
the man who fills his quiver with them!" ESV

Oh, the beauty of a houseful of children! It doesn't matter whether they are boys or girls. They each are a blessing to those who live in that home. Nor does it make a difference how they became a part of that household.

They may have been birthed by you, or been brought through adoption into your home, or they could have been borrowed from other houses. Foster children become ours too as they pass through the doors to the house and our hearts. Each different, each fresh and new, each a blessing. When they sit at your dinner table and eat your dinner, they become yours in every sense of the word.

We thank God for the children he placed in our home through all those ways! Our love for each has been true. It has been full. It has been free. There is no greater pleasure than to have them around, then and now. To be given the life to get to know their children is an extra blessing to us. To be given the years to see their kid's children is a joy more than our hearts can express. Look at those God sent your way. Praise him for each. They are your heritage from the Lord.

October 17

PSALM 23:5C

"…My cup runs over …" ESV

There are so many times in this life when I have felt this small phrase from the lovely twenty-third Psalm applied to more than what it does here. You know, when the day holds more on my agenda than I can do or even think about doing! There have been those days when my body was tired, my soul was just plain weary and my mind was totally out of gear. Ever feel that way? Ever try to be an overcomer when there was not even a great desire to be one? Yeah!

There are times when I have to experience the law of unintended consequences. I will set a date on my calendar way in advance of the time. Weeks flash by and other things get in line near or on that same date. No one intends that to happen. It just does. I think it happens to all of us pretty regularly, doesn't it? And then we must start calculating just what must be done, in what order, that each thing can be attended to reasonably. What do you do when that happens to your calendar? Do you panic or fret or even break down and cry? None of those responses can make any difference in getting it all finished.

This is the perfect time to go to the Lord first. You can even confess that you messed up the date and your ability to do what you accepted to do. It would be wise to take time to ask him for clear directions and sound thinking. Those few minutes talking with him will not be wasted, child of God. You'll notice I said "talking WITH him." Conversation is a two- way street. When you've poured out your heart, then be still and quiet for a while and listen. He may bring some of his words from his Word to your mind that will place clarity and peace over your calendar. He can order your day for you while you listen. Try it, friend. You might like having his help!

October 18

"I will sing of steadfast love and justice; to
you, O Lord, I will make music." ESV

Your love that never wavers, that stands firm forever, that cannot falter is the bright joy of my day. Though my voice is not beautiful, I can still sing of this love that you have so freely given to me, your child. It stands as a bulwark against anything that would come against me in any day that you have named as mine on this earth. Your love is mine, today and forever. How can I not sing your praises!

Your justice is also an important part of your love for me. I learned so many years ago that there can be no mercy if there is no justice. When man stands before the judge in these earthly courts, there must be the possibility of his being condemned, or there can be no mercy freely given to him. It is the very action that can be taken against him of imprisonment that makes the judge's mercy, when extended, so wonderful to hear.

Therefore, while my voice is weak, my heart is strong for your love and justice, because I desire to be where you would have me to be in this life, that is, forgiven and redeemed by the blood of the Lamb. You are my Restorer, my Mercy, my Love and I will make music to you today. My music will be from the piano, but still "sung" to you by my fingers of appreciation. Where is the music only you can make to the Lord, friend? Sing with your voice, your hands and your life every day to our great God.

October 19

PSALM 63:6-8

"… I remember you upon my bed, and meditate on you in
the watches of the night; for you have been my help. And
in the shadow of your wings I will sing for joy. My soul
clings to you; your right hand upholds me." ESV

The days of deep hurt and depression fold over my life sometimes and I feel that I am coming apart at my seams, unraveling at great speed. There is more than I can attend to, there is a loneliness that overtakes my heart and I cry out to my God. It happens! Not too often, but it does happen and then nights are longer than should be as I move through them to the morning light. It seems so far away when my mind cannot think because my brain is not ready to deal with any one thing that is weighing me down. As the troubles pile up and the energy goes down, I am in need of a touch from my God.

Then I think of this verse, reminding me to remember him on my bed and to meditate on him while the night terrors are upon me. While I return to the Word, my God brings comfort and shows me how he has lifted me to rest under the shadow of his wings. I can rest there away from those troubles that I wrestle with each day. I can sing again of the joys of the Lord as I think back to his deliveries in my past. I can rejoice at his faithfulness even in the night seasons, while I listen to the time being called out by the clock that ticks away the hours. I bring to mind the idea that all clocks tell time one second at the time. I can handle one second at the time! I cling to you, but it is your right hand, your mighty hand that upholds me as your child. If you are a child of God's too, trust him to hold you up today, His hand is able!

October 20

PSALM 100:4-5

"Enter his gates with thanksgiving, and his courts with praise! For the Lord is good; his steadfast love endures forever, and his faithfulness to all generations." ESV

This is the last portion of Psalm One Hundred that I learned at my mother's knee when just about three years old. She didn't wait for me to go to school to read on my own. She literally poured the Word into my brain before anything else could get in there! How wise of her!

When I approach the house of God, I am glad that I am there. Sometimes I am extremely tired from a busy week or perhaps, not feeling too well physically which age brings. But when I enter those doors and begin to hear the music of praise and thanksgiving, the Lord opens my heart to hear his goodness and his love sung in strong heartbeats. There is where I find enjoyment among his people, renewal for my weariness and strength for my weakness.

The beauty of knowing that his word confirms that his love is mine forever and that his faithfulness will never run out for his creation is joy indeed. Your word strengthens my heart and calms my fears that another generation will come to be that cannot see your handiwork or your faithfulness. How delighted I am to see that will never be! You will be here for all generations to know if they choose to do so.

Again, it's always about choices, isn't it? We must make them every day about all kinds of things. But the most important is to choose to see God, to choose him over all others and to live in thanksgiving and praise of him. Today is the day you have, the only day you have, that is before you to make the wisest and best choice you ever made. As I've said before, choose wisely, my friend.

October 21

PSALM 102:7

"I lie awake; I am like a lonely sparrow on the housetop." ESV

Occasionally, I find myself "borrowing trouble from tomorrow" as I flip over and over in my bed, rolling from thought to thought in my head. It seems I have put my mind in gear before I put my heart to sleep in the Lord! There is no one thing that is bothering me. I just cannot stop the mind games of "tomorrow" from playing in the front of my brain! They need to be rolled back to the very back where God takes care of them until I wake.

But instead, I sit up there on the top of the house, so to speak, as the sparrow does, huddled against the wind that he fears will topple him from his perch. I suppose that's it: I fear something, but I'm not too sure what! I waste sleep time, renewal time, by fearing an unknown.

The morning brings a whole new light to my thinking and I realize that I have sinned, not in being concerned about a thing, but in being a worry wart about nothing.

When these nights happen to you, take time to understand that God wants you to be wise and think through your concerns. But he does not want you pushing your limits with worrying. When sleep is lost, it can never be regained. When time I am afraid, I will trust in you, Lord, the Word tells me. Even when I do not know or cannot name what I am fearing, you call to me to trust you. You have not left your throne or me! Thank you, Lord for your steadfast love, today and tomorrow. I love you, Lord!

October 22

PSALM 100:1-3

"Make a joyful noise to the Lord, all the earth! Serve the Lord
with gladness! Come into his presence with singing! Know
that the Lord, he is God! It is he who made us and we are
his; we are his people and the sheep of his pasture." ESV

The role my mother played in my coming to know the Lord is primary in my salvation and my learning to walk daily in praises with him. This is the very first Psalm she taught me long before I could read. It was taught by rote, of course, but the day came when I could read on my own what I had been reciting for years. I learned it at my mother's knee. That's where most of my formative years were set in motion: at her knee, occasionally over it!

It didn't require my having a lovely voice to praise God. It didn't require that I be able to read or fully understand about God. It did require that I trusted mother for my learning of many things, the Bible being one of the very first. How wise of her! Books were important to her. The Bible was most important of all. She just finished the sixth grade in school, was married at fifteen and a mother at eighteen. Her life rushed on, but she was faithful to do what she could to make certain her children learned to read, go to college and know about God.

What she had learned about her God was that he was her Creator, he was her Shepherd in life and she trusted him with it all. Each of her children did learn to read, go to college and learn about her God. What is the legacy you are leaving for your children? What are they learning at your knee? Those early few years are so important for you to be teaching them about your God. Choose to start today. It's not too late.

October 23

PSALM 94:18-19

"If I say, 'My foot is slipping,' your faithful love
will support me, Lord. When I am filled with
cares, your comfort brings me joy." HCSB

How many times have you realized that your foot was slipping and you were going to fall, and you were totally fearful of the fall? It happens to all in this life. None of us are immune from the slippery slopes of living in a fallen world. We need something more in this life to be able to walk in faith. Our God has provided this "something more" from the storehouse of his steadfast, faithful love. That love lifts us when we feel the pressures of seeing our frailness and failures, our fears. He is all we need to keep pressing on toward his goal for us.

But how can we know when the cares that bring unsteadiness to our heart are too often more than we think we can respond to in faith? His comfort is there for us as we struggle with the load between family, work and community. He is aware of our desire to keep going. He knows our weaknesses and frailties. He cares that we want to be obedient to his words. So, he intervenes with us to remind us that he is aware, he knows and he cares. His love is superimposed onto our minds as we recount the ways he has loved us in the past and his faithfulness to us in that never- ending love. But, if we do not remember, if we don't rethink them when we are falling, we will not bring to mind the faithfulness he has left as a trail behind us. We need to look back to see his handiwork in our own lifetime to realize his faithfulness is waiting even now. Do a little time in the remembrances of your life. Then do some big- time praises for his love expressed along that way you traveled and trust him for your future. He cares about your cares! He brings comfort and cheer to you. Accept his joy!

October 24

PSALM 31:12

"I have been forgotten like one who is dead; I
have become like a broken vessel." ESV

When the heart is broken, the head is low and the mind is warping
with all the jumbles of thoughts running through it, seek out your
Lord. When you walk and the feet grow weary and the hands are
weak, turn to God with a listening ear for his still small voice of love.
When you fear and you're not sure just what you fear, move into his
word to receive his encouragement there.

Everyone has times that are like these. You are not alone. It just
seems that way. We all feel broken, shamed, mixed up, weary and
weak. That's why God prepared his word for us to have. We would
not make it without his love letters to us. They have been preserved
to sustain us and to be our reason for going on into life, no matter
how hard the road is.

Today is a good day to begin fresh with a small portion of his
instruction to you. The Proverbs are a great place to start. Each one
has strong messages to faltering folks. You can move into the Psalms
that give strength for each day and share how others have felt when
they have failed too. Read what you can remember and then think
about it as you hurry through your busy day. As the Lord opens
your understanding, you will rejoice that you have learned his words
meant just for you! It all begins with one choice. Be wise. He is waiting for you to meet him there.

October 25

PSALM 63:6-8

"When I remember you on my bed, I meditate on You in the night watches. Because You have been my help, therefore, in the shadow of your wings I will rejoice. My soul follows close behind you; Your right hand upholds me." NKJV

As I lie down each night I remember my God on my bed as sleep begins to overtake me. I think about all the times you, Lord, have been there when no one else was. I remember the lonely nights when watching over one of my children as they have been sick while my Buck was with the other ones at home. I am at peace because you have been faithful and strong for me. You have steadfastly been my hope, my help. Therefore, I will rejoice no matter what you have allowed into my life, because I know I can trust you with my all. Your wings overshadow my life with care and protection.

Also, I will try not to run ahead of you. I will follow close behind you with my hand reaching up for your right hand, your hand of blessing to guide me through these next moments. That right hand is sure and strong. It is ever there waiting for me to receive your hand as you stoop down for your child's little hand.

You are too wonderful for me. You are my thoughts as I drift into peaceful sleep each evening at the close of my busy day. Praise you for the loving time you spend with me as the day folds itself together into darkness. You attend to my night. It is enough for me.

October 26

PROVERBS 12:25

"Anxiety in the heart of a man causes depression.
But a good word makes it glad." NKJV

How different the world we move around in, you know, the family and friends we are in contact with continually, would be if we simply learned this verse. It is not great words, or fancy speaking that make the heart of one suffering from anxiety or depression glad. It is just a simple, good word.

We all have ones who are dear to us who need a good word that can lift their spirits and take them out of the dark place where their minds and heart travel to when they are depressed. We all also, have anxieties that oppress us often, meaning we all can use that good word ourselves once in a while. Choose this day to speak a good word to those God has placed in your life who would enjoy a good word.

You don't have to "fix' their lives. You don't have to even talk about their problems; you don't have to do anything else to make them glad. There are times when only a good word will do it for you. Let the Lord take your word and let him open the heart and mind of those who need to hear it. One of the best things you can do for another is to accept that they are where they are right now. Don't judge their pain. Don't try to approve of what they feel. Just approve of them, the person, because they are God's creation.

He didn't promise we would never experience this thing called depression. He said he would be with the one who does. Let them speak to you how they need to when their anxieties overcome them. Be God's blessing to them with that easily spoken good word.

October 27

PROVERBS 14:4

"An empty stable stays clean, but there is no income
from an empty stable." TLB (paraphrase)

This is one of two Proverbs Big Buck and I have built our household on through the years. We would love to have a clean and "presentable" home all the time. But we have learned over the years, if you want to have folks be able to drop in easily and comfortably, you must be willing to have a little clutter from those folks who love being at your house.

You will be loading your dishwasher with dishes, and the washing machine with many towels and dish cloths and picking up happy kid's toys. But you will also be smiling at the memories of big, and little, faces who were sitting around your table or in the living room laughing and talking for hours. We wouldn't trade any one of those precious memories to be able to possess that house beautiful place.

If you desire that your home be an asset in the Kingdom of God and a place where his love is shared easily, you are going to have to shovel some manure out the door when all is quiet again. What a great "income" the years of shoveling that manure out the door has been to our memory banks! Thanks to all of you who have "graced" our house with your presence and have helped to turn that house into a home where forgiveness and mercy have been available to all. This mama loves you.

Take today and think about your household that could become a channel of God's blessings to others.

October 28

PROVERBS 12:18

"There is one who speaks rashly, like a piercing sword;
but the tongue of the wise brings healing." HCSB

Have you ever witnessed an exchange between two folks that caused you to ponder just how it all took place? You know, where one speaks to the other with the quick retort and you can actually see the hearer flinch with the pain received with the rash words. Often, the speaker has no idea of the hurt inflicted on the friend.

Enter a third person who steps to the plate and speaks words of wisdom to that same hearer and healing takes place immediately! I have seen it happen so many times. And often, the rash speaker will still not understand the stinging words that brought pain. Don't worry over that speaker! God will attend to that one! Mama has seen that too. Mama has been that rash speaker as well.

So, for today, pause a moment before you speak and settle your mind and heart instead of delivering those types of words from the tip of your tongue. And then, start to learn how to be that one who speaks wisdom, peace and love. Your world needs your kindness. Your family and friends desperately need your approval of them, not of their actions, but of them as part of God's plan and purpose. You have the power to send messages of life to each one. Just do it!

October 29

PROVERBS 22:1A

"A good name is to be chosen rather than great riches." ESV

As the years go by and you watch folk's behavior it is easier to see why this is so important: to have a good name. Their actions continue to reveal their true character to others. It is possible to fool some people many times and quite simple to fool a lot of people some time. But sooner or later, the real you will come around, and that name begins to stick to you for a lifetime. It is very difficult to remove that bad name, to outlive the stupid things said and done in years long gone.

It would be much wiser to begin with the desire to build a good name as a young person. It takes less to start with than trying to overcome a bad name. People are willing to forgive, but when the actions that hurt and destroy a name continue, folks get tired of the request to forgive and they just walk on to others to spend their time. Learn that it is good to think first, to give room to others first and to make allowances for ones around you to be the center of attention first. That leaves less room for you to make mistakes.

The final thought is to remember how rich it makes you to have a good name. It is better to have than great riches of silver and gold. It is better to have than many possessions to store away. A good name is on the lips of others, for they see your behavior and glorify your Father in heaven because of you! He has made you wise! So, friends, watch your mouth, the actions your body takes and the ungodly thoughts your mind exposes. They will show up!

October 30

There is one who scatters, yet increases more; And there is one
who withholds more than is right, But it leads to poverty." NKJV

In the minds of human beings, this seems to be impossible. But let
us think about it a bit. I have known folks who are always willing
to share whatever the Lord has given them with the people around
them. One would think that would make the giver have a lot less.
But that is not the way it works, friend. It is the opposite.

Theoretically, it is always possible to divide any given thing you
possess, if you had the equipment to do it and the will to try! Of
course, we know not all things would be good to divide. But there
are so many more that we hold on to and refuse to share that it
would not really leave us with less if we chose to share. Most often, it
is about making the choice to divide it with one in need.

Over the years, there have been multiple times when the food
on our table was not "enough" for all sitting at that table. We pull
out the chairs, seat all who are there, ask God's blessings on that food
and start serving it. When the meal is over, the eaters go away full
and happy. I'm not certain how God does that but I am sure he is
the one who did it!

When you are down to your last dollar and another desperately
needs food, that dollar won't buy much you think. But do the same.
Share the dollar, ask God to bless the dollar and watch as your dollar
buys "enough" for that person. Trust him with whatever he has given
you and share, share, share.

October 31

PROVERBS 31:10

"An excellent wife who can find? She is far
more precious than jewels." ESV

How hard it is for men to come upon this wonderful woman of excellence! To read the following verses makes one realize there probably is no one woman who fills all of these characteristics. She truly would be a wonder woman! But there is hope for all of us girls to be many of these with the help of the Lord. We really can't fill this bill apart from him!

But the idea I want to probe is this: Men, wait for the woman our God has prepared just for you! And in the meantime, work on becoming the man God created you to be. You will have a hard-enough time doing that without jumping into a relationship that is not for you. Women, learn to listen to our God on becoming the very best you can be, just what God has created you to be, a woman of excellence regardless of what your future holds with or without another person. We would all be wise to develop our own skills for living a good life before entangling ourselves with others.

That waiting business is the difficult part, isn't it? Humans don't enjoy waiting on anything or anyone. We are too often as children, demanding our own way in most everything we approach in life. That is not good for us nor for the folks around us! Learn to wait on the Lord before you dive into the things you think you must have and do. Waiting is a good thing!

November 1

JEREMIAH 3:22

"Return, O faithless sons; I will heal your faithlessness." ESV

We all fail to stand faithful to the Lord at times, but many of us deliberately walk away into the world without a second glance. We are still "sons," but we are wayward ones who need to return to him quickly. It is not wise to continue to stay apart from the very one who loves us without reservation, who desires us to come home to him before it is too late, that we must receive the pain that comes from such choices. There is an accounting day for everyone.

But God's love for us offers an opening that we may hear his call, to return to him so that he can restore us to fellowship with him. He promises to heal our unfaithfulness!

What a thought to comprehend! He has the ability to heal us! He can and will restore us! Oh, blessed God of our fathers! We need not be so foolish as to stay away from our God when he calls. We need not be presumptuous on his forgiveness and love. They are there for us, but he will not be toyed with so.

Look to your life and take stock of your whereabouts. He knows where you are! Do you? Or have you wandered, never really meaning to go so far, and have not gained understanding of the road back? He will make it plain for you. He calls and he lights the path to himself for you. Look up and return to your Father now, today. It is the only day you have! Healing is there. He does not mind giving it to you, for he loves you.

November 2

PROVERBS 13:20

"The one who walks with the wise, will become wise, but
the companion of fools will suffer harm." HCSB

My mother and father always told me to watch out for those whom I chose to make close friends, for I would have a strong tendency to become as they were. If they were wise, I would gain wisdom from them. If they were foolish, I would become more like them. The longer I walked with either one, the more I would be the same as they were.

This proverb speaks well to this same thought. We really do have a pull toward those with whom we spent much time. The more we are there, the stronger that pull is. It takes some wisdom and strength on our part to walk away from those people. We don't like to start something new. We fear being alone, so we stay with the bad companionship. To keep standing in the way of an oncoming truck even when we know what the danger is, is a very poor choice!

Our Lord has promised to walk with us through this life, even when we must walk by ourselves for a distance. Keep walking away from the foolish and stay on the straight path to the Lord's hand extended for your delivery. You must make the choice though. God will not make it for you! That's today's opportunity: choose wisely!

November 3

PROVERBS 25:21-22

"If your enemy is hungry, give him food to eat, and if he is thirsty, give him water to drink; for you will heap burning coals on his head, and the Lord will reward you." HCSB

Rest assured this is not telling you to reap vengeance on your enemies! That is God's only. So, if this is not about vengeance, just what does it say? How do I receive God's blessings when dealing with those who would harm me?

Food and water are two of our basic needs to maintain life. We cannot last very long without either one. Even our enemies need both! The easy part would be to give what we received at those hands that meant to hurt us. The harder part is to give what is good for those hands! And when we give as God has given to us, that is, kindness in mercy and grace, we also give pause to that enemy to think about what was done to us. They have the opportunity to feel the heat of shame that would be felt if there were hot coals shoveled on their hanging heads.

God gives a promise with this behavior. He has said he will give reward, blessings to us! What a difference the Lord makes. If we could remember to act as he acts when reacting to harmful behavior, what a difference we could make in our world! Our realm of influence would be amazed at such giving, because the world says to retaliate to hurt done to us. God says to be kind, even to our enemies. Next time you feel the cutting words or harmful actions by someone who hates you, give that cup of water or piece of bread instead of reacting to the hurt.

November 4

PROVERBS 24:17-18

"Don't gloat when your enemy falls, and don't let your heart rejoice when he stumbles, or the Lord will see, be displeased, and turn his wrath away from him." HCSB

We are never to be glad at another's fall or stumbling. We are to have compassion even on those who don't like us. We are to be as the Savior was toward others in our world. We are to give kindness and grace where needed. That doesn't mean we don't have enemies who would harm us and not take care to protect ourselves and our family. It does mean we can let God deal with those who displease him as he sees fit. After all, he keeps perfect score on everyone.

Develop a disposition that is pleasing to the Lord by following his words that give glory to him. He wants us to delight in him and rejoice in him. We can do this when we trust him to do as he desires in his world. We do not have to enter into his discipline of others by laughing or having fun at their expense. It is his job. He needs no help from us!

Instead, let's pray for those who persecute us and pray that God will open the eyes of the lost to see him, to hear his word and to respond in acceptance of his Son. We will never change those opposed to God. But we can be a part of seeking his face concerning them. Let your God live in you with all the grace and love that he can instill in you. He wants all to know him. Be a part of sharing him with his world.

November 5

2 COR. 9:6

"Remember this, a farmer who plants only a few seeds
will get a small crop. But the farmer who plants
generously will get a generous crop." NLT

Growing up on a farm was an education in itself about everything. What is planted germinates. What is watered does well. What is fertilized does better. What is harvested goes into the barn (bank!), and the amount planted mostly controls how much you get to harvest. Of course, weather conditions, labor force and market prices can hinder the harvesting of any crop. But the one big factor to a farmer is the seed he puts in the ground. Few seeds, small harvest!

When deciding on a piece of land to plant, the farmer decides what will be a good crop for the type of soil, the water supply and the money it will take to bring that crop to harvest. But the biggest decision is the number of acres out of that land he will plant. This determines the amount of seed he will need. In other words, he counts all the cost. Remember though that the object of farming is to plant, care for and harvest a whole crop.

The same is true for a believer. When we consider obeying the Lord's desire for us to share with our fellow believer, it is good to remember to be generous too, for as we sow in sharing with others, so shall we reap. Plant many seeds among the ones around us in circumstances of need. One day we may be in those same kinds of situations. Look in kindness on others and put yourself in the same walk of life being experienced by them. Kindness always brings a joy your way. Generosity always brings its own reward, not always in the same coin, but always a sweet spirit for your own life. Sow, friend, sow those seeds that will spring into a blessing for you and the others.

November 6

PROVERBS 22:6

"Train up a child in the way he should go; even when
he is old he will not depart from it." ESV

We are to speak to our children, whether as young ones or even
youths in an age appropriate way, making the terminology fit their
ability to understand. They are much more likely to remember and
respond positively if done this way. Children are famous for wanting
their own way and youths are known for being foolish and unwise.
But we are the ones charged with the discipline and teaching of them
in such a way as to give them an opportunity to hear and understand
our motives.

We need to make the punishment fit the crime, as they say. Make
it appropriate for their age and ability to do. We need to remember
that discipline is meant to correct the thinking and actions of the
child or teen not to inflict pain or humiliation. That doesn't mean
you must never apply the "rod of correction" to applicable parts. It
does mean it is not meant to do bodily harm to the student (which
he is, in your care!). It is to be a last resort, meaning communication
has broken down and they are no longer hearing you!

Fathers and mothers, grandparents when needed, make certain
you teach in the same way the Lord has taught you. He applies the
consequences of your actions to you when you miss his commandments. We reap them when we fail to hear and follow the Lord's
word, don't we? He forgives and restores. You must also forgive and
restore the one in your household. And remember, your love is never
removed, even when the child's actions are severe. Your approval is
always theirs whether you approve of their actions or not. God is
firm but loving. You be the same: firm but loving.

November 7

LUKE 11:24-26

"When the evil spirit leaves a person, it goes into the desert,
searching for rest. But when it finds none, it says, 'I will return
to the person I came from.' So, it returns and finds its former
home is all swept and in order. Then the spirit finds seven other
evil spirits more evil than itself, and they all enter the person
and live there ... that person is worse off than before." NLT

All the world hates a vacuum. Just have a machine suck the air out of a can and it will collapse. Reforming ourselves is not the way to go to overcome evil. Sweeping and making order does not work for long. The human condition is to realize we miss the perfect mark and continue into evil ways so easily. Often, we fall even farther into evil. If we are to be overcomers, we must learn (it is a life-long process) to fill our "vacuum" with the things of God, leaving no room for our first state to come crashing back. This will take the power of the Holy Spirit to fulfill the new creation we are in Jesus. The Word gives us the knowledge of what to do and be. Our prayer life gives the communion with God that enables us to want to do and be. And fellowship with other believers gives the encouragement, knowing they will stand with us in our hour of need. Don't be empty. Don't just sweep the place of your life and try to set things in order. Instead, be filled with the Holy Spirit and let him order your day, moment by moment. Our God is able!

November 8

PROVERBS 14:29

"Whoever is slow to ager has great understanding, but
he who has a hasty temper exalts folly." ESV

It is a fact for my family in the household I grew up in, that we all
are rather impulsive and quick tempered. I have had many opportunities to see it expressed to my dismay! Over the years I have tried
to realize the family trait and to overcome how quickly we speak or
act and how quickly we regret it. Ever identify with us? Perhaps you
too have a quick retort all ready when another irritates you. It sits
there just below the surface of your heart making a way up the chute
before you've even thought about it! I guess that's probably one of
the problems; thinking about it! If we could just stop and think first.

This is something God has entered the cure on with me. He
doesn't want my mouth open before his Holy Spirit has engaged my
spirit to be as I should be, righteous, not "right" in the eyes of the
world. That's a wise idea. Let not haste intercept my life with anger
and hail down the other person with babblings instead of passing on
kindness and peace.

I want to understand before I begin the process of speaking. I
desire to hear the other person's words and what that one is really
saying before I attempt to answer too hastily. I would have much less
to ask forgiveness for if I were a little slower on the draw! I do not
want to play the fool and harm the name of the Lord in so doing.
Watch your feelings; your words chosen in haste will hurt you before
it harms others. Grow understanding. It is available to you in great
amounts if you simply slow down your tongue and speed up your
love of the Lord.

November 9

PROVERBS 29:18A

"Where there is no vision (no revelation), the people perish;
but he that keepeth the law, happy is he." NKJV

These words are speaking of a people who have no revelation from God. In dry situations as these, a people have no guidance to depend upon or follow for safety and to be able to live productive lives. It takes guidance for all humanity. We have a problem with throwing off any restraint when there are no rules to follow as we interact with others.

But I would like to apply this thought to your family as well. When the family has no parameters that hedge it in, it is too easy to stretch over into the other member's space, causing damage to that one in our way. When we have no rules that curb our own desires, we start behaving as though might makes right and power moves to enforce our ideas. But chaos ensues and life become intolerable.

But there is one other aspect I'd like to have you think about and start making for your household. Do you and your family have a mission statement, a statement with few words that gives all of you the reason why you exist and how you do things there? If not, consider drawing up one soon. It is simple to do. Just why are you who you are? Do you belong to the Lord and follow his word? If so, that makes it even easier to do. Keep is short. Keep it simple. Keep it truthful. That way, all of you, even young ones can recite it quickly when making decisions about behavior. It will keep you from throwing off restraint and will cause you to think about your name, your family's name, as you make choices. It's always about choices, isn't it?

November 10

PROVERBS 14:23

"In all toil there is profit, but mere talk tends only to poverty." ESV

In my many years, I have seen that this is true, but I have also seen that the profit is not always equal to the effort put out! There are some jobs that require much more energy and willingness to get your hands down right dirty and have sweat on your brow (and running through your hair and down your back). These do not always pay in cash. Some pay only in the satisfaction of a job well done. I have also found that some of these jobs get put off with the phrase, "I'll get that done when I have more time, when I get around to it." That usually means never, because mere talk tends to bring poverty when we don't get around to it!

I had a Sunday School student who brought me a present one Sunday that squelched my best excuse for not doing anything. In her hand was a round pot holder that had the one word, 'roundtoit' written across the front. It was "front and center" for me in that one moment! Guess I used that term once too often.

Laughter is a beautiful thing. It can rise up in you as a wave rises up just before it hits the shore and out your mouth the same way that wave runs up the shoreline, bringing a sound to our ears as nice as the wave brings. It can add corrections to us without harming our self-value. It causes us to hear rightly and enjoy what we hear from another. To laugh brings joy to our hearts in spite of our sadness in life. It can wash our face with a youthfulness that has been lost in the hard days. And the ability to laugh at oneself when we find ourselves being funny is a joy indeed. So, laugh, my friends, you are far funnier more often than you can imagine!

November 11

EPHESIANS 6:2

"Honor your father and mother, which is the first
commandment with a promise, so that it may go well with
you and that you may have a long life in the land." HCSB

The older I get the more I like this verse! It is good to have children who honor us even when we displease or anger them, even confuse them. We find it a blessing to be treated with this kind of behavior from our kids, grown though they be. Our children are in what is called the "sandwich generation." Meaning they are caught between their children's needs and their aging parents. It is hard for the two of us to believe we are the aging parents part of this equation!

Also, the older I get the more I understand the many things my mother said and did in those last years of her life. They didn't make a whole lot of sense at the time I thought. She said she didn't enjoy shopping anymore because the legs hurt or she got too tired, or the clothes didn't look right on her aging body anymore. Yes, I understand now! She used to lean on the sink while she brushed her teeth or on the kitchen counter when peeling a potato. I wondered why. I know now! She liked for the grandkids to drop by for a few minutes regularly. I get it now. It does get lonely when you sit around and watch TV very much.

But the best part of this honoring thing is to be treated with acceptance of the many weird things we say or do! We even surprise ourselves sometimes when our thoughts finally make it out to our mouths and spill over with ramblings! It has reached the place where it takes both of us to carry on one side of the conversation! Thanks, kids for loving us anyway and laughing behind our backs at our silliness. The best that I can say to each of you is this: you, too, will one day be where we are! The promise from God is good for you when you honor us.

November 12

HEB. 13:1-2

"Let brotherly love continue. Do not neglect to show hospitality
to strangers, for thereby some have entertained angels unawares."

It is true that our citizenship is in heaven when we belong to the Lord.
We are living each and every day on that road to that wonderful destination where there will be no needs. We will each have everything
we need in that place. But until then, we must walk the road that is
laid before us in a fallen world, understanding that there are extreme
needs in every heart here on earth. Since that is so, let us continue
to give love toward one another that is normally reserved for those
we call brothers. Thanksgiving is soon to be shared with those we
call family. This year let us be kind & share our worldly goods with
others, even strangers. You do not have to be given the spiritual gift
of hospitality to do this. So it might be a little out of your comfort
zone. That's all right. Who knows but what one of those strangers
just might be a heavenly being! You never know...Mama said!

November 13

PROVERBS 14:27A

"The fear of the Lord is a fountain of life …" ESV

When I look in the night sky at the heavenly bodies scattered across it, I am amazed at their vast expanse. When I sit down with a new born baby and hold that little one close, it is beyond understanding how God brings life to that little one, unique and lovely. When I walk down the aisle of a church, sit and look around, where a bride and groom are preparing to link their lives as one, I am surprised every time how handsome he is, how lovely she is and how joy lights their faces as they see each other down that aisle, having eyes for each other only.

When I go to worship in my church and walk down that same isle to greet the other worshipers, it is a delight to know we are sitting at the feet of our Jesus together, to learn his words of instruction and encouragement. As I touch the hand of another believer and sing the songs of praise for the wonder of his name, I realize we are joining together that his name may be glorified. I stand in awe of him and his mighty works!

And there rises to meet me with all my needs fulfilled a fountain of life with each experience. It is not a river flowing by me. It is not a pool for me to sit beside. It is not a pond to look over to the other side. It is a fountain springing up forevermore for me to receive nourishment and strength as I raise my hand in joy for it. It fills me with a new- found sense of life each day. It is from my Father to me fresh every moment of my day. It can be yours too. Every morning it brings laughter to me in the face of sadness. It brings strength when I am weak. It sends up movement when I believe I cannot make one more step. It is yours for the asking too. Accept his fountain of life today. It never runs dry nor gives out.

November 14

ROMANS 7:24,25A; 8:1

"Wretched man that I am! Who will deliver me
from this body of death? Thanks be to God through
Jesus Christ our Lord! … There is therefore now no
condemnation to those who are in Christ Jesus." ESV

When I take a really good look, an honest approach to myself, I
know the sin that so easily besets me at every turn. Who can make
any difference in this life of mine? Only Jesus, when he is my Lord
and Savior. He is the agent of change through his Holy Spirit that he
has sent to be mine to finish this course we call life.

The time slides by so quickly as we enter each day and end each
too. We let the moments carry us through and don't seem to realize that the day is gone until we stop at the closing to see what we
missed. That's the way life is lived, one moment at the time. It does
not come as a full day, one day at a time. It comes stealthily, wandering through our minds as we stay so busy with the mundane
things, those that won't make any difference tomorrow. And we too
wander through the mundane with no thought for tomorrow even
glimmering through the corners of our thoughts. We head on, only
to find that sin has invaded while we were asleep at the wheel that
turns only once each day.

Today is the day for changes. Make a list and put the Name of
Jesus at the top. Place the Word of God second and then call a friend
who knows Jesus too; ask for strength to aid you as your accountability on listening to your Jesus. He is your Savior! The friend is your
arms held wide to remind you of the change you've made. There is
no condemnation where Jesus is your Deliverer.

November 15

RUTH 2:5-7

"… Boaz asked his foreman, 'Who is that young woman over
there?'… the foreman replied, 'She asked me this morning if she
could gather grain behind the harvesters. She has been hard at
work ever since, except for a few minutes rest in the shelter.'" NLT

Before our spring garden started "picking", we made a small patio
area in the front yard. The mechanics of it were finished, but the
"decorating" of it was not. I had not put the flowers or shrubs around
the edge yet. And you know Mama; it isn't finished until that's done.
I LOVE flowers and shrubs! I asked my grandson to help. No, I'm
not proud when I know I need help. So, early that next day at seven
in the morning, here he comes, eats breakfast with his Poppi and we
start the planting and moving of heavy potted flowers into the place,
finishing the edging around those pots.

What does all this have to do with Ruth and her gathering of
grain. I could have thought, I'm too old to do this kind of hard work.
I should hire it done by a professional. A woman shouldn't have to
do this physical work! But, if I had, I would have missed four hours
with my precious grandson. There wouldn't have been opportunities
to drop a word into his heart or mind, or to listen to his heart about
what's in his world, his life. If I had been above "menial" work, that
is, dirty work, tiring work, I would have missed a most productive
time in his life.

And, as with Ruth's rewards, I also received "grain" from that
grandson's interaction with me. Also, like Ruth, some of those
rewards will be for a time in his future when I can no longer "be
there" for him. He will remember a word fitly spoken that day to
him with all of my love and encouragement. For Ruth, the rewards
for serving her mother-in-law, Naomi, by gathering grain for them
both, went far into their futures.

In the distant future, Ruth became the great (many times over) grandmother of Jesus. I have no idea what God's plans are for this young man, but I know I want to be used in his life for good to aid God's road for him. I really enjoyed the precious moments we had together that day. I listened to his hopes, dreams and thoughts he holds close to himself rather than sharing with others.

Perhaps, God will give you the chance to share life and work with a young one soon. Be willing to be a little sore from what it costs you to "be there" for that one. I was sore too, but pleased with my rewards.

November 16

1 JOHN 1:7A

"But if we walk in the light, as he is in the light, we
have fellowship with one another..." NIV

Early every Wednesday morning, about 5:30, Big Buck goes to the
restaurant to have breakfast with several other younger men. Me, I
just wanted to go back to bed! But this is one morning he does not
sleep late at all. In fact, some times, he doesn't sleep too well waiting
for the time to come so he can get up! It's always the same fellows,
the same restaurant, the same table, the same food. But it is a joy to
the big man.

These young men are not brothers, but you can see they love one
another that way. There is a Proverb that says how wonderful when
brothers get along. That's the way these guys are. They seldom miss.
When any of them do miss, I know that one is really sick. This time
is so strengthening for Buck. I think it must be for them too. It is
powerful when men hold each other to a higher plain of conduct, to
a greater challenge of going above the cost of duty. Duty will drive
you only so far. Love will move you all the way that it takes to reach
a fellow believer's need. Duty is a demand. Love is a gift.

I'm not always certain how much light is shed abroad at that
table. But, at least, they haven't been thrown out...yet. Take a few
moments today to give a strong encouragement to another one. Meet
a friend for breakfast or lunch. You may find they strengthen you too.

November 17

ZECHARIAH 4:6

"… This is the word of the Lord to Zerubbabel: 'Not by might,
nor by power, but by my Spirit,' says the Lord of hosts." ESV

The ability to be an overcomer of life's hard knocks is a gift from the Lord of hosts. It is given through the Holy Spirit of God to those who are called by him to be his spokesperson to his world, who are chosen to do a specific work. He enables us to do work far beyond our human capabilities and to become a light to those around us by answering that call and being obedient to his word.

Zerubbabel was to rebuild the house of God. God told him he would, not only lay the foundation of the house, but would complete this house. Nothing would stand in his way to stop the work. Many people tried to stop the forward progress but God gave Zerubbabel the encouragement needed to know that it was God calling him and commissioning him for this specific job. This was the Lord of the heavenly hosts who equipped the man to go forward and do as he was told.

God still calls today for those who are willing to be his spokesperson in his world. He equips those who accept the opportunity. He will encourage you. He will send his Spirit to follow through on his call to you. It is not about results as we humans look for results. It is about being faithful to obey the call. God will attend to his results in his time in his way. What is God sending you to do? Don't miss the chance to see it through to completion. It is by his Spirit that you will overcome the obstacles before you.

November 18

SONG OF SOLOMON 4:11A

"Your lips drip nectar, my bride; honey and
milk are under your tongue ..." ESV

When your spouse irritates you in any way, could they still say this about your tongue? Or would it more apt to be that they find the honey bees hiding under there sitting on ready to sting them back as quickly as they can? Would here be sweet milk held in your mouth or would it be what old folks from year's past would have called "clabber"? That is, sour milk!

Every mate, at one time or another, possibly more often than not, brings anger to the other half of their union. It is part and parcel of marriage. We each act in accord with our feelings and behave badly. That is the human condition that all suffer with in this fallen world. But what can one do about such a state of affairs?

I have found that when my spouse rubs me the wrong way, I can reverse my feelings about it by turning around and making it a caress in my thought process. I change my thinking and change my actions. Of course, I know it was not meant to be a caress! But I also know it was not meant to destroy me either. I am learning to give grace where grace is needed, not deserved, because my mate has given grace to me so many times. The more I see myself as I really am, the easier it becomes to give forgiveness whether asked for or not! After all, we plan to be together until there is only one of us left!

Check your tongue to see what lies under it: the nectar of honey and sweet milk or the sourness and sting of anger? Today is a good day to practice the sweet tongue!

November 19

ROMANS 14:11

"For it is written: 'As I live,' says the Lord, 'Every knee shall bow to Me, and every tongue shall confess to God.'" NKJV

When you hear or read, or see on television how sinful and depraved our world is, do not be dismayed. Our God is aware, he is strong enough to attend to this world, and he is going to do just that one day in the future. It is not a surprise to him when humans are so vile to each other. God knew before he even laid the time line how we would behave. He gave us free will, the ability to choose. Oh my, there's that word again! It is always about a choice, isn't it?

Today is a good day to remember this promise that one day this world will be different because all will one day bend the knee to our Lord and all will confess to our God.

Don't be afraid of what the future holds. It will be hard, harder than we can even imagine. But our God will be there with us in all things. He has promised never to leave us as orphans in our storm. Thank God for these comforting words that I recall wherever I am in life. It doesn't matter what our leaders are like or what folks around us are either. What matters is that your name is written in the Lamb's Book of Life. You be faithful to God!

Trust God that one day, maybe not today or tomorrow, but one day, he will set all things right. Until then we are to occupy his world with the Good News of Jesus. Instead of being upset over how things are, share him with those who are next to you. You are where you are for a purpose. Let him prepare you to speak in love to those who need Jesus before that day of the Lord. Open your mouth and let the Spirit fill you with his words.

November 20

SONG OF SOLOMON 5:1A,3

"I slept, but ... a sound! My love is knocking. Open to
me ... I had put off my garment; how could I put it on?
I had bathed my feet; how could I soil them?" ESV

This verse tells me so much about the inner workings of our mind
when we are at ease in our mind and body and don't want to be bothered by anyone, not even the one we say we love more than all others.
The bottom line is that we are all so self-centered that we really want
life as we want it: easy!

This young bride was all cleaned up. She had been showered,
shampooed and had her pretty little P.J.'S on, already lying down
and at ease. She was all about her this one night! Her mind was in
gear to be set on herself all evening. Nothing wrong with that, you
say. Probably not. Except... that her love was waiting at her door
with his heart in his hand looking for her touch, her acceptance of
him as the one and only for her. He thought she was ready for him!
Oops!

Now, it's nice when the spouse is thoughtful about such things,
but it is better when each is able to respond with thoughtfulness for
the other's need.

Many years ago, in a couple's Bible Study, a young, engaged two
were answering a question about being able to say, "Not tonight,
dear," when the young man responded to her, "How do you know
you wouldn't find that being well loved could ease your headache?"
Besides laughter, there was genuine wisdom in his response. Don't
jump to conclusions ahead of your answer! Tonight, look at your
spouse with compassion for that special one's needs. Love as never
before.

November 21

RUTH 1:16

"Entreat me not to leave thee, or to turn away from following after thee; for where thou goest, I will go; and where thou lodgest, I will lodge: thy people will be my people, and thy God, my God. Where thou diest, I will die, and there I will be buried; the Lord do to me, and more also, if anything but death part thee and me." KJV

Through the many years of playing the piano at weddings, I have heard these words quoted over and over. I feel it is more beautiful and poetic than the newer versions. Therefore, I have used it here to show the wonder of two people expressing their lifelong love for each other so beautifully. The most beautiful part to me though is that these words were spoken to a mother-in-law, not a lover.

It reveals that the Lord enjoys a whole family relationship when two people in love decide on marriage! Remember that when you're choosing someone with whom to spend the rest of your life. When you marry, you marry the whole family, for better or worse! They do not stop being that other person's parent. Choose to accept the family, warts and all. And then realize that you and your love are your own household too. You can make choices that work for the two of you in that personal household.

But these lovely words do show what it is like to love someone forever. It reveals a deep love that is not frayed by the storms that will come. It declares a love that will be from life to death. If you cannot love the one you are considering to marry that deeply, stop where you are. Rethink and start the process over to see where you are lacking. Better to refrain now than to move forward into a terrible mistake. When it is sorted out, then move into a time of learning from the Lord what real love is and how long it must last... forever! If you are in marriage already, look to the Father to see how to choose to make it a forever love. His instructions are available in his word. Search out, read and learn to love.

November 22

PROVERBS 25:11

"A word fitly spoken is like apples of gold
in settings of silver." NKJV

What a wonderful thing to know that my words can be beautiful, healing, kind, gentle, moving and helpful to others. What a way to celebrate Thanksgiving, when family and friends gather at your home, or you go to theirs, remember to speak in such a way as to let your words be like apples of gold in settings of silver. Let your speech be such that, when they turn them over in their minds even when long gone from the Great Feast, they will be warmed and encouraged by the very memory of being with you.

The question is: how can we do this simple sounding way of speaking? Here are some ideas. When a relative is quite opinionated about any given subject, remember it is not your place to set the whole world right about how you see it. You can always ask questions that will reveal how that one came to that conclusion instead of correcting that conclusion! When another friend is critical about a dish on the table, tell the one who brought that dish what is good about it. When an aunt gives unbidden advice to a young family member, choose to give grace to the one being advised and give the same grace to the nosy aunt by smiling and laughing over the "spilled milk" of criticism. It can't be taken back but it can have some of the sting removed with a touch on the shoulder, a "Now, now, Auntie!" Even when sports arrive at the table conversation, your team does not have to be the dominant players over all the others. Give room at the table to have more than one "best" team. As for politics, it's Thanksgiving! Give it a rest. It doesn't matter at all!

When considering how to respond to anyone else, remember to think through how this will matter in twenty minutes, twenty days, or even twenty years! If it really doesn't make a difference in later life, share peace and joy on this one day. It is a day for sharing golden words in silver settings. All will go away being thankful for you!

AMOS 4:5A

"And offer a sacrifice of thanksgiving …" NKJV

The Thanksgiving holiday is upon us. What will your list of things for which you are thankful have on it? Here are mine:

1. Early in life we learned that God does not always give us a yes to our pleas. But what he built in us through those experiences was a strong desire to shelter children and be a part of God's revealing of his goodness, even when it looks as if he has forgotten us. He is still gracious and loving even when it is only silence we hear.

2. When all others desert you, choosing not to stand with you, he is still there and cares. His plan is still intact for you.

3. That age and time take care of most things. If you take your time and let "this too shall pass," there is a border to the pain. There is a personality that events take on that can cloud the issues, keeping us looking at the wrong things. Time is your friend. It will help keep your perspective focused toward the future not the past.

4. That even in the deepest difficulties there is often an amusement about many things. Look long and hard to see it and smile.

5. That when our first baby girl died, I was given the opportunity to hold her one time, realizing her short life gave us a dimension to our days that we can still look forward to seeing her again, trusting God for this.

6. That when Buck lost his job, it was not a problem to God either. He brought another one in two weeks and sent, by mail, a hundred dollars to last those two weeks. We still do not know from where it came.

7. That when all seemed lost, it was not, because God was not! The graveside was not a place where he abandoned us.

8. And last of all, he has given grace for each day as that day unfolded, never early, nor late with his mercy, bringing grace equal to the day's need. God moves into each day as you do, not in yesterday nor tomorrow. Just today. He has been faithful. May I be so too.

November 24

ROMANS 1:16

"For I am not ashamed of the gospel, because it is God's power for salvation, to everyone who believes …" HCSB

It is so important for we who name the name of Jesus as Lord and Savior to be not ashamed of his gospel. We are to share this Good News with all whom we are given the opportunity. We are to be ready to speak in truth about our Jesus, to share his love and compassion for the world he created. We are to have the truth embedded into our hearts so that it comes easily to mind when confronted with those who would oppose it.

The only way we can be ready with this truth is to know the Word of God well. When do you sit down and study the Gospel of Christ? When do you commit it to your mind to be called forth when appropriate? If you need to start with this, there is no better time than right now. Choose a place where you can think. Choose a time when you won't be constantly interrupted. It need not be a great amount of time to begin. Start with five to ten minutes. You must train yourself to study longer if you are out of the habit of doing so. As you go, the Lord will increase your desire to know the Word and him. He can fill you with a hunger to read his messages to you. It will become a personal joy for you with him.

As always, today is the day to begin. It is the only day you have! Begin with one of the four Gospels to learn more about Jesus himself while on earth. Then you can progress to the letters of Paul or the other disciple's writings. It is easier than you think. Today, friend, today!

November 25

ROMANS 8:35, 37

"What shall separate us from the love of Christ? Shall
tribulation, or distress, or persecution, or famine, or
nakedness, or peril, or sword? Nay, in all these things we are
more than conquerors through him that loved us." KJV

Oh, the sheer joy, the unspeakable wonder, of knowing that Christ's love for us is forever with the power to survive anything the world or the Enemy can throw at us. We are one of God's children, never to be forgotten or forsaken. He has ensured us of the power of the Holy Spirit to carry us over and through any adversity or difficulty. We have the assurance of his ability to save, to preserve and to deliver us to the Father intact and safe. His assurance includes our being more than conquerors in this life. It is not an assurance of never being hit with the sorrows and pains of living. It is the giving to us a peace for going through this world that we all must experience this side of heaven.

To be more than conquerors is to me an expression of walking in faith forward, without having to look behind as I move in response to his call to obey. It is trusting him when I can't see around the bend of my tomorrow. It is knowing he is committed to me and my choice to follow his way in this life. He is my past, my present and my future. May his will be ever before me as I answer his call to, "Come!" I thank him for his plan for me, for his world and for his heaven. His call to you is the same, "Come!"

November 26

ROMANS 8:38, 39

"… I am convinced that nothing can ever separate us from God's love. Neither death nor life, neither angels nor demons, neither our fears for today nor our worries about tomorrow—not even the powers of hell can separate us from God's love. No power in the sky above or in the earth below—indeed, nothing in all creation will ever be able to separate us from the love of God that is revealed in Christ Jesus our Lord." NLT

The key to understanding how infinite God's love for us, when we belong to him through Jesus, is the last thought… the love that is revealed in Christ Jesus our Lord. It is by him that we are loved and kept together with him. It is his commitment to those he has given new life to in response to our accepting his free, but costly, gift of salvation. It is not about us. It is all about him. It is exciting to realize that neither angels nor demons can break that bond he has made to us. He is the keeper of that company of the believers. We are safe in his hand where he has promised to deliver us to his Father one day, pure and holy as he is. By his power, we are made to be his vessels of honor and glory as we obey his call to share that love. Look around today and chose to be a channel of blessing, poured out for that one who needs this love. Count on him giving you the power of the Holy Spirit to become this channel for allowing his love to flow through to your personal world.

November 27

REVELATION 7:9

"After this I looked, and behold a great multitude that no one
could number, from every nation, from all tribes and peoples
and languages, standing before the throne and before the Lamb,
clothed in white robes, with palm branches in their hands." ESV

When I cut back my Areca Palms each year so they are neat and
beautiful, I think about this verse that describes a scene in Heaven.
There will be a date in the future, known only to our God when we
will be called home, everyone who knows our Lord Jesus as Savior.
What a day that will be!

The thing that is special about the two palms that I have, planted
here when we moved into the house in Parrish, is that they were
planted by my mother in her yard in Palmetto in 1959 at the birth of
our second daughter, Alicia. We were staying there with her for a few
days after the safe and successful delivery by C-section. (Remember,
we lost the first baby girl at birth.) It was a day to remember when
our arms brought her home that morning. Our God was so gracious
to us!

I hold the lowly little palm branch in my hand as I remove it
from the tree. And I think at how wise God is in everything, even
raising this little plant to importance in his kingdom. We will use the
small and insignificant palm branch to praise and honor our God. It
was so in Jesus' day of entry into Jerusalem as well. All things will
bring glory to him one day! Make certain your name is written in
that Lamb's Book of Life so you will be there with me. Then you can
wave those palm branches that you didn't even have to cut! Mama's
just saying…

November 28

PSALM 143:5B

"… I meditate on all Your works; I muse on
the work of Your hands." NKJV

Everywhere I go, each place I visit, whether in a town, city or the country, I see God's handiwork. It's in the face of an elderly man. It is found in a baby's delighted eyes when seeing a ball bounce for the first time. It is in the way a manicured lawn sparkles in the bright sunshine.

It is seen every time I pick up a flower or watch the birds fly over in a formation known only to them.

But most of all, I enjoy star-gazing on a cool night in a Florida winter when the air is crisp and the country side is free of lights that cities have. There is nothing quite like seeing such expanse over me. And each works in its ordained order. How amazing! It seems such a simple thing to sit and watch these twinkles of light so far away. The Word says that my God knows the names of all of them! I "muse," that is, I think deeply in wonder at his creation that defies description with words from our language. I conclude that God must have a separate set of words that are saved just for this when we see him face to face.

How your joy in this life could be increased with taking such a small amount of your precious time to look around at the wonders of his world, to see them fresh and new as though they were created just for you. We can reach out and touch his universe with our hearts when we bless his Name by seeing what he has made for us.

November 29

PSALM 5:8. PHILIPPIANS 3:14

"Lead me, O Lord, in your righteousness … Make
the way straight before my face …"

Today, as I hoed the last of the Pole beans in the garden, I noticed again how long the rows were and yet how straight Buck had made them before the days of lasers. I remembered how it is that farmers can do that. It is the same way we as believers walk that straight path of the Lord. I cannot look down at the ground. I cannot look back behind myself. I cannot look to either side. I must keep my eyes on the goal at the end of the row. The tractor driver would have placed stakes at the end of the row before he even began to get on the tractor. There would have been a "flag" tied on the top of the stake so he could easily see that "goal" at the end. When he mounted his tractor, started the engine, put it in gear and moved down the row, he kept his eye on that far "goal" until he reached it. Then he could look around and see that the row was straight.

It would be a good idea to keep our eyes on the goal God has placed before us, the high calling, the upward call of God in Christ Jesus. Do not be distracted by the world around us, nor the call of those who would entice us to waver to one side or the other, not even to those who would ask us to turn around and go back to another way of life. Keep your eyes on your "goal." He will be faithful to lead you in his righteousness all the way to the end. Bless you as you respond to his call.

November 30

ROMANS 10: 9-10

"… if you confess with your mouth that Jesus is Lord and believe in your heart that God raised him from the dead, you will be saved. For with the heart one believes and is justified, and with the mouth one confesses and is saved." ESV

How easy it is to be saved! But it does mean I must accept the knowledge of Jesus's Lordship and his being resurrected from the dead. This is not a head knowledge, this is a heart knowledge. When I learn these facts about Jesus, I must receive them into my heart that raises them to my mouth from my heart and my head. As I confess, he saves me, all on his own by the power of his Holy Spirit. He is the master of my soul!

One of the following verses explains that, as I call on the Name of the Lord, I will be saved. Simple, isn't it? But so many miss it! Because many have a hard time recognizing their own sin and need. We are so cloudy in our thoughts as to feel we need no one to save us. Pride gets in our way and we lift up our hearts to believing we are all that we need. What a sad state of affairs!

If you know one or have a loved one who thinks this way, pray that the Lord will woo them with his strong arms of love and reveal to them their desperate need. And then, share your Jesus with them by sharing just what he has done in and for you. They cannot accept what they never hear. Be the Bible they read as they watch you live depending on Jesus alone because you believed and confessed.

December 1

ROMANS 8:37

"No, in all these things we are more than conquerors
through him who loved us." ESV

There will be obstacles in life. There will be opposition to face. There will be mountains to make it to the top and to cross over. There will skills to gain and master, hard though they be. There will be decisions to live through and in which to find good. There will be times when it is easy and a great many times when we will fail to meet the mark we have set for ourselves. There will be fears to surmount and there will be hardness and difficulties to gain victory over regularly. It is a fact of this life!

The Apostle Paul accepts that these will be. He also accepts that we have a Savior who is aware of what this life is like here on his earth. After all, He lived here too. In the verses that follow this assurance of being conquers, he outlines all that can come against us while we journey here. And the best of all, is that nothing listed can overcome us! We are not just conquerors. We are more than conquerors!

We can meet the obstacle. We can stand against the opposition. We can start to climb that mountain that seems to separate us from him, depending on his assurance to keep climbing, putting one foot in front of the other as we go. We can take the time to prepare for skill-mastery and can learn the necessary ones to perform our calling. We can rise to live through our decisions that need overcoming to be able to continue upward. We can recognize the times that are failings and accept missing the mark as part of pressing on to the next one.

At the presence of fear, we can direct it to the Lord who knows all about us. And we can be victorious as we lean on him to sustain us through any hardship or difficulty. They are facts, but he has said we can be conquerors. No, more than conquerors! Stretch and reach out for the prize that lies before us, content in his love never leaving nor his victory being unattainable. These words are our assurance in him, not ourselves.

December 2

PSALM 141:3

"Set a watch, O Lord, before my mouth;
keep the door of my lips." KJV

O Lord, it is so easy to let my mouth, my lips, get in gear before my brain is engaged! So, for today, just today, because I can't handle future days yet, answer this prayer for me. Set that watch strong and keep my lips shut until you have put my heart into movement for others. Let me see where that one is walking, that one it is so easy to criticize, to complain about regularly.

Turn your mirror toward me that I may see myself as you see me, in need of help! Touch me with your grace that I may pass it on to that other one who needs it too, just as I have needed it from your hands. Make me a channel of blessing to those whom I meet, those with whom I interact. Pour yourself through me to them. May I become a door of hope, a window of love that you may be seen clearly. And when you do open my lips, let it be to praise you and to give joy to my world. Let it be so, Lord.

December 3

ROMANS 8:28

"And we know that all things work together for
good to them that love God, to them who are
the called according to his purpose." KJV

When we face the hard rocks of real life, it becomes apparent that God has a hand, a part, even in this too. Though it hurts and becomes a weight that seems to be more than we can bear, though it pulls us into a sadness that cannot be relieved by any avenue, we still know that he is ultimately in full control. He has promised mercy, grace sufficient for the day, the right timing for all that he allows into our hearts and that he is aware what is going on in our days and nights. He is not ignorant of our pain. And he cares. His word proclaims he will never leave us nor forsake us. But there are times when it "feels" as though he has. It feels that we are alone.

But listen to his words here.

He has promised that all things will "work" for good (that's not just sitting around, folks!) for the "called," those that love him. Praise him for his word and for the testimonies of those who have walked this same road. We have walked this way of pain and found that God gives purpose even to pain. He doesn't lightly let his children hurt. But having received such pain, we can hold you to our hearts, remembering our own time of knowing our lives would never be the same again. We can still identify the emptiness of unrelieved sorrow as we see your pain. We are the evidence of his never-ending love and tenderness through this life.

December 4

ROMANS 12:1-2

"Therefore, brothers, by the mercies of God, I urge you to present
your bodies as a living sacrifice, holy and pleasing to God; this
is your spiritual worship. Do not be conformed to this age, but
be transformed by the renewing of your mind, so that you may
discern what is the good, pleasing and perfect will of God." HCSB

To my friends, my children, my grand-children and great-grand-children, to friends I have not met yet: I beg you, urge you, to choose to offer your bodies to God as a Living Sacrifice. This is your reasonable choice. It is the best one you will ever make. It means you will choose daily some things not to do and many things to do as you live out this journey that you will experience only once.

When you make the choice early, you save yourself many poor choices down the road. When I made the decision long ago not to drink alcohol, there were many times in many places where I did not have to consult with myself even once before refusing the pretty glass filled with pretty colors of drinks. It was made already! When I set the thought in my mind and heart to be honest, kind, generous and a friend to others, it placed in motion the responses to the actions of others before I had to choose.

God desires for you to live for him every day. It is not too late. Decide this one day to be honest, kind, generous and a friend to others, and move into a joy that comes only from him. He holds his hand out for your offering. Only you can give your body to him for holy and pleasing worship.

December 5

ROMANS 5:6-8

"For while we were still weak, at the right time, Christ died
for the ungodly. For one will scarcely die for a righteous
person—though perhaps for a good person one would
dare even to die—but God shows his love for us in that
while we were still sinners, Christ died for us." ESV

Unbelievable fact. Amazing truth. Our Lord Jesus loved us so much he died for us while we were unworthy sinners, ungodly people who cared for nothing but ourselves. That's love, true love, unmerited love, amazing love that revealed God to us. There is no greater love than he showed in this fact of dying for us in our place at our accounting.

We stand saved by his grace through our faith. Our salvation is given to us as his pure love, expressed through his blood at his death, paid the total price of our mountains of sin. He left nothing unpaid on our account ledger when he died for us. He did it once and never again will he die for anyone. He has finished the debt. He is risen to life eternal, making eternal life available to us. He is the only one who can offer that to all.

It is beyond human understanding that one could love so. It is a God thing. He is worthy of our love, our praises, our follow-ship of him. Today is the day of salvation offered to all. Accept while you have today. He understands that you are a weak and ungodly sinner. That's why he came: to give you this opportunity for eternal life. It can be had in no other way. He is the Way!

December 6

ROMANS 6:12

"Let not sin therefore reign in your mortal body,
to make you obey its passions." ESV

It is so easy to let the normal way of life move on into the choices that are not even thought about, much less prayed about, before we start into obeying those desires. Desires are strong and move along rutted channels where we've listened to them and went along with them for too long. Those ruts in our brain get deeper as the years go by, for we dig them with repetition. If you would cause them to be filled in, there must be new routes made in there.

They say that if you want to change a habit, you must make a new habit to take its place. That avoids leaving a vacuum that must be filled. Sounds reasonable. So, let's explore the idea of stopping our mortal bodies from hearing only the call of our passions. What could be replacing those desires to give those ruts an opportunity to "heal", to fill in with better ways? When I am tempted with an old passion, what can I do?

The first thing that comes to mind is what does the Word of God have to say about this particular desire. The second is to pray openly, honestly and diligently to your Father who cares deeply about you. The third is to call a friend or family member who also cares about you enough to be an accountability partner. There you have it! That is the three- legged stool that every believer must stand on to make changes in the life choices that have been poor. The Word, the Prayer life and the Fellowship of the believers is where we can have the strength to change. Life is hard. We need the Father's instruction. We cannot do without the prayer channel to him. We desperately need one another to encourage us. Be a help to others and depend on them to help you too.

December 7

"Turn my eyes from looking at worthless things;
and give me life in your ways." ESV

There are always in front of me the things that others see as valuable and needed, things to be greatly desired. But I must learn early that I cannot have it all and do it all. I must decide, pick, choose from among them those that will add to my life instead of taking away. I must know that everything is not good for me, nor profitable. So, I need ways of finding the valuable and worthy as opposed to the worthless. How can I make such choices well?

The key is in the second part of the verse. I need the Lord first and foremost in my life. I need to know him well, in an intimate way that can be achieved only by knowing his word well. I need to believe that he has my best in his heart for me. I want to be able to follow his directions clearly because they have been preserved for me clearly. The whole 119th Psalm is a great way of learning these attributes of God and his love, his care for me. Read it all, dear friend. You will find your heavenly Father's instructions, his love and plans for you, as well as, his truth shared so trustworthily. There are no muddy waters there. It is as clear as a pool of water with a mirror at the bottom looking directly back at you. You will find yourself and your God explained, verse after verse.

You can see those things that are worthless because you can measure them against the truths found. When you have the plumb line to cast against the wiggly line, you can see where the crooked and perverse lie. It is your assurance of the straight and narrow, the tried and true of God's plan for his creation. You will be able to tell the difference speedily. Take the time to start reading the word in this place. It is worth it. It is profitable. It is good for you.

December 8

"My soul melts away for sorrow; strengthen
me according to your word!" ESV

Everyone's life has days of weeping for the loss that occurs in each life. But for some, there is a time when the heart, the soul of man, melts away to nothing, spilled upon the ground in front of him as he experiences a pain that is beyond describing to others. It has no words that can be spoken that will let another understand the depths of that pain.

When the sorrow is more than you can bear, when the anguish is from the bottom of your being to the top of your existence, it takes something else to be grasped by any other person. Sometimes our God is the only one who can come even close to understanding that darkness that enfolds you, that covers and blocks out the very air you breathe. It is then, when you must come to the word of God for comfort, for peace that is beyond human understanding.

And here is where the Psalmist comes too. He asks the Lord to strengthen him with the word of God. He pleads for God to lift up his soul to the shoulders of his promises he has made to men who follow the him with all their hearts. He says he has melted into the floor around him and there is no comfort apart from God's word. He depends on these promises that God made long ago. He knows where to find his comfort and he goes directly to God and the word of God. You can too, fellow believer. The word has all you need to survive the pains of sorrow. Go to him today and find rest for your soul.

December 9

PSALM 119:55A

"I remember Your name in the night, O Lord ..." NKJV

When the night is covering me as I wait upon the Lord in my difficulty, when the darkness is overwhelming me, when I know I have met my match in the Enemy and am faltering before him, these are the times I need you, Lord. The Enemy is stronger than I. He is wearing me down with his moment by moment sitting over my shoulder reminding me of my failures, mistakes and downright sin. He seems never to go away. The night is long, Lord. The darkness is deep. The Enemy is there...so "there."

Where are you, Lord? Where have you gone? Why have you left me alone in this? What? You say you have not left me? I am not alone? But, Lord, it seems I'm so alone! I am weak and plain lonely. I am tired and weary. Where are you, Lord? What? You say you are right here? Where? In your Word, Lord? Your Word? Yes, your Word reminds me you are stronger than the Enemy!

Ah, yes, I remember your Word upon which you have caused me to hope! You are my comfort. Yes, I have sung songs of your statutes in the day, Lord. But it is night now. What? That doesn't make any difference, Lord? Your Words are true even in the night seasons? Oh, yes, I remember now. I remember your name in the night, Lord. Your name! And there is strength in that name. There is comfort and joy as I cry out to your name. You are my portion even in the long nights, even when the darkness is too deep. You lift me above my night and let me sing as though it is day. Thank you, Lord. At midnight, I will rise and give thanks to you... Thank you, thank you again. I see you now in your Word. I remember.

December 10

PSALM 119:133

"Keep steady my steps according to your promise; and
let no iniquity get dominion over me." ESV

There are certain sins that keep coming up in our lives. We try to overcome them and we fail too often. We wonder why and try again only to slip into that same sin again. Here is a clue to being an overcomer in this particular sin. We too often work on it by ourselves, trying to get better, do better and be better. But it is not about our strength in these matters. It is about depending on God for our ability to break this from our steps. The Bible is not a self-help book. It is a surrender to the Lord, all of our being, that he will send the Holy Spirit to be our Helper in this.

His word is for us to read, to ponder over, to learn from and to see his works in us that give us the power to be victorious over sin. We can't do it alone. So, he has made a way for us. Thank you, Lord, for your mercy in this. Thank you for your promises to me for every day. I can pray your word back to you when my heart cannot express the right ones. You have preserved your word to be for all generations to have, to know who you are and to receive your salvation. You have left nothing out but have given us all we need in the Lord Jesus. Again, thank you, Father. Turn to our Jesus too, and receive!

December 11

PSALM 139:16

"Your eyes saw my unformed substance; in your book were
written, every one of them, the days that were formed
for me, when as yet there was none of them." ESV

When I am the least bit wary of the future that lies before me, I like to go to this beautiful verse that tells me how God formed me, watched me develop and saw my beginning and my ending before any one part had even occurred yet! It is one of the most comforting set of words I have ever read. It brings stillness and cheer to my being to lay back in the arms of my God and allow him to move me toward every day that he has already written into his book for me. What peace here. What joy is mine as I rest in his Word of his knowledge of me.

When you are lonely, worried, pushed toward the unknown and your heart trembles at the very thought of the next few hours or days, turn to this Psalm and reread it over and over again. Stay a while and bask in the strength of our Father who made you and delivered you. He has not left you there to lie in your need. He has brought you to this day. He will see you through it too.

December 12

PSALM 139:1

"O Lord, You have searched me and known me." NKJV

It was an amazing moment when I read this verse for the first time as a young person. It was more than my heart could bear with which to start my day. To realize that my God, the All-Mighty, All-Knowing, Ever-Present God of all creation has searched me, the real me, the sinful me, the one who falters so often, has known me intimately and still loves me, is more than I can grasp.

The verses that follow reveal there is no place I can go that he is not there ahead of me. There is no thing I do, say or think that you have not already known about and still love me. You understand me! And you still laid your hand upon me in spite of such knowledge. I accept your love with an overwhelmed heart at such knowledge. You made me and you are pleased with your product, for you are continually leading me forward to your perfect plan for me.

There has never been a newborn baby that you did not make, beautifully and wonderfully. You watched each one as that one became a part of your plan. May you be praised and honored with our speech and our love. And you have written all the days you have allotted to me in your book before any ever were.

Friend, your life, each day you have, is written in his book. Turn to him today. He loves you too. You are a part of His plan.

December 13

PSALM 139:23-24

"Search me, O God, and know my heart! Try me and
know my thoughts! And see if there be any grievous way
in me, and lead me in the way everlasting!" ESV

There are so many times when I realize that I need the Lord looking
over me and my thoughts, for the thought is the father of the deed. It
begins in there, somewhere deep in my brain where I don't let many
people see very often. You know the place, where we don't always
filter the words and deeds that give birth down in there. Those words
and actions that are far less than our God would want there to be
in us.

I must let him open my mind, my heart and my desires for me
to admit the faults that are coming forth when unbidden even. He
sees them all the time. But I need to know that they are there and
unwatched that they will spill out the mouth and do harm to me
and those around me. When he does, he can cleanse me from the
thoughts that grieve him. He can take me by my hand and walk me
through the fog to see the light of his face. It makes my way so easy
to see then. He leads me in his way everlasting. Praise him for his
mercy and grace that convict me, clear away the stubble from my
thoughts and restores the right way for my eyes to see and my heart
to follow. Thank you, Lord. Let him clear your thoughts too. Let
him search you with his love light that brings goodness to you from
the hand of One who loves you immensely.

December 14

PSALM 139:1-2

"O Lord, you have searched me and known me!
You know when I sit down and when I rise up;
you discern my thoughts from afar." ESV

What an amazing reality that my God, my Lord, observes and searches out the "Me" that I am! He truly has known me intimately and has looked into the very depths that make "Me" the unique person I am. No one else can know "Me" that well. No one else has been created by him that is just like "Me". He has made "Me" the only "Me" there is!

He can even know my thoughts from "afar"; wherever his being is, he is still close to "Me." How carefully he attends to the "Me" that I alone am whether I feel him close or not. His word tells me so. Therefore, I accept that knowledge. He is aware of my rising up or my sitting down every time I do. There is nothing he misses about "Me."

The same is true for the "You" that you alone are, unique and delightful indeed. He has missed nothing about "You" either. He knows You. He searches the "You" daily and knows your thoughts also from afar. He sees when "You" rise and when "You" sit. Today is a day for thanking him for such wonderful attention to "You." "You" are special in his creation and he has plans for the "You" that he made. Look to him for this plan, his ideas about what "You" are here to be and to do. Run today's race he has set before you. Don't worry or stress about tomorrow's. You are not there yet! See to today's journey.

December 15

PSALM 139:11-12

"If I say, 'Surely the darkness shall fall on me' (to cover me),
even the night shall be light about me; Indeed, the darkness
shall not hide from You, but the night shines as the day; the
darkness and the light are both alike to You." NKJV

This is a most welcome knowledge for me. The very idea that God sees all in all in every hidden place is wonderful indeed. To know that nothing is ever unavailable for him to know gives me strength to go on, even into the darkness ahead. He sees and is not hampered by any event there, dark or not.

Lord, you walk in the light and you give light to your children to move in obedience to you. The world around us may be dark, may be hard to go forward into for the fear that very darkness brings to us. But you can shed light over any event in our lives. The night is as the day to you. How marvelous are your works for your children!

Today may be heavy with darkness for you, friend. But remember, the Lord sees into your night as if there did exist no darkness at all. Trust him with everything you have. Do not fear anything or anyone. Fear only the Lord, your God. He has a plan for you. Read his word and follow him every day, for his plan is best. It is born out of his love.

December 16

PSALM 71:17-18

"O God, from my youth you have taught me, and I still proclaim your wondrous deeds. So even to old age and grey hairs, O God, do not forsake me, until I proclaim your might to another generation, your power to all those to come." ESV

For the last years of my life this has been my life verse from God's word. He gave it to me while I was flying over the Atlantic Ocean returning from Morocco, North Africa, after a trip there where I and some friends simply prayed from one end of the country to the other as we enjoyed the rare beauties of that land. We proclaimed the name of Jesus all those years ago and came back flying the flag of Christ's Kingdom as I came off that plane to family and friends here.

The gracious Lord used many ways of teaching me about himself. There was first and foremost my mother, as well as, father. But more so, my mother, for at her knee I heard the first words of his greatness, his love and the opportunity to be forgiven from the failed attempts at doing life my way. Even young, we have a tendency to try ourselves, don't we? In my memories, God wore my mother's face, I think! She knew him intimately. And her greatest calling was to share that knowing with her kids. We all became Christ Followers, all were sinners, but all knew him and his forgiveness too. What a legacy to pass to us. She couldn't do it for us, but she was faithful to give us that knowing of him.

He used blessed Sunday School teachers too, faithfully knowing my Jesus and faithfully sharing with me that gift. How I love those who believed and taught with a joy from him that passed my Jesus' love on in words, and by loving me with a complete and forgiving spirit. Now, it is my turn to finish my race by sharing this knowledge of God's mercy and grace with you. You are my purpose and joy. Thank you for the time we have spent together on these pages of encouragement and love. May my God bring goodness and mercy into your household every day that you read one of these devotions. They are meant just for you! Your Mama loves you.

December 17

PSALM 119:105

"Thy word is a lamp unto my feet, and a light unto my path." KJV

As the days of aging keep slipping under my feet so that they are slower and unsteady, I realize these words are still true for my life, whether my physical feet are halting or not. There is no way I can ever repay or thank my mother enough for teaching the word to me long before I could read. I know now how many hours she spent while doing the work of a woman during the post - World War Two era, a time when everything was done by hand and from "scratch." I am amazed at her diligence and strength that, though tired and weary from having a family of six, working in the fields, sewing all we wore, she would still take time doing all those things to teach me at her knee in the most gentle and natural way to assure that I knew his words.

All these years later, that word is still my guide, my assurance of direction and straight paths to explore and live in God's world. She was faithful. She was a natural at the "knee desk" of learning. Even at the piano, mother would encourage me to practice, to stay with it until I mastered a piece and to enjoy the gift she was making available to me. My mother gave me a lamp that would open my mind to his plan. She turned on a light that would never go out by running out of oil or because it was blown out by the world's pull. It is forever truth. Mothers and fathers, teach your children the word that in years to come it will still be their lamp, their light to leave the way clear before them. Though I be slow and unsteady now, the path is still very much clear all because she cared enough to pay the price in her days with me.

December 18

PSALM 139:2

"You know when I sit down or when I stand up ..." HCSB

What, Lord? You know every time I stand or sit? Why, Lord? What's eventful about my every move? Standing or sitting? Wow! Every little move I make is in your vision and you care about it...when I am excited and jump to the occasion going on? When I am tired and plop down exhausted? When I worry and give in to it as I sag into my chair? When I run to the door to see my loved one coming up the walk? When I move over in a quick up-down movement to make room for my child, grandchild, even my great grand kids? Lord, you see it all and take note of my thoughts as I do each of these movements.

You see each of my emotions as I respond to these times. As I've already said: Wow! Lord, you are my God! I will stand to worship you. I will sit to pay honor to you in prayer and thanksgiving. I will bow my head in yielding to your will for me. Thank you. Take this, my day and honor yourself through me all day. Kids, he knows when you sit and when you get up too. Rise to worship. Sit in prayer and thanksgiving. Bow to yield to his will for you. Take time to respond to his call to you.

December 19

PSALM 139:2B

"You understand my thoughts from far away." HCSB

Where else is there a friend such as you who can understand my very thoughts before I utter them? There is no other who knows me so well. As well as Buck knows me after seventy-three years, even the love of my life does not know me this well. Now, he's often able to know just what I am going to say before I say it. But not all the time.

Lord, you not only know what is running around in my mind, you understand it. You mean, Lord, when I am thinking beautiful thoughts, you see? And when I am mulling over those ugly thoughts, you understand how I feel, why I feel that way and though you would not want me to think those, you still love me and understand my feelings that made those thoughts so easy to come. Thank you. You gave me the ability to feel emotions, even strong ones … all of them. But you didn't leave me in the midst of them either. You gave me a freewill so I don't have to make choices based on those emotions. You love that I can work through my feelings by the power you gave in your Holy Spirit.

Thank you again. It doesn't matter that you are far away in one sense. You still know and understand. You're omniscient, knowing it all anyway. But to me personally, the best part is that you really understand deep down in me. I love you, Lord, for understanding in compassion for your child.

December 20

PSALM 139:13-14A

"For it was You who created my inward parts; You knit me together in my mother's womb. I will praise You because I have been remarkably and wonderfully made." HCSB

Lord, when I even try to think of the way your care for me is done, it is more that I can mull in my small mind. As I remember the beginning of this Psalm, the fact that you "know" me, "search" me and you still care for me knowing all about me, is a fact I have trouble encompassing in there where I live. That too is more than I can hold in my thoughts with any deep understanding. That kind of care is too high for my earthly mind to grasp. To understand with my heart how you hug me tight and lay your blessed hand on my shoulder to steady me throughout my day is beyond any love I have ever known. It is pure and perfect. It is for now and forever. It is freely given and over me all the time. That too us more than I can hold. But what I can hold in my little brain is the fact that your Word tells me how you think and feel about me!

I yield to your love for this one day. Not because I can grasp or understand, nor reach it with my smallness. I yield because your Word tells me so. In my condition you knew I would need help to become a new creation in Christ Jesus. Therefore, you sent to me and your whole world whom you loved completely, a Savior. God became a Man and dwelt among men. You provided in your perfect, complete love everything we would need. Thank you, Lord Jesus. I celebrate your birth because you celebrate me! Jesus loves me, this I know!

December 21

1 JOHN 4:10-11

"Love consists in this: not that we loved God, but that He loved us
and sent his Son to be the propitiation for our sins. Dear friends,
if God loved us in this way, we also must love one another." ESV

Christmas is only a few days away and we look for ways to do nice
things for others, a way to be kind and loving to them who are dear
to us. The Season just brings that to the surface, doesn't it? That's
not the sort of love God expressed for us when he sent his Son to his
earth to redeemed his children. He gave it all because he loved with
a pure and sacrificial love, complete and unconditional, not just you
and me, but all the world! What love shown to humans who could
do nothing to gain favor with God!

Choose today to show real love toward those around you,
whether they deserve it or not, whether they are loving in return
or even if they are unkind, unjust or unlovely themselves. When
shopping for groceries, goods, presents or lovely decorations, take
a moment to notice those around you as they too are doing these
things. See if they need a hand with bags, carts or packages. Offer
instead of waiting for them to ask. They very probably won't ask for
help. Most of us don't. We struggle with our lives and go home with
disappointments and pain, wishing just someone, anyone, would
have given a little help.

It's Christmas, you know! The world doesn't really know how to
celebrate it. Show them how! Give love from a genuine heart filled
to the brim by your Savior. His love was over the top. Let yours be
so also.

December 22

ECCLESIASTES 11:7A

"Truly the light is sweet…" NKJV

In the middle of one night I got out of bed to make a bathroom run and walked by my dark Christmas tree still up several days after the holiday. I love the lighted tree, all sparkly and colorful, bright and shiny with glass, crystal and golden ornaments. But this tree was dark in a dark room. But it was so different when totally dark. It wasn't the first time I had seen it without lights. But it was the first time I really thought about the fact that it is light that gives the tree its beauty, its life.

I went back to bed thinking about this. I lay there wandering though the items on that tree in my mind. I knew each one. They were mostly years old. They were still on the tree. They were as real as they could be. They were still in the same places on the limbs. There were as many as before…all the same. But they were empty when I looked because they had no life! The outside lamp post by our walk-way revealed the outline of each thing through the French doors. But the glow of that tiny light only showed their lifelessness.

Of course, that set me to thinking about the lesson from his own word of the Light of the World, that lights the door to eternity in Jesus. Oh, how pertinent to us that we share that Light of the World within our realm of influence where God has placed us, giving the opportunity for that Light to open the Door of heaven to others. You are right now where God has placed you because God has a plan for your little light to shine.

I was up early the next morning. As I reached for the light switch, I was delighted to see the dark tree shimmer and shine for me as it responded to the electricity moving through it. May we be as faithful to shine when our Lord turns us on with his life, his Light.

December 23

JOHN 1:14

"And the Word became flesh and dwelt among us,
and we have seen his glory, glory as of the only Son
from the Father, full of grace and truth." ESV

Never will I ever be able to grasp such love as this, that God became a man and came to live among us on the earth, to walk where we must go, to experience what we must live through and to become the answer to God's price for our redemption: Perfection for our sinfulness. We will one day get to see him and thank him for such grace, mercy and love. But until then, we have only to share his grace, mercy and love with those whom he has placed in our realm of influence.

There are those around you who have sinned too. Just as you have. They need to know that Jesus paid their price for redemption too. He marked your sinful state, "Paid in full!" Be certain you share that knowledge with them. Show them how he forgave you. Reveal the love, the unconditional love, that he shed on you to them with a willing heart and a set mind to lift them instead of shoving them deeper into the pit that holds them. God's forgiveness is available for them too.

Turn your entire life over to completely yielding to his Holy Spirit's leadership. You'll still be doing the things you must but you will be sharing Jesus every where you do those things. He wants to use you to light your world with his Light. He wants to share his Bread with the hungry by your hands. He wants to be merciful through your compassion and care. Open your hearts to fulfill his call just as God opened his heart to send his world a Savior. Celebrate Jesus with obedience to the Word, Emmanuel, for God is with us!

December 24

MICAH 5:2

"But you, O Bethlehem Ephrathah, who are too little
to be among the clans of Judah, from you shall come
forth for me, one who is to be ruler of Israel, whose
coming forth is from old, from ancient days." ESV

At Christmas time, we all know the story of Jesus coming from little Bethlehem, the tiny little town where Jesus was born. Yes, we all know, but we don't really appreciate the depth of that fact. God is not one who chooses from the great always. He had a plan from of old, from ancient days of exactly the place where his Son would be born. It was not by any accident. It was his perfect plan.

We think in our hearts that God couldn't possibly choose to use us. We are too little, too young, too old, to weak, too whatever. You get the idea. We look at ourselves and just know he wouldn't use us. He has to have better, bigger, wiser, or smarter to use. But your God has a call for you. That's right. YOU! You're not misunderstanding. He calls you by name when he calls. Listen to his call. Read his word to see how he calls and why he says your name, not another's.

He put the very Son of God in little Bethlehem. You must not try to limit our God with what he wants you to do in his Plan. You can't change his mind when he motions for you to get up and go. Your only choice is to obey or disobey. It is always about choices, isn't it?

December 25

PSALM 107: 30

"Then are they glad because they are quiet; so he
bringeth them unto their desired haven." KJV

Now, I realize I am taking this out of context but I think you will
understand before I am finished. This is Christmas Day. It started
very early, about six in the morning, when our young grandson called
for us to come to his house to see all he got for Christmas under his
tree. By seven the phone rang again with the seven-year-old wanting
the same thing: come! So, we jumped in the car and hurried to each
child's home "to see." That's what you do when they are willing to
share with you on Christmas. Many grandparents don't have the
luxury of being called to "come see."

By ten-thirty that day the family was beginning to gather for
present exchange and snacking before a late Christmas dinner. As
they all collected around the house and porch, we all caught up
on each other, snacking all the time, waiting for the meal later. We
laughed, we talked, we played board games, we remembered year's
past. And then, dinner was served on the Christmas china and tea
poured in the Christmas crystal which many of them had given me
over the many years. It was, as always, a special day.

They are all gone now. The house is quiet and we are tired. But
it's a good tired. You know, when though everything hurts, you have
enjoyed it all. And he has brought us to our desired haven…a sofa
and chair, to be followed by the king-sized bed shortly. The end of a
beautiful Christmas Day. Thank God for the wonderful day and for
the blessed quiet of Christmas over!

December 26

2 CORINTHIANS 9:15

"Thanks be to God for his unspeakable gift." KJV

Christmas is a wonderful time, a time to remember, to understand more than others what a gift our Lord Jesus is to us. When we celebrate this gift each year, let us think beyond the usual way of honoring him. Here is my gift to you about my celebration of his birth.

The Greatest Gift was:

Birthed, not bought.

"Bowed" to His Father, not "bowed" with ribbon on top.

Wrought to do His Father's will, not wrapped to hide His identity.

Right-priced: free to all, but costly!

Complete, not "batteries-not-included."

A fisher of men, not Fisher Price.

Laid in a manger, not a mansion.

Wrapped in swaddling clothes, not Christian Dior

Not a game, though He has a "no credit card monopoly" on heaven.

Is eternally our Savior and is better that the Energizer Bunny

Not a stuffed lamb, but the Lamb of God.

The reason for the Season.

With the "Super Bowl" right behind this Season, keep Christmas in first place. There is no "play-off" for a winner here! May we raise our voices of praise to the One who ran the whole field, played all four quarters, both offense and defense, with no fumbles, no penalties, no interceptions and made the only score, winning for all time for all mankind the opportunity of salvation from His score, His Sacrifice, His Gift. This gift can be yours too. His Name is not Wilson, not Manning, not even Tebow nor Brady. His Name is Jesus! Celebrate his coming.

December 27

PSALM 55:4-6

"My heart is very pained within me...fearfulness
and trembling are come upon me, and horror has
overwhelmed me. And I said, 'Oh, that I had the wings
of a dove! For then would I fly away and be at rest.'"

King David was a mighty warrior, a strong ruler, a man of faith in his great God, but when his enemies were at his door and were seemingly able to destroy him, he cried out to his God for relief, for help from the One he had trusted in better times to be there in the worst of times. It is really in these types of times that we need God the most, for we are children of weakness, frail and tired. How we wish we had the wings of a dove with the ability to fly away into the sky for peace and rest when there are no words to tell another what we are feeling, when the pain is more than we can bear without his intervention. Everything in us yearns for relief. The pain is a weight bearing down on our soul. The word won't come out and yet we feel as if we will burst if they don't. Our hearts pound. We are totally overcome with grief as we know how very real the grave is. Everything says we are alone in this grief. But then, as King David remembered too, we are not alone anymore. We have a Savior who is able to overcome all things he allows in our lives. Not that he removes them. But that he is there. We also have each other, siblings in the faith, who will stand with us, even by the graveside. The day we set our hearts on Jesus, the day we turned from our life as we knew it and reached out for his gift of life, that very day, we became no longer alone. It's not about how these events happen in life but about who will stand with us through them. And first on the list is the One who saved you already. The others are for even more strength. Depend on the Savior. He will never leave you nor forsake you.

December 28

PSALM 92:12A, 14

"The righteous shall flourish like a palm tree…They shall still bear fruit in old age. They shall be fresh and flourishing." HCSB

God's calling of me has not stopped just because I am old now. He won't stop his calling on your life either. As long as he gives breath, he intends for his children to worship him, love him, honor and share his name. So, there's not as much as in the past that I can still do. There is still much to be done that I can do!

I can make a call, write a note, send an email, buy a small gift, encourage others with the knowledge that they can make it each day though the day is long. I can smile wherever I go, whether in my grocery, doctor's office or the Post Office. Even on the road driving, I can smile, especially there! I can refrain from gossiping or judging others when I have no idea what's going on in their hearts or lives. I can refrain from being critical of others too. I can reach out with a soft answer to their tears and soothe the spirits of one who is hurting.

Choose today (yes, there's that word again!) to begin a new work with God. Depend on him to show you the way to speak, to share, to lift, to answer, to strengthen and to give joy to those whom your life touches this day. And smile BIG! It improves your countenance all the way to beauty. This mama believes in you!

December 29

2 TIMOTHY 4:6-8

'For I am now ready to be offered, and the time of my departure is at hand. I have fought a good fight, I have finished my course, I have kept the faith; henceforth there is laid up for me a crown of righteousness, which the Lord, the righteous judge, shall give me at that day; and not to me only, but unto all them also that love his appearing." KJV

The Apostle Paul, talking to his young friend and youthful pastor-in-training, Timothy, knew he was at the end of his journey, but not even Paul knew when the Lord would call him by name to his reward at the feet of Jesus. But he was ready! He trusted his Lord would know the exact time of his calling. Paul took some of his precious breath that he had remaining to leave Timothy some strong words of wisdom from one farther down the lane of life. Take time to read the whole chapter. To Timothy, Paul's example was to be ready, to fight a good fight, to finish the course, to keep the faith and to trust the Lord for the crown of righteousness AT THAT DAY. And only God knows the exact day, the very moment he will call. But he will call each of us, by our own name and we will answer that call. Our days are numbered. We each have an expiration date stamped on us somewhere. Thank God he stamped it there in his providence and we can't see it early! Thank God for his faithfulness, his trustworthiness that he will not be late, nor early. Even Paul just knew it was close, "at hand" as he described it. Fight the good fight, finish your course, keep the faith and be ready. Trust him for your crown of righteousness.

December 30

PSALM 61:1-3

"Hear my cry, O God, listen to my prayer; from the end
of the earth I call to you when my heart is faint. Lead
me to the rock that is higher than I, for you have been
my refuge, a strong tower against the enemy." ESV

Everyone has times in life when the fear of the future is more than can be accepted and understood. We feel this can't be God's plan because it hurts so much. But this verse tells there will be times when my heart is faint, when I can't go on, I believe. No matter where I am on this earth, God is aware and cares about my pain. I cry out as I experience that pain. I call on my God from wherever I am and plead with him to hear. I am overwhelmed.

And then, I know. He does hear. He does desire my heart to be replenished with the grace to go on into that unknown future, that walk that seems too hard to make. He has been and still is my rock that is higher than I. He has been and will continue to be, my refuge before me, able to receive me into its shelter. And that rock is stronger than I as well. Its tower hides me from any enemy that is bearing down on my life. He is my dwelling place forever and there are no holes in his tower when he closes the door behind me.

My circumstance may not change but my vision of it does. I see it now as a battle he must fight. I do not battle alone. Thank you, Lord for your mercy that covers me with your mighty hand. Run to his tower, friend. Cry to our God for he listens to our every breath. Your name is on his lips. He is your rock.

December 31

2 PETER 1:12-15

"Therefore, I will always remind you about these things, even
though you know them and are established in the truth you
have. I consider it right, as long as I am living in this bodily
tent, to wake you up with a reminder, knowing that I will
soon lay aside my tent, as our Lord Jesus Christ has also shown
me. And I will make every effort that you may be able to
recall these things at any time after my departure." HCSB

Yes, I consider it a privilege to remind you, even though you already
know many of the things I have recorded in this book, that you
sometime will need being waked up. That wake up call will be by
someone much older than yourself who has walked that same road
you are heading down, or who has experienced the same battle you
are living through right now.

At eighty years old, I have walked those side trails in my past
and have made the mistakes you are contemplating right now. Let
me assure you it is not a tangent you want to head onto, for it takes
you so far away from the God who loves you enough that he sent his
only Son to save you. Yes, you! Take this advice and turn around as
quickly as you can and reenter the straight and narrow that the Lord
has called you to travel.

At eighty, I know the time is short for me. That's how life is.
Even if I live another fifteen or twenty years, all the way to one
hundred, that is such a short time. And I am certain the body and
the mind will not be as productive or sharp as it has been in the
first eighty! So, while there is life for me, I will keep telling you that
our God is able. Our God is mighty and will see to it that your life
is bound for glory with him because Jesus bought it with his blood
and you accepted his free gift. There will be difficult times. That's
the way it is in a fallen world. But our Lord has overcome the world
and will set all things right. Trust him and praise him. He is worthy!
Remember my words to you long after I am gone. This devotional

book was written that you might be strengthened in the word, that you would be encouraged that you are not alone in your struggle and that God has equipped you to be able to persevere all the way to the end. Press on, dear children. Your mama loves you!

About the Author

Jacqueline Vera Jo (Burnett) Strickland

Born May 18, 1937 Palmetto (Gillette Community), Florida

Graduated Manatee County High School, 1955, Bradenton, Florida

Graduated Manatee Community College, Magna Cum Laude, Associate of Arts, 1962, Bradenton, Florida

Taught private piano lessons at 18 years old, still teaching at 79 years old.

Married to Lee "Buck" Strickland February 29, 1956

She has five children: Deborah Hope (deceased), Alicia Love, Elizabeth Helene, Sarah Yvonne, and Daniel Leon

She has many grandchildren and great-grandchildren and those that call her mama or mimi.

Made in the USA
Lexington, KY
20 December 2019